T0301103

A Recipe for Every Day of the Year

An Hachette UK Company
www.hachette.co.uk

The authorized representative in the EEA is Hachette Ireland,
8 Castlecourt Centre, Dublin 15, D15 XTP3, Ireland (email: info@hbgi.ie)

First published in Great Britain in 2024 by Hamlyn,
an imprint of Octopus Books Ltd
Carmelite House
50 Victoria Embankment
London EC4Y 0DZ
www.octopusbooks.co.uk

Distributed in the US by
Hachette Book Group
1290 Avenue of the Americas
4th and 5th Floors
New York, NY 10104

Distributed in Canada by
Canadian Manda Group
664 Annette St.
Toronto, Ontario, Canada M6S 2C8

ISBN: 978-0-6006-3826-1

A CIP catalogue record for this title is available from the British Library

Printed and bound in the UK

10 9 8 7 6 5 4 3

Publisher: Lucy Pessell
Designer: Isobel Platt
Editor: Feyi Oyesanya
Assistant Editor: Samina Rahman
Production Controller: Sarah Parry
Illustrations: Bárbara Malagoli

This FSC® label means that materials used for the
product have been responsibly sourced.

MIX
Paper | Supporting
responsible forestry
FSC   FSC® C104740
www.fsc.org

A Recipe for Every Day of the Year

A year of timeless, trusted and seasonal recipes

Francesca Huntingdon

hamlyn

Introduction

Welcome to a wonderful year in the kitchen. From winter warmers to summer sizzlers, here are 365 recipes – plus an extra one for leap-year luck – to inspire you.

This book offers everything from showstoppers and crowd-pleasers to family favourites and simple one-bowl suppers. You'll find ideas for breakfasts and brunches, light meals and snacks, main meals and sweet treats. Whether you're looking for soups, salads or sandwiches, or cocktails, cakes and casseroles, they're all here.

With some extra-special recipes for celebrations such as Diwali, Christmas and Valentine's Day, and with dishes from all over the world, you can take your tastebuds on a culinary adventure all year long.

There are a variety of vegan, vegetarian, dairy-free and gluten-free options and, where possible, the recipes reflect the changing seasons to help you use fruit and veggies when they are at their best.

Good food deserves a delicious drink to complement it, so scattered throughout the book you'll find additional recipes for both alcoholic and non-alcoholic drinks.

HOW TO USE THIS BOOK

You'll find two separate contents lists in this book.

The first lists all the recipes according to meal type, and are marked as being suitable for vegans (vg) or vegetarians (v).

Please note that if you are cooking for vegetarians, there are some cheeses that may not be suitable because they contain animal rennet. Always check the labels and seek vegetarian-friendly alternatives where necessary.

The second lists the recipes by celebrations, festivities and moveable feasts. The dates on which many special celebrations, such as Easter, Eid and Shavuot fall varies from year to year, so this is a quick guide to all the suitable recipes.

CONTENTS BY MEAL

MAINS

DESSERTS

DRINKS

CONTENTS BY CELEBRATIONS

Citrus Baklava (v)	112
Thumbprint Cookies	119
Chocolate & Beetroot Fudge Cake (vg)	155
Sri Lankan-Style Lamb Curry	171
Mango, Coconut & Lime Lassi (v)	187
Royal Lamb Biryani	188
Rosemary Lamb Kebabs	250
Haddock, Tomato & Tamarind Fish Curry	296
Gulab Jamun (v)	334
Mint Choc Chip Cheesecake (v)	341
Spinach & Red Lentil Soup (v)	359
Vegetable Samosas (v)	363
Goan Prawn & Coconut Curry	368
Creamy Lamb Korma	398
Clove & Cardamom Spiced Cookies (v)	399

PASSOVER

Kale Soup with Garlic Croutons (v)	25
Carrot & Apple Nut Roast Parcels (vg)	45
Lemon Chilli Chicken	106
Chocolate Walnut Brownies (v)	127
New Potato & Green Bean Pasta with Pesto (v)	145
Lamb Chops with Olive Couscous	216
Carrot & Feta Potato Cakes with Eggs (v)	401
Pea & Potato Tikkis (vg)	409

SHAVUOT

Kale Soup with Garlic Croutons (v)	25
Beetroot, Orange & Goats' Cheese Salad (v)	97
Pea & Asparagus Risotto (v)	130
Garlic Mushrooms with Potato Rösti (v)	132
Corn Cakes with Smoked Salmon	173
Baked Ricotta Cheesecake (v)	182
Summer Vegetable Fettuccine (v)	209
Courgette & Herb Risotto (v)	221
Vegetable Moussaka (v)	292
Wild Mushroom Lasagne (v)	321
Baked Mushrooms with Taleggio & Pesto (v)	355
Spinach & Red Lentil Soup (v)	359
Lemon & Green Veg Pasta Salad (v)	367

DIWALI

Mango, Coconut & Lime Lassi (v)	187
Gulab Jamun (v)	334
Vegetable Samosas (v)	363
Clove & Cardamom Spiced Cookies (v)	399

ROSH HASHANAH

Freeform Apple & Mixed Berry Pie (v)	19
Pan-cooked Eggs with Spinach & Leeks (v)	24
Halloumi with Pomegranate Salsa (v)	253
Honey Cake (v)	301
Leeks Milanese (v)	315
Pumpkin, Beetroot & Goats' Cheese Bake (v)	344
Spinach & Red Lentil Soup (v)	359

HALLOWE'EN

Pumpkin, Beetroot & Goats' Cheese Bake (v)	344
Clove & Cardamom Spiced Cookies (v)	399
Pumpkin Pie (v)	374
Beef Pumpkin & Ginger Stew	390

CHRISTMAS

Sticky Gingerbread (v)	27
Orange & Caraway Seed Cake (v)	62
Triple Choc Cookies (v)	100
Roast Lamb Stuffed with Rice & Peppers	143
Caramel Chocolate Fondants (v)	172
Beef Skewers with Satay Sauce	270
Roast Chicken with Herbs & Garlic	300
Chicken, Bacon & Sage Meatballs	325
Pork & Apple Balls	342
Sausages with Sprout Colcannon	356
Chocolate Mousse with Honeycomb (v)	387
Bubble & Squeak Cakes with Poached Eggs (v)	396
Bûche de Noël (v)	404
Turkey & Chestnut Soup	407

January

GOOD TO EAT THIS MONTH

broccoli * Brussels sprouts * cabbage * carrots *
cauliflower * celeriac * Jerusalem artichokes * kale
* leeks * mushrooms * onions * parsnips * potatoes
* sweet potatoes * apples * blood oranges * pears *
rhubarb * Seville oranges * rosemary * sage

DATES TO LOOK FORWARD TO THIS MONTH

New Year's Day
Chinese New Year
Burns' Night

It's the start of a whole new year. After the sparkly lights and
festive excitement of the previous month, January can feel dark
and gloomy. But it's a time to take a cue from nature, still in a
deep slumber, to use this time to cocoon, regroup and make plans
for the year. So get those comfy socks on, draw the curtains and
light some candles.

After a month perhaps of excess, many of us make resolutions
to get healthier, so this month you'll find plenty of health-boosting
recipes to help ward off winter colds, including the **Gingered
Pear Juice** on page 43 and the **Kale Soup** on page 25.

There are also comforting cold-weather treats, like the **Sticky
Gingerbread** on page 27 and the **Chicken Puff Pie** on page 46.

Root vegetables that began their season last autumn are at their
best now and perfect for the hearty stews and soups we crave at
this time of year, like the **Celeriac & Apple Soup** on page 17.

Seville oranges from Spain will appear in the shops this month.
They only have a brief season, from the end of December to
mid-February, but what a promise of sunshine they bring to a
dark month. Use them to make the traditional **Dark Oxford
Marmalade** on page 37.

• BREAKFASTS •

All-Day Breakfast Wrap

SERVES 4 • PREP & COOKING TIME 20 minutes

- 375 g (12 oz) pork sausagemeat
- 1 tablespoon vegetable oil, plus extra for greasing
- 250 g (8 oz) mushrooms, sliced
- 2 large eggs
- 2 tomatoes, deseeded and diced
- salt and black pepper
- 4 large soft flour tortillas

After a late night seeing in the New Year, enjoy the comfort of a fry-up, cleverly wrapped in a soft tortilla for cutlery-free eating. All you need alongside is your favourite sauce for dipping. Ready in just 20 minutes, this will go down a treat.

- Divide the sausagemeat into 4 long, flat sausages. Place on a greased baking sheet and cook in a preheated oven, 200°C (400°F), Gas Mark 6, for 15–18 minutes, turning once, until cooked through.

- Meanwhile, heat the oil in a frying pan and cook the mushrooms for 4–5 minutes, until softened and golden. Transfer to a bowl and keep warm. Place the frying pan back over a medium heat.

- Crack the eggs into a bowl and beat lightly. Stir in the chopped tomatoes, season with salt and pepper and pour into the hot frying pan. Stir gently until it starts to set, then cook for 1–2 minutes, until the base is golden and the omelette is just set. Slide on to a chopping board and slice thickly.

- Place 1 baked sausage in the centre of each tortilla, then top with some mushrooms and strips of omelette. Roll tightly and cut in half diagonally. Serve hot with brown sauce, barbecue sauce or tomato ketchup.

v

• LIGHT BITES •

Celeriac & Apple Soup

SERVES 6 • PREP & COOKING TIME 40 minutes

- 25 g (1 oz) butter
- 1 celeriac, about 500 g (1 lb), peeled and coarsely grated
- 3 dessert apples, peeled, cored and chopped
- 1.2 litres (2 pints) chicken or vegetable stock
- pinch of cayenne pepper, or more to taste
- salt

TO GARNISH
- 2–3 tablespoons finely diced dessert apple
- paprika

Low in carbs and high in nutrients, celeriac – with its nutty, celery flavour and velvety texture – creates a beautifully smooth and warming soup. Add the sweetness of apples and you have a flavoursome and comforting midweek meal or elegant first course.

• Melt the butter in a large saucepan and cook the celeriac and apples over a moderate heat for 5 minutes or until they have begun to soften.

• Add the stock and cayenne pepper and bring to the boil. Reduce the heat, cover the pan and simmer for 15–20 minutes or until the celeriac and apples are very soft.

• Purée the mixture in a blender or food processor until it is very smooth, transferring each batch to a clean saucepan. Alternatively, rub through a fine sieve.

• Reheat gently. Season to taste and serve garnished with the finely diced apple and a dusting of paprika.

V

· MAINS ·

Dhal Makhani

SERVES 4 • PREP & COOKING TIME 1 hour 20 minutes, plus soaking

- 125 g (4 oz) dried split black lentils
- 500 ml (17 fl oz) boiling water
- 3 tablespoons butter
- 1 onion, finely chopped
- 3 garlic cloves, crushed
- 2 teaspoons peeled and finely grated fresh root ginger
- 2 green chillies, split in half lengthways
- 1 teaspoon ground turmeric
- 1 teaspoon paprika, plus extra for sprinkling
- 1 tablespoon ground cumin
- 1 tablespoon ground coriander
- 200 g (7 oz) cooked or canned red kidney beans
- 500 ml (17 fl oz) water
- 200 g (7 oz) baby leaf spinach
- salt
- large handful of chopped coriander
- 200 ml (7 fl oz) single cream

This lentil dish really delivers both on flavour and health benefits. It's full of zingy spices and provides plenty of fibre, protein, iron, vitamins and antioxidants. Don't forget to start the prepping the evening before by soaking the lentils. Serve with hot parathas or naan bread.

- Place the black lentils in a sieve and wash under cold running water. Drain, place in a deep bowl and cover with cold water. Leave to soak for 10–12 hours.

- Rinse the lentils then place in a saucepan with the measured boiling water. Bring to the boil, reduce the heat and simmer for 35–40 minutes or until tender. Drain and set aside.

- Meanwhile, melt the butter in a large saucepan and add the onion, garlic, ginger and chillies. Stir-fry for 5–6 minutes and then add the turmeric, paprika, cumin, ground coriander, kidney beans and reserved lentils.

- Add the measured water and bring the mixture to the boil. Reduce the heat and stir in the spinach. Cook gently for 10–15 minutes, stirring often. Remove from the heat and season with salt. Stir in the chopped coriander and drizzle over the cream. Sprinkle over a little paprika and serve immediately

V

• DESSERTS •

Freeform Apple & Mixed Berry Pie

SERVES 6 • PREP & COOKING TIME 50 minutes, plus chilling

- 275 g (9 oz) plain flour, plus extra for dusting
- 75 g (3 oz) icing sugar
- 125 g (4 oz) unsalted butter, softened, diced
- 2 eggs
- a little milk or beaten egg, to glaze
- caster sugar, to decorate

FOR THE FILLING
- 2 cooking apples, about 500 g (1 lb), cored, peeled and thickly sliced
- 175 g (6 oz) frozen mixed berries (no need to defrost)
- 50 g (2 oz) icing sugar
- 2 teaspoons cornflour

The great thing about this charmingly rustic-looking pie is that you don't have to worry about any fiddly fitting the pastry into a tin – simply pile up the fruit filling in the middle and shape the pastry up around it. Serve it warm with plenty of vanilla ice cream or custard for dessert heaven.

- Put the flour on a large board or straight on to the work surface, add the icing sugar and butter, then make a dip in the centre and add the eggs. Begin to mix the eggs and butter together with your fingertips, gradually drawing the flour and sugar into the mix until it begins to clump together and you can squeeze the pastry into a ball. Knead the pastry lightly, then chill in the refrigerator for 15 minutes.

- Mix together the apples, frozen mixed berries, icing sugar and cornflour for the filling.

- Roll out the pastry on a lightly floured surface until it forms a rough-shaped circle about 33 cm (13 inches) in diameter.

- Lift it over a rolling pin on to a large greased baking sheet. Pile the fruit mix high in the centre of the pastry, then bring the edges of the pastry up and around the fruit, shaping into soft pleats and leaving the centre of the fruit mound exposed.

- Brush the outside of the pie with a little milk or beaten egg and sprinkle with caster sugar. Bake in a preheated oven, 190°C (375°F), Gas Mark 5, for 20–25 minutes until the pastry is golden and the fruit tender.

V

• BREAKFASTS •

Spiced Dried Fruit Compote

SERVES 4 • PREP & COOKING TIME 30 minutes

- 4 ready-to-eat dried pears or apple rings
- 4 ready-to-eat dried figs
- 8 ready-to-eat dried apricots
- 8 ready-to-eat dried prunes (about 75 g/3 oz)
- 600 ml (1 pint) fresh orange juice
- 1 cinnamon stick
- 1 star anise
- brown sugar, to taste

TO SERVE
- Greek yogurt
- ground cinnamon

In winter, when there is less seasonal fruit to choose from, dried fruit comes to the rescue. Serve this compote for breakfast with a dollop of Greek yogurt, as here, or for dessert with vanilla ice cream.

- Place the dried fruits in a saucepan with the orange juice and spices and bring to the boil. Reduce the heat, cover and simmer for 25–30 minutes until the fruits are plump and tender and the liquid syrupy.

- Check the liquid occasionally during cooking, adding a little water if necessary. Taste the liquid and add a little sugar if required. Remove the spices.

- Spoon into 4 bowls and serve with spoonfuls of Greek yogurt sprinkled with a little ground cinnamon, if liked.

• LIGHT BITES •

Caribbean Chicken Patties

MAKES 4 • PREP & COOKING TIME 1 hour, plus chilling

- 2 tablespoons sunflower oil
- 250 g (8 oz) boneless, skinless chicken breast, diced
- 250 g (8 oz) butternut squash, deseeded, peeled and cut into small dice
- 1 small onion, chopped
- 2 garlic cloves, finely chopped
- ½ small Scotch bonnet chilli, deseeded and finely chopped
- 1 red or orange pepper, deseeded and diced
- 1 teaspoon mild curry powder or paste
- 2 tablespoons chopped coriander
- beaten egg, to glaze
- black pepper

FOR THE PASTRY
- 250 g (8 oz) plain flour
- 1½ teaspoons turmeric
- 125 g (4 oz) white vegetable fat, diced
- 2½–3 tablespoons cold water
- salt

Turmeric adds a glorious sunshiny colour to the pastry encasing the chicken and vegetable filling in these patties. The Scotch bonnet chilli will be seriously fiery so remember to wash your hands after chopping it.

- Make the pastry. Add flour, turmeric, a little salt and the fat to a mixing bowl, and rub the fat in with your fingertips or using an electric mixer until you have fine crumbs. Gradually mix in enough of the measured water to form a soft but not sticky dough. Knead lightly, then wrap in clingfilm and chill while making the filling.

- Heat the oil in a frying pan, add the chicken and butternut squash and fry for 5 minutes until the chicken is just beginning to brown.

- Add the onion, garlic, chilli and pepper and fry for 5 minutes until the vegetables are softened and the chicken cooked through. Add the curry powder, coriander and a little pepper and cook briefly, then take off the heat and leave to cool.

- Cut the pastry into 4 pieces, roll each piece out on a lightly floured surface and trim to an 18 cm (7 inch) circle. Divide the filling between the pastry circles, brush the edges with beaten egg, then fold in half and press the edges together well, first with your fingertips, then with the prongs of a fork, until well sealed.

- Transfer to an oiled baking sheet, brush the patties with beaten egg and bake in a preheated oven, 190°C (375°F), Gas Mark 5, for 20–25 minutes.

· MAINS ·

Spaghetti & Meatballs with Tomato Sauce

SERVES 4 • PREP & COOKING TIME 30 minutes

- 500 g (1 lb) minced beef
- 5 garlic cloves, crushed
- ¼ teaspoon dried oregano
- 1 tablespoon chopped parsley
- 2 tablespoons grated Parmesan cheese
- 2 tablespoons olive oil
- 1 onion, diced
- a small pinch of dried chilli flakes
- 2 × 400 g (13 oz) can chopped tomatoes
- 100 ml (3½ fl oz) red wine
- 1 teaspoon sugar
- 2 tablespoons chopped basil leaves
- 375 g (12 oz) spaghetti
- Parmesan cheese shavings, to serve

This is sure to become a go-to recipe for a midweek family meal. For really tender meatballs, get your clean hands in the meatball mixture and mix together thoroughly – the more you squeeze and mash the mince, the better.

- Mix together the minced beef, 2 of the crushed garlic cloves, the oregano, chopped parsley and grated Parmesan in a mixing bowl. Roll into walnut-sized balls.

- Heat 1 tablespoon of the olive oil in a frying pan and fry the meatballs for 10–12 minutes, turning frequently.

- In another frying pan, heat the remaining olive oil and sauté the onion, remaining crushed garlic and chilli flakes for 3–4 minutes, then add the chopped tomatoes, red wine, sugar and basil and simmer for 8–10 minutes.

- Meanwhile, cook the spaghetti in a saucepan of boiling water according to the packet instructions until al dente.

- Transfer the meatballs to the tomato sauce and cook for a further 3–4 minutes, until cooked through.

- Drain the spaghetti and serve the meatballs spooned over the top. Serve sprinkled with Parmesan shavings.

VG

• DESSERTS •

Banana Fritters

SERVES 4 • PREP & COOKING TIME 20 minutes

• sunflower oil, for deep-frying
• 4–5 bananas or plantains
• caster sugar, to serve (optional)

FOR THE BATTER
• 125 g (4 oz) self-raising flour
• 1 teaspoon baking powder
• 2 teaspoons sugar
• ¼ teaspoon salt
• 25 g (1 oz) freshly grated or desiccated coconut
• 175 ml (6 fl oz) water

Fried to golden perfection, crispy on the outside and soft on the inside, these are a real treat. Eat them warm with your fingers just as they are or add a dollop of vanilla ice cream.

• Make the batter by mixing the flour, baking powder, sugar, salt and coconut in a bowl. Add the measured water and mix it with a fork or spoon until smooth.

• Heat 7 cm (3 inches) of oil in a nonstick wok or saucepan over a medium heat. While it is heating, peel the bananas or plantains, cut each banana into half lengthways, then cut them into 5 cm (2 inch) slices. Halve the plantains lengthways and then slice each length in half. The oil is ready when a little batter sizzles when dropped in.

• Coat the banana or plantain slices with the batter and then lower them carefully into the hot oil, 6–7 pieces at a time. Cook over a medium heat for 6–7 minutes until golden brown. Remove the fritters from the oil with a slotted spoon and drain on kitchen paper.

• When all the slices are cooked, arrange them on a serving dish and serve at once, sprinkled with sugar, if liked.

Make the most of your leftovers...
Bananas freeze really well, so don't waste overripe bananas. Peel them, then pop into freezer bags. Add them frozen to smoothies, or defrost and mash for **Banana & Honey Flapjacks** on page 32.

V

• BREAKFASTS •

Pan-cooked Eggs with Spinach & Leeks

SERVES 2 • PREP & COOKING TIME 10 minutes

- 25 g (1 oz) butter
- 1 leek, thinly sliced
- ¼ teaspoon dried chilli flakes
- 300 g (10 oz) baby spinach leaves
- 2 eggs
- 3 tablespoons natural yogurt
- pinch of ground paprika
- salt and black pepper

A speedy choice for brunch for two that combines soft-set eggs with sweet leeks and wilted spinach, this health-packed dish works well for a quick midweek dinner too. Delicious accompanied by fresh crusty bread.

- Heat the butter in a frying pan, add the leek and chilli flakes and cook over a medium-high heat for 4–5 minutes until softened. Add the spinach and season well, then toss and cook for 2 minutes until wilted.

- Make 2 wells in the centre of the vegetables and break the eggs into the well. Cook over a low heat for 2–3 minutes until the eggs are set. Spoon the yogurt on top and sprinkle with the paprika.

v

• LIGHT BITES •

Kale Soup with Garlic Croutons

SERVES 8 • PREP & COOKING TIME 1 hour

- 50 g (2 oz) butter
- 1 onion, chopped
- 2 carrots, sliced
- 500 g (1 lb) kale, tough stalks discarded
- 1.2 litres (2 pints) water
- 600 ml (1 pint) vegetable stock
- 1 tablespoon lemon juice
- 300 g (10 oz) potatoes, sliced
- pinch of grated nutmeg
- salt and pepper
- 2 kale leaves, thinly shredded, to garnish

FOR THE GARLIC CROUTONS
- 90–125 ml (3½–4 fl oz) olive oil
- 3 garlic cloves, sliced
- 6–8 slices wholemeal bread, crusts removed, cut into 1 cm (½ inch) cubes

With four times the vitamin C content of spinach, plus vitamins K and E, kale is amazing for you, particularly for boosting your immune system to ward off winter colds. It's definitely worth making the croutons to add a garlicky crunch.

- Melt the butter in a large saucepan, add the onion and cook over a medium heat for 5 minutes or until soft. Add the carrots and kale in batches, stirring constantly. Cook for 2 minutes until the kale has just wilted.

- Pour in the measured water and stock, then add the lemon juice, potatoes and nutmeg. Season with salt and pepper. Bring to the boil, then reduce the heat, cover and simmer for 30–35 minutes until all the vegetables are tender. Add a little water if the soup is too thick.

- Make the croutons while the soup is cooking. Heat the oil in a large frying pan, add the garlic and cook over a medium heat for 1 minute. Add the bread cubes and cook, turning frequently, until golden brown. Remove with a slotted spoon and drain on kitchen paper. Remove and discard the garlic. Add the shredded kale to the pan and cook, stirring constantly, until crispy.

- Reheat the soup gently. Serve in warm soup bowls, garnished with the croutons and crispy kale.

· MAINS ·

Classic Coq au Vin

SERVES 4 • PREP & COOKING TIME 2 hours

- 25 g (1 oz) plain flour
- 8 mixed chicken thigh and drumstick joints
- 2 tablespoons olive oil
- 375 g (12 oz) shallots, halved if large
- 125 g (4 oz) smoked streaky bacon
- 2 garlic cloves, finely chopped
- 4 tablespoons brandy or Cognac
- 300 ml (½ pint) cheap Burgundy red wine
- 200 ml (7 fl oz) chicken stock
- 2 teaspoons tomato purée
- fresh or dried bouquet garni
- salt and black pepper

FOR THE GARLIC CROUTONS
- 25 g (1 oz) butter
- 1 tablespoon olive oil
- 1 garlic clove, finely chopped
- ½ stick French bread, thinly sliced

This French dish of chicken braised low and slow in a glossy red wine sauce, laced with brandy and served with golden garlic croutons, is deservedly a classic. It's hearty, timeless comfort food.

- Mix the flour on a plate with a little seasoning, then use to coat the chicken joints. Heat the oil in a large shallow flameproof casserole (or frying pan and transfer chicken to a casserole dish later), add the chicken and cook over a high heat until golden on all sides. Lift out on to a plate.

- Fry the shallots and bacon until golden, then stir in the garlic and return the chicken to the casserole. Pour over the brandy or Cognac and when bubbling flame with a long taper. As soon as the flames subside, pour in the red wine and stock, then mix in the tomato purée and bouquet garni.

- Season, then cover the casserole and transfer to a preheated oven, 180°C (350°F), Gas Mark 4, and cook for 1¼ hours until tender.

- When the chicken is cooked, pour the liquid from the casserole into a saucepan and boil for 5 minutes to reduce and thicken slightly, if liked. Return the liquid to the casserole.

- Heat the butter and oil in a frying pan for the croutons, add the garlic and cook for 1 minute, then add the bread slices in a single layer. Fry on both sides until golden.

- Serve the coq au vin in shallow bowls topped with the croutons.

V

• DESSERTS •

Sticky Gingerbread

SERVES 12 • PREP & COOKING TIME 1 hour

- 225 g (7½ oz) plain flour
- 1 teaspoon bicarbonate of soda
- 2 teaspoons ground ginger
- 75 g (3 oz) slightly salted butter
- 125 g (4 oz) light muscovado sugar
- 75 g (3 oz) golden syrup
- 75 g (3 oz) black treacle
- 125 ml (4 fl oz) buttermilk
- 1 egg, beaten
- 75 g (3 oz) sultanas

FOR THE GLAZE
- 3 tablespoons ginger marmalade or jam
- 1 teaspoon water

This old-fashioned favourite is a cake loved by kids and adults alike. Dark, soft, and squidgy, the addition of treacle gives real depth of flavour. You can also serve it warm from the oven with some whipped cream or vanilla ice cream for dessert.

- Put the flour, bicarbonate of soda and ginger into a bowl.

- Put the butter, sugar, golden syrup and treacle into a saucepan and heat gently without boiling until the butter has melted. Remove from the heat and stir in the buttermilk, then beat in the egg. Add to the dry ingredients with the sultanas and beat well to mix.

- Spoon the mixture into a greased and lined 20 cm (8 inch) square cake tin or shallow baking tin, spreading the mixture into the corners. Bake in a preheated oven, 160°C (325°F), Gas Mark 3, for about 30 minutes or until risen, just firm to the touch and a skewer inserted into the centre comes out clean.

- Leave to cool in the tin (the cake might sink slightly in the centre), then transfer to a board and peel off the lining paper.

- Make the glaze. Put the marmalade or jam and measured water in a small saucepan and heat gently. Press through a sieve to remove any lumps and brush over the gingerbread, then cut into bars.

VG

• BREAKFASTS •

Nutty Homemade Muesli

SERVES 4 • PREP & COOKING TIME 25 minutes, plus cooling

- 100 g (3½ oz) shredded dried coconut
- 100 g (3½ oz) flaked almonds
- 100 g (3½ oz) blanched hazelnuts
- 100 g (3½ oz) sunflower seeds
- 250 g (8 oz) buckwheat flakes
- 250 g (8 oz) millet flakes
- 100 g (3½ oz) dried cranberries
- 100 g (3½ oz) sultanas

Full of good things and no nasties, homemade muesli makes sure you start your day the right way. You can vary the dried fruit: try dried apricots, chopped dates, goji berries or currants. Store in an airtight container for up to 1–2 weeks.

- Spread the coconut out in a thin layer on a baking sheet. Toast in a preheated oven, 150°C (300°F), Gas Mark 2, for about 20 minutes, stirring every 5 minutes to make sure it browns evenly.

- Toast the flaked almonds, hazelnuts and sunflower seeds in the same way, but be careful not to allow the seeds to burn. Leave to cool, then roughly chop the hazelnuts.

- Mix together all the ingredients in a large bowl until well combined.

V

· LIGHT BITES ·

Oatcakes

MAKES 20 • PREP & COOKING TIME 40 minutes

- 125 g (4 oz) medium oatmeal
- 75 g (3 oz) plain flour
- 4 tablespoons mixed seeds, such as poppy seeds, linseeds and sesame seeds
- ½ teaspoon celery salt or sea salt
- ½ teaspoon black pepper
- 50 g (2 oz) unsalted butter, chilled and diced
- 5 tablespoons cold water

These seeded oatcakes are the perfect vehicle for all kinds of toppings, from cheese and smoked salmon to nut butter or hummus. Stored in an airtight container, they will keep for a week.

- Put the oatmeal, flour, seeds, salt and pepper in a bowl or food processor. Add the butter and rub in with the fingertips or process until the mixture resembles breadcrumbs.

- Add the measured water and mix or blend to a firm dough, adding a little more water if the dough feels dry.

- Roll out the dough on a lightly floured surface to 2.5 mm (⅛ inch) thick. Cut out 20 rounds using a 6 cm (2½ inch) plain or fluted biscuit cutter, re-rolling the trimmings to make more. Place slightly apart on a large greased baking sheet.

- Bake in a preheated oven, 180°C (350°F), Gas Mark 4, for about 25 minutes until firm. Transfer to a wire rack to cool.

· MAINS ·

Gravadlax with Dill Sauce

SERVES 4–6 · PREP & COOKING TIME 25 minutes,
plus 2–3 days marinating

- large handful of dill
- 1 tablespoon mixed peppercorns, roughly crushed
- 2 tablespoons salt flakes
- 2 tablespoons golden caster or light muscovado sugar
- 500 g (1 lb) piece of thick salmon fillet, skinned

FOR THE DILL SAUCE
- 2 tablespoons Dijon mustard
- 4 teaspoons golden caster or light muscovado sugar
- 3 tablespoons sunflower oil
- 1–2 teaspoons white wine vinegar
- 2 tablespoons chopped dill
- black pepper

For a healthy, light meal for January, cure your own salmon, Scandinavian-style. It needs to sit in the fridge for a few days, but the results are elegant and clean-tasting. Serve with brown bread and a little salad garnish.

- Tear half the dill into pieces on to a plate. Add the peppercorns, salt and sugar and mix together. Coat both sides of the salmon in the dill mixture then transfer to a large strong plastic bag with any mixture from the plate. Seal the bag and stand in a shallow dish. Cover with a chopping board and weigh down with an unopened bag of flour, bags of sugar or cans. Marinate in the refrigerator for 2–3 days, turning twice a day.

- On the day of serving, make the sauce by mixing the mustard and sugar together in a small bowl. Gradually trickle in the oil, little by little, whisking continuously until thickened. Thin the sauce with vinegar to taste. Stir in the chopped dill and season with pepper.

- When ready to serve, lift the salmon out of the marinade, drain, put on a chopping board. Sprinkle with the remaining dill, torn into pieces. Cut into thin slices with the knife at a 45-degree angle to the fish. Arrange on serving plates with spoonfuls of the sauce.

V

• DESSERTS •

Pear & Almond Tart

SERVES 8 • PREP & COOKING TIME 1 hour 15 minutes, plus chilling

- 450 g (14½ oz) chilled ready-made sweet shortcrust pastry
- 125 g (4 oz) unsalted butter, softened
- 125 g (4 oz) caster sugar
- 125 g (4 oz) ground almonds
- 2 eggs, lightly beaten
- 1 tablespoon lemon juice
- 3 ripe pears, peeled, cored and thickly sliced
- 25 g (1 oz) flaked almonds
- sifted icing sugar, for dusting

FOR THE CHOCOLATE SAUCE
- 100 g (3½ oz) chopped plain dark chocolate
- 50 g (2 oz) diced unsalted butter
- 1 tablespoon golden syrup

Serve this with vanilla ice cream or, for an indulgent treat, with homemade chocolate sauce.

- To make the chocolate sauce, melt the chocolate, unsalted butter and golden syrup together in saucepan over a low heat. Leave to cool slightly before serving.

- Roll out the pastry on a lightly floured surface until a little larger than a 25 cm (10 inch) tart tin. Lift the pastry over a rolling pin, drape into the tin, then press over the base and sides. Trim off excess pastry with scissors so that it stands a little above the top of the tin. Prick the base with a fork and chill for 30 minutes.

- Line the tart with nonstick baking paper, add baking beans and bake in a preheated oven, 190°C (375°F), Gas Mark 5, for 15 minutes. Remove the baking paper and beans and bake for a further 5–10 minutes until the pastry is crisp and golden. Leave to cool completely. Reduce the oven temperature to 180°C (350°F), Gas Mark 4.

- Beat the butter, sugar and ground almonds together until smooth, then beat in the eggs and lemon juice.

- Arrange the pear slices over the pastry case and carefully spread over the almond mixture. Sprinkle with the flaked almonds and bake for 30 minutes until the topping is golden and firm to the touch. Remove from the oven and leave to cool.

- Dust the tart with sifted icing sugar and serve.

V

• BREAKFASTS •

Banana & Honey Flapjacks

SERVES 4 • PREP & COOKING TIME 30 minutes

- 25 g (1 oz) light muscovado sugar
- 175 g (6 oz) unsalted butter
- 1 tablespoon clear honey
- 1½ tablespoons golden syrup
- 1 large banana, mashed
- 300 g (10 oz) rolled oats
- 75 g (3 oz) dried banana chips, roughly broken

When breakfast has to be grabbed on the go, these super-easy flapjacks are ideal. They're also great with a cup of tea in the afternoon and for school lunchboxes.

- Place the sugar, butter, honey and golden syrup in a saucepan over a medium heat and heat, stirring occasionally, until the butter has melted and the sugar dissolved. Remove from the heat.

- Stir in the mashed banana and oats and mix well. Spoon half of the oat mixture into a lightly greased 22 cm (8½ inch) square cake tin, sprinkle over the banana chips and top with the remaining oat mixture. Press down and level the top.

- Bake in a preheated oven, 180°C (350°F), Gas Mark 4, for 20–22 minutes until golden.

- Remove from the oven and cut into 12 bars while still hot. Leave to cool in the tin.

• LIGHT BITES •

Pea & Lentil Soup with Crispy Cured Ham

SERVES 4 • PREP & COOKING TIME 10 minutes

- 50 g (2 oz) butter
- 3 spring onions, sliced
- 1 garlic clove, crushed
- 600 ml (1 pint) hot ham or vegetable stock
- 400 g (13 oz) can chickpeas, rinsed and drained
- 400 g (13 oz) can green lentils in water, rinsed and drained
- 200 g (7 oz) frozen peas
- 3 sage leaves, chopped (optional)
- 1 tablespoon olive oil
- 4 slices of Black Forest or Parma ham
- salt and black pepper

When it's cold outside, curled up in front of the fire with a bowl of thick, hearty soup is the place to be. Quick to prepare, using convenient canned lentils and chickpeas, this is sure to become a go-to recipe for the winter months.

- Melt the butter in a large saucepan and cook the spring onions and garlic over a medium heat for 1–2 minutes, until softened.

- Add the stock, chickpeas, lentils, peas and sage, if using. Simmer for 5–6 minutes, until the peas are tender.

- Meanwhile, heat the oil in a large frying pan and fry the ham until crispy, turning once. Drain on kitchen paper.

- Blend the soup to the desired consistency, season to taste then ladle into bowls and crumble some of the ham on top.

• MAINS •

Chilli Con Carne

SERVES 4 • PREP & COOKING TIME 1 hour

- 2 tablespoons vegetable oil
- 2 onions, chopped
- 1 red pepper, deseeded and cut into cubes
- 2 garlic cloves, crushed
- 500 g (1 lb) minced beef
- 450 ml (¾ pint) beef stock
- ½–1 teaspoon chilli powder
- 475 g (15 oz) canned red kidney beans, drained
- 400 g (13 oz) can chopped tomatoes
- 1 tablespoon tomato purée
- 1 teaspoon ground cumin
- 250 g (8 oz) long-grain white rice
- salt and black pepper

TO SERVE
- soured cream
- red chilli flakes
- Cheddar cheese, grated
- finely chopped spring onion

This is one to leave bubbling away low and slow to get the best flavour. Be generous with the toppings as they make all the difference. Great for a casual get-together, it can be made ahead and gently reheated and quantities are easily upped for a crowd.

- Heat the oil in a saucepan over a low heat. Add the onions and red pepper and gently fry, stirring now and then, for about 5 minutes until soft. Add the garlic and cook for another 1 minute until opaque.

- Increase the heat slightly and add the meat. Fry until just brown, stirring and breaking up the meat with a wooden spoon. Pour in the stock, then add the chilli powder, beans, tomatoes, tomato purée, cumin and a dash of salt and pepper.

- Bring to the boil, then cover, reduce the heat to as low as possible and simmer very gently for 50–60 minutes, stirring occasionally so that it does not stick to the bottom of the pan.

- Cook the rice, towards the end of the chilli's cooking time, in lightly salted water, according to the packet instructions, then drain.

- Pile up the rice on each of 4 serving plates, dollop on the chilli and top with the soured cream. Scatter over the chilli flakes, grated Cheddar and spring onion and serve immediately.

V

• DESSERTS •

Brioche Bread & Butter Puddings

SERVES 4 • PREP & COOKING TIME 40 minutes, plus soaking

- 8 slices of brioche
- 3 eggs, lightly beaten
- 50 g (2 oz) caster sugar
- 250 ml (8 fl oz) milk
- 250 ml (8 fl oz) double cream
- ½ teaspoon ground mixed spice
- 25 g (1 oz) butter, melted
- 1 tablespoon demerara sugar

Ideal for entertaining, you can make these ahead – they benefit from standing to soak up the cream mixture – and pop them in the oven just before you sit down to eat your main course.

- Cut the brioche slices diagonally into quarters to form triangles. Arrange, overlapping, in 4 × 250 ml (8 fl oz) baking dishes.

- Whisk the eggs, caster sugar, milk, cream and spice in a separate bowl. Pour over the brioche slices, pushing them down so that they are almost covered. Drizzle over the butter and scatter over the demerara sugar. Leave to soak for 30 minutes.

- Set the baking dishes in a large roasting tin. Pour in enough boiling water to come halfway up the sides of the dishes. Bake in a preheated oven, 180°C (350°F), Gas Mark 4, for 30 minutes until set and the top is lightly golden.

V

• BREAKFASTS •

Prune, Apple & Cinnamon Smoothie

MAKES 400 ml (14 fl oz) • PREP TIME 5 minutes, plus standing

- 65 g (2½ oz) ready-to-eat prunes
- pinch of ground cinnamon, plus extra to serve
- 350 ml (12 fl oz) apple juice
- 3 tablespoons Greek yogurt
- ice cubes

Cinnamon goes so well with the dried prunes in this smoothie which is good for digestive health and filled with essential vitamins. It's a great choice for breakfast on a busy morning.

- Roughly chop the prunes. Put the prunes and cinnamon in a large bowl, pour over the apple juice, cover and leave to stand overnight.

- Put the prunes, apple juice and yogurt in a food processor or blender and process until smooth.

- Pour the smoothie into a large glass over ice cubes, sprinkle with extra cinnamon and drink immediately.

V

• LIGHT BITES •

Dark Oxford Marmalade

MAKES 5–6 jars • PREP & COOKING TIME 2 hours 10 minutes

- 1 kg (2 lb) Seville or regular oranges (about 6)
- 1.8 litres (3 pints) water
- juice of 1 lemon
- 1.75 kg (3 lb) granulated sugar, warmed
- 250 g (8 oz) dark muscovado sugar, warmed
- 15 g (½ oz) butter (optional)

The trickiest part of making marmalade is knowing when it has reached setting point. An easy way to tell is to drop a teaspoon of marmalade on to a saucer that's been chilled in the fridge or freezer. The marmalade will quickly cool to room temperature. Push the marmalade gently with your finger – the skin will wrinkle if it's ready. If it's not, return to the heat and boil it again and re-test in a few minutes.

- Cut each orange into 6 wedges, then thinly slice. Tie the orange pips in a square of muslin. Add oranges and pips to a preserving pan, pour over the measured water and add the lemon juice. Bring slowly to the boil, then simmer gently, uncovered, for about 1½ hours until reduced by almost half.

- Add the sugar and heat gently, stirring occasionally, until dissolved. Bring to the boil, then boil rapidly until setting point is reached (10–20 minutes).

- Lift out the muslin bag, squeezing well. Skim with a draining spoon or stir in butter if needed (this will help to break up any foamy scum on the surface).

- Ladle into sterilized, warm, dry jars, filling to the very top. Cover with screwtop lids.

- Label and leave to cool.

• MAINS •

Mediterranean Fish Stew

SERVES 4–6 • PREP & COOKING TIME 1 hour 15 minutes

- a large handful of live mussels
- 800 g (1 lb 9 oz) mixed skinless white fish fillets, such as pollack, haddock, halibut, bream, gurnard or mullet
- 4 tablespoons olive oil
- 1 large onion, chopped
- 2 small fennel bulbs, trimmed and chopped
- 5 garlic cloves, crushed
- 3 pared strips of orange zest
- 2 × 400 g (13 oz) cans chopped tomatoes
- 2 teaspoons caster sugar
- 4 tablespoons sun-dried tomato paste
- 500 ml (17 fl oz) fish stock
- 1 teaspoon saffron threads
- 250 g (9 oz) cleaned squid tubes, cut into rings
- salt and black pepper

It might be January but you can enjoy the tastes of a Mediterranean summer in one glorious bowlful here. If you like, serve with garlic toasts: drizzle olive oil over slices of ciabatta and grill on both sides until golden, then rub with a clove of garlic while still hot.

- Scrub the mussels. Scrape off any barnacles and pull away any beards. Discard those that are damaged or open and do not close when tapped firmly. Check over the fish for any stray bones and cut into chunky pieces. Season with salt and pepper.

- Heat the oil in a large flameproof casserole and fry the onion for 5 minutes. Add the fennel and fry, stirring, for 10 minutes. Add the garlic and orange zest and fry for 2 minutes. Add the tomatoes, sugar, tomato paste and fish stock. Crumble in the saffron and bring the stew to a gentle simmer. Cook gently, uncovered, for 15 minutes.

- Lower the thickest, chunkiest pieces of fish into the stew. Reduce the heat to its lowest setting and cook for 5 minutes. Add the thin pieces of fish and the squid to the stew. Scatter the mussels on top and cover with a lid or foil. Cook for a further 5 minutes or until the mussel shells have opened. Ladle into large bowls, discarding any mussel shells that remain closed.

V

• BREAKFASTS •

Quinoa Porridge with Raspberries

SERVES 2 • PREP & COOKING TIME 30 minutes

- 600 ml (1 pint) milk
- 100 g (3½ oz) quinoa
- 2 tablespoons caster sugar
- ½ teaspoon ground cinnamon
- 125 g (4 oz) fresh raspberries
- 2 tablespoons mixed seeds, such as sunflower, linseed, pumpkin and hemp
- 2 tablespoons honey

Super-charge your morning with a simple recipe that's absolutely packed with goodness – protein, fibre, vitamins and healthy fats all combine in a sustaining breakfast bowl. For a vegan version, use almond milk and replace the honey with maple syrup.

- Bring the milk to the boil in a small saucepan. Add the quinoa and return to the boil. Reduce the heat to low, cover and simmer for about 15 minutes until three-quarters of the milk has been absorbed.

- Stir the sugar and cinnamon into the pan, re-cover and cook for 8–10 minutes or until almost all the milk has been absorbed and the quinoa is tender.

- Spoon the porridge into 2 bowls, then top with the raspberries, sprinkle over the seeds and drizzle with the honey. Serve immediately.

V

· DESSERTS ·

Cranachan

SERVES 4 • PREP & COOKING TIME 10 minutes

- 50 g (2 oz) medium oatmeal
- 2 tablespoons whisky
- 250 ml (8 fl oz) double cream
- 250 g (8 oz) raspberries
- 3 tablespoons honey

Every 25th January Scotland celebrates poet Robert Burns. So dust off your tartan and whip up this traditional Scottish dessert, a simple and delicious concoction of oats, fresh raspberries, cream and – vital, this one – whisky.

- Place the oatmeal in a nonstick frying pan over a medium heat and dry-fry for 2–3 minutes, stirring continuously, until toasted. Transfer to a plate to cool.

- Meanwhile, whip the whisky and cream with a hand-held electric whisk in a bowl until it forms soft peaks. Place a handful of the raspberries in a separate bowl and crush with a fork.

- Stir the oatmeal, honey, crushed raspberries and remaining raspberries into the whisky cream. Spoon into 4 glasses and serve immediately.

• LIGHT BITES •

Butter Bean & Anchovy Pâté

SERVES 2–3 • PREP TIME 8 minutes

- 425 g (14 oz) can butter beans, drained and rinsed
- 50 g (2 oz) can anchovy fillets in oil, drained
- 2 spring onions, finely chopped
- 2 tablespoons lemon juice
- 1 tablespoon olive oil
- 4 tablespoons chopped coriander
- black pepper

Whip up this pâté in under 10 minutes to serve as a light lunch with some crisp vegetable crudités, or serve as a starter with some toasted **Sunflower Seed & Rye Bread** from page 75, or with the **Oatcakes** on page 29.

- Place all the ingredients, except the coriander, in a food processor and blend until well mixed but still rough in texture. Alternatively, mash the beans with a fork, finely chop the anchovies and mix the ingredients together by hand.
- Stir in the coriander and season well with pepper.

• MAINS •

Salmon with Tamarind Sauce & Pak Choi

SERVES 4 • PREP & COOKING TIME 40 minutes

- vegetable oil, for oiling
- 450 ml (¾ pint) boiling hot water
- 4 chunky salmon steaks, about 200 g (7 oz) each
- 1 tablespoon tamarind paste blended with 175 ml (6 fl oz) cold water
- 2–3 tablespoons light soy sauce
- 15 g (½ oz) fresh root ginger, peeled and grated
- 2 teaspoons caster sugar
- 2 garlic cloves, crushed
- 1 mild green chilli, thinly sliced
- 1 teaspoon cornflour, mixed into a paste with 1 tablespoon cold water
- 250 g (8 oz) pak choi
- 8 spring onions, halved lengthways
- 15 g (½ oz) coriander leaves, chopped

Celebrate Chinese New Year with this deliciously healthy fish dish. Certain dishes are eaten at Chinese New Year for their symbolic meaning and fish symbolizes increased prosperity.

- Oil a roasting rack or wire rack and place over a roasting tin. Pour the measured hot water into the tin. Lay the salmon steaks on the rack, cover tightly with foil and cook in a preheated oven, 180°C (350°F), Gas Mark 4, for 15 minutes or until the fish is almost cooked through.

- Meanwhile, place the tamarind paste mix in a small saucepan. Stir in the soy sauce, ginger, sugar, garlic and chilli and heat through gently for 5 minutes.

- Add the cornflour paste to the tamarind mixture and heat gently, stirring constantly, for about 1–2 minutes until thickened.

- Quarter the pak choi lengthways into wedges and arrange the pieces around the salmon on the rack with the spring onions. Re-cover and return to the oven for a further 8–10 minutes or until the vegetables have wilted.

- Stir the coriander into the sauce. Transfer the fish and greens to serving plates, pour over the sauce and serve.

VG

• BREAKFASTS •

Gingered Pear Juice

MAKES about 300 ml (½ pint) • PREP TIME 5 minutes

- 2 cm (¾ inch) piece fresh root ginger
- 5 pears, about 750 g (1½ lb) in total
- large pinch of ground cinnamon
- ice cubes

Put a zip in your step with this sweet pear juice that has a kick of spice from the ginger. And it's good for you too – the pear will provide fibre and vitamins, while ginger is loaded with antioxidants.

- Peel the ginger. Add to a juicer with the pears and juice. Stir in the cinnamon.

- Pour the juice into a glass over ice and serve immediately.

· LIGHT BITES ·

Salt Cod Croquettes

SERVES 4 • PREP & COOKING TIME 1 hour, plus soaking

- 250 g (8 oz) piece of salt cod
- 400 g (13 oz) potatoes, peeled and quartered
- 1 egg yolk
- handful of flat-leaf parsley, chopped
- 2 tablespoons finely grated Parmesan
- 2 garlic cloves, crushed
- generous squeeze of lemon juice
- 100 g (3½ oz) dried breadcrumbs
- olive oil, for oiling and drizzling
- salt and black pepper

These crispy and fluffy bite-sized snacks are the perfect finger food. If feeding a crowd, be sure to make lots as they're very moreish. Great served with lemon wedges for squeezing over, plus some mayo for dipping.

- Soak the salt cod in cold water in the refrigerator for 24–48 hours, depending on its thickness, changing the water at least twice. Drain, then place the fish in a saucepan and cover with fresh cold water. Heat just to boiling point, then remove the pan from the heat and leave to stand for 15 minutes. Lift the fish out, reserving the cooking water. Flake the fish, removing the skin, and set aside.

- Bring the salt cod cooking liquid to the boil, add the potatoes and cook for 15 minutes until tender. Drain well, then return to the pan and mash until smooth.

- Stir the salt cod, egg yolk, parsley, Parmesan and garlic into the mashed potato and add a generous squeeze of lemon juice. Season well. Using your hands, form the mixture into small egg shapes.

- Place the breadcrumbs on a plate. Roll each ball in the breadcrumbs until well coated. Place on an oiled baking sheet and drizzle over more oil. Place in a preheated oven, 200°C (400°F), Gas Mark 6, for 15–20 minutes until golden, crisp and cooked through.

VG

• MAINS •

Carrot & Apple Nut Roast Parcels

SERVES 4 • PREP & COOKING TIME 1 hour

- 3 tablespoons rapeseed oil
- 1 onion, finely chopped
- ½ red pepper, finely chopped
- 1 celery stick, finely chopped
- 1 carrot, peeled and coarsely grated
- 75 g (3 oz) chestnut mushrooms, trimmed and finely chopped
- 1 green apple, cored and grated
- 1 teaspoon yeast extract
- 50 g (2 oz) fresh white breadcrumbs
- 75 g (3 oz) mixed nuts, such as pistachios and blanched almonds
- cooked chestnuts, finely chopped
- 2 tablespoons pine nuts
- 2 tablespoons chopped flat-leaf parsley
- 1 tablespoon chopped rosemary
- 1 tablespoon wholemeal plain flour
- 8 sheets of filo pastry

Colourful vegetables, sharp apple, crunchy nuts and fragrant herbs wrapped up in layers of crisp filo pastry – this is a vegan delight that will win over even the meat eaters! Serve with green beans and roasted cherry tomatoes.

- Heat 1 tablespoon of the oil in a frying pan, add the onion, red pepper and celery and cook over a gentle heat for 5 minutes until softened. Add the carrot and mushrooms and cook for a further 5 minutes until all the vegetables are tender.

- Remove the pan from the heat and stir in the grated apple, yeast extract, breadcrumbs, nuts, chestnuts, pine nuts, parsley, rosemary and flour. Season with salt and pepper and mix together.

- Brush one sheet of filo pastry with some of the remaining oil, then place a second on top. Spoon one quarter of the nut mixture on to one end of the filo pastry and roll up, tucking in the ends as you roll to encase the filling. Put seam side down on a baking sheet. Repeat with the remaining pastry and filling to make 4 rolls. Brush the tops with the rest of the oil.

- Bake the parcels in a preheated oven, 190°C (375°F), Gas Mark 5, for 20 minutes until golden and crisp.

• MAINS •

Chicken Puff Pie

SERVES 4 • PREP & COOKING TIME 2 hours

- 8 chicken thighs
- 300 ml (½ pint) dry cider
- 300 ml (½ pint) chicken stock
- 2 small leeks, sliced
- 50 g (2 oz) butter
- 50 g (2 oz) plain flour
- 1 tablespoon chopped tarragon
- 2 tablespoons chopped parsley
- 500 g (1 lb) puff pastry
- flour, for dusting
- 1 egg, beaten, to glaze
- salt and black pepper

Soft leeks and chicken in a cider-laced sauce, topped with a golden puff pastry lid. This is just what you need on a cold night, with some creamy mashed potatoes and a glass of something warming.

- Pack the chicken thighs into a saucepan, pour over the cider and stock, then season. Cover and simmer for 45 minutes.

- Lift the chicken on to a plate, and simmer the leeks in the stock for 4–5 minutes. Strain the leeks, reserving the stock in a measuring jug. Make up the stock to 600 ml (1 pint) with water, if needed.

- Wash and dry the pan, then melt the butter in it. Stir in the flour, then gradually whisk in the stock and bring to the boil, stirring until thickened. Mix in the herbs and season.

- Dice the chicken, discarding the skin and bones. Put into a 1.2 litre (2 pint) pie dish with the leeks. Pour over the sauce.

- Roll out the pastry on a floured surface until a little larger than the top of the pie dish. Cut 4 strips about 1 cm (½ inch) wide and stick along the rim with a little egg. Brush the top of the strip with egg, then press the pastry lid in place. Trim off the excess and crimp the edge. Cut leaves from the excess and add, if you like.

- Glaze the pastry lid and bake in a preheated oven, 200°C (400°F), Gas Mark 6, for 30 minutes until golden.

• DRINKS •

Hot Chocolate

SERVES 4 • PREP & COOKING TIME 15 minutes

- 100 g (3½ oz) good-quality plain dark chocolate, broken into small pieces
- 25 g (1 oz) caster sugar
- 750 ml (1¼ pints) milk
- a few drops of vanilla extract
- pinch of ground cinnamon
- 3 tablespoons Kahlua or other coffee liqueur (optional)
- mini marshmallows, to serve

A hug in a mug on a cold day and heaven for chocolate lovers, this velvety hot chocolate includes an optional dash of liqueur and is finished off with mini marshmallows.

- Put the chocolate and sugar in a heavy-based saucepan. Pour in the milk, then add the vanilla extract and cinnamon.

- Cover and gently heat, whisking once or twice, until the chocolate has melted.

- Continue heating until the mixture is steaming hot, but do not allow to boil. Stir in the Kahlua or other coffee liqueur, if using.

- Ladle the hot chocolate into 4 large cups or mugs and top with a few mini marshmallows. Serve immediately while steaming hot.

February

GOOD TO EAT THIS MONTH

beetroot * broccoli * Brussels sprouts * cabbage
* carrots * cauliflower * celeriac * kale * leeks *
mushrooms * onions * parsnips * potatoes * spring
onions * sweet potatoes * apples *blood oranges *
lemons * oranges * pears * rhubarb * rosemary * sage

DATES TO LOOK FORWARD TO THIS MONTH

Superbowl
Valentine's Day

It's the shortest month of the year. It's still dark and sometimes dreary but we're into late winter now and get a boost from the gradual, but noticeable, lengthening of the days. And the lovely sight of delicate snowdrops gives a welcome sign that spring is on the way.

This month's recipes include warming soups, curries, stews and puddings, including the **Rhubarb & Ginger Slump** (page 53), made with the forced rhubarb that is in the shops and markets now.

Nothing says 'I love you' like a home-baked cake, so this 14th February give the **Red Velvet Cupcakes** on page 63 instead of roses. And if you're watching the Superbowl, the **Nachos with Chipotle Sauce** on page 58 are sure to score as a viewing snack.

Citrus from sunnier climes is excellent this time of year and the bright colours of oranges, limes and lemons brighten up our fruit bowls while providing cold-defying vitamin C. The blood orange season runs from December to May but they are most plentiful in the UK in January and February. Try the **Blood Orange Sorbet** on page 71 – the glorious sun-going-down colour of it will remind you that summer is coming.

The unsung hero of so many dishes, spring onions are in season now and get their moment in the spotlight in the unusual **Watercress Pesto** on page 118.

V

• BREAKFASTS •

Moroccan Baked Eggs

SERVES 2 • PREP & COOKING TIME 45 minutes

- ½ tablespoon olive oil
- ½ onion, chopped
- 1 garlic clove, sliced
- ½ teaspoon ras el hanout
- pinch of ground cinnamon
- ½ teaspoon ground coriander
- 400 g (13 oz) cherry tomatoes
- 2 tablespoons chopped coriander
- 2 eggs
- salt and black pepper

Ease yourself into the weekend with this lovely recipe. It features ras el hanout, a spice blend of fragrant spices popular in North African cuisine. Add a little finely chopped chilli if you'd like extra heat.

- Heat the oil in a frying pan, add the onion and garlic and cook for 6–7 minutes until softened and lightly golden. Stir in the spices and cook, stirring, for a further 1 minute.

- Add the tomatoes and season well with salt and pepper, then simmer gently for 8–10 minutes.

- Scatter over 1 tablespoon of the coriander, then divide the tomato mixture between 2 individual ovenproof dishes. Break an egg into each dish.

- Bake in a preheated oven, 220°C (425°F), Gas Mark 7, for 8–10 minutes until the egg whites are set but the yolks are still slightly runny. Cook for a further 2–3 minutes if you prefer the eggs to be cooked through. Serve scattered with the remaining coriander.

V

· LIGHT BITES ·

Speedy Minestrone

SERVES 4 • PREP & COOKING TIME 30 minutes

- 2 tablespoons olive oil
- 1 onion, chopped
- 1 carrot, peeled and chopped
- 1 celery stick, chopped
- 1 teaspoon tomato purée
- 2 garlic cloves, finely chopped
- 400 g (13 oz) can chopped tomatoes
- 750 ml (1¼ pints) hot chicken or vegetable stock
- 2 thyme sprigs, leaves stripped
- 125 g (4 oz) ditalini pasta
- 400 g (13 oz) can cannellini beans, rinsed and drained
- ½ head of Savoy cabbage, shredded
- salt and black pepper
- grated Parmesan cheese or vegetarian hard cheese, to serve*

This hearty winter warmer is great for using up whatever is lurking in the fridge. You can replace the cabbage with spring greens or kale. It tastes even better the next day and freezes well so you could double the quantities and make a big batch.

- Heat the oil in a large saucepan, add the onion, carrot and celery and cook over a low heat for 10 minutes until really soft.

- Stir in the tomato purée and garlic, then add the tomatoes, stock and thyme and simmer for 10 minutes.

- Add the pasta and beans to the soup and cook for a further 10 minutes or until the pasta is cooked through. Add the cabbage 5 minutes before the end of the cooking time and cook until tender. Season well.

- Ladle into bowls and serve scattered with the Parmesan.

*For guidance on vegetarian cheeses, see page 5.

• MAINS •

Hoisin Duck Pancakes

SERVES 4 • PREP & COOKING TIME 30 minutes

- 4 boneless duck breasts, about 200 g (7 oz) each, skinned
- 2 teaspoons ground white pepper
- 2 garlic cloves, crushed
- 1 teaspoon peeled and grated fresh root ginger
- ½ teaspoon Chinese five-spice powder
- 2 teaspoons sesame oil
- 1 tablespoon groundnut oil
- 100 ml (3½ fl oz) hoisin sauce, plus extra for dipping
- 2 tablespoons sweet chilli sauce
- 8 spring onions, shredded
- ½ cucumber, halved, deseeded and cut into thin matchsticks
- 12 Chinese rice pancakes

Great for a build-it-yourself dinner. Place the duck, pancakes and spring onion mix on the table, give each diner a little bowl of hoisin sauce for dipping and let everyone dig in and construct their own.

- Cut the duck breasts into thin strips and place in a bowl.

- Mix together the white pepper, garlic, ginger, five-spice powder and sesame oil in a small bowl.

- Add the groundnut oil to a large nonstick wok or frying pan and heat over a high heat. Add the duck and spices and stir-fry for about 3–4 minutes until the duck is just cooked through but still slightly pink in the centre, then add the hoisin sauce and sweet chilli sauce and cook, stirring, for 1–2 minutes until the duck is well coated with the sauce.

- Transfer the duck to a serving dish. Arrange the spring onions and cucumber in a bowl.

- Warm the pancakes according to the packet instructions, then serve for each person to top with some of the duck, spring onions and cucumber, roll up and eat straight away with extra hoisin sauce to dip into.

V

· DESSERTS ·

Rhubarb & Ginger Slump

SERVES 4–6 • PREP & COOKING TIME 45 minutes

- 750g (1½ lb) rhubarb, trimmed and cut into chunks
- 1 tablespoon self-raising flour
- 50 g (2 oz) granulated sugar
- 2 pieces of stem ginger in syrup, drained and chopped, plus 2 tablespoons syrup from the jar

FOR THE TOPPING
- 100 g (3½ oz) self-raising flour
- 75 g (3 oz) butter, softened
- 75 g (3 oz) granulated sugar
- 4 tablespoons milk
- 1 egg, beaten

Tart rhubarb and warm stem ginger bubble beneath a golden cakey topping to make this winter warmer that everyone will love. If you happen to have an orange in the fruit bowl, you could add the finely grated zest to the rhubarb and ginger mixture.

- Place the rhubarb, flour, sugar and ginger in a shallow ovenproof dish and toss together. Cover with foil and place in a preheated oven, 190°C (375°F), Gas Mark 5, for 15 minutes.

- Meanwhile, place the ingredients for the topping in a bowl and beat until smooth. Take the rhubarb from the oven, remove the foil and spoon over the topping.

- Return to the oven for 25 minutes or until the topping is puffy, golden and cooked through.

VG

· BREAKFASTS ·

Apricot & Prune Muesli

SERVES 4 • PREP TIME 10 minutes, plus cooling

- 75 g (3 oz) whole hazelnuts
- 75 g (3 oz) rolled oats
- 75 g (3 oz) bran-based breakfast cereal
- 2 tablespoons sunflower or mixed seeds (optional)
- 75 g (3 oz) ready-to-eat dried apricots, sliced
- 50 g (3 oz) ready-to-eat dried prunes, chopped

This recipe serves 4 but it will keep for up to a week in an airtight container so you could double up the quantities and make a big batch. To ring the changes, replace the bran cereal with puffed wheat.

- Place the hazelnuts in a small, dry frying pan and heat gently for 4–5 minutes, shaking the pan occasionally, until lightly toasted. Tip into the bowl of a mortar, crush lightly with a pestle and set aside to cool.

- Meanwhile, combine the oats, bran cereal, seeds and dried fruits. Add the toasted hazelnuts and mix well.

V

• LIGHT BITES •

Broccoli & Almond Soup

SERVES 6 • PREP & COOKING TIME 30 minutes

- 25 g (1 oz) butter
- 1 onion, roughly chopped
- 500 g (1 lb) broccoli, cut into florets, stems sliced
- 40 g (1½ oz) ground almonds
- 900 ml (1½ pints) vegetable or chicken stock
- 300 ml (½ pint) milk
- salt and black pepper

TO GARNISH
- 15 g (½ oz) butter
- 3 tablespoons flaked almonds
- 6 tablespoons natural yogurt

Tasty, filling and full of good-for-you fibre, protein, vitamins and minerals, this soup can be on the table in 30 minutes – ideal for those winter nights when you get home tired and hungry. Delicious with a thick slice of the **Mixed Seed Soda Bread** on page 256.

- Heat the butter in a saucepan, add the onion and fry gently for 5 minutes until just beginning to soften. Stir in the broccoli until coated in the butter then add the ground almonds, stock and a little salt and pepper.

- Bring to the boil then cover and simmer for 10 minutes until the broccoli is just tender and still bright green. Leave to cool slightly, then purée in batches in a blender or food processor until finely speckled with green.

- Pour the purée back into the saucepan and stir in the milk. Reheat then taste and adjust the seasoning if needed.

- Heat the 15 g (½ oz) butter in a frying pan, add the almonds and fry for a few minutes, stirring until golden.

- Ladle the soup into bowls, drizzle a spoonful of yogurt over each bowl, then sprinkle with the almonds.

v

• MAINS •

Sri Lankan Tomato & Egg Curry

SERVES 4 • PREP & COOKING TIME 30 minutes

- 1 tablespoon groundnut oil
- 1 onion, finely chopped
- 10 curry leaves
- 3 garlic cloves, finely chopped
- 2 teaspoons peeled and finely grated fresh root ginger
- 2 fresh green chillies, finely chopped
- 3 tablespoons medium curry powder
- 400 g (13 oz) can chopped tomatoes
- 8–12 eggs, hard-boiled and peeled
- 6 tablespoons finely chopped coriander leaves
- salt

This gently spiced curry is a handy one to have up your sleeve as it uses favourite standbys, a can of chopped tomatoes and eggs. Serve with plain rice, chapatis or naan breads.

- Heat the oil in a large nonstick frying pan and add the onion, curry leaves, garlic, ginger and chillies. Stir-fry over a medium heat for 6–8 minutes.

- Sprinkle over the curry powder and stir-fry for 1–2 minutes until fragrant. Stir in the chopped tomatoes, season to taste and stir to mix well.

- Add the eggs and bring to the boil. Reduce the heat and simmer gently for 4–5 minutes. Remove from the heat and stir in the coriander. Halve the eggs and serve immediately.

VG

• DESSERTS •

Carrot & Apple Muffins

MAKES 12 • PREP & COOKING TIME 40 minutes

- 300 g (10 oz) self-raising flour
- 1½ teaspoons bicarbonate of soda
- ½ teaspoon salt
- 1½ teaspoons ground cinnamon
- 1 teaspoon ground ginger
- 75 g (3 oz) raisins
- 150 g (5 oz) light muscovado sugar
- 1 tablespoon poppy seeds
- 275 ml (9 fl oz) almond milk
- 100 ml (3½ fl oz) olive oil, plus extra for oiling (optional)
- 1 tablespoon cider vinegar
- 1 dessert apple, cored and coarsely grated
- 1 carrot, peeled and coarsely grated

Start your day with a freshly baked muffin. These gently spiced muffins have grated apple and carrot which makes them lovely and moist. Store the muffins for up to 2–3 days in an airtight container, or freeze.

- Line 12 holes of a muffin tin with paper cases or lightly oil and line the bases with discs of baking parchment.

- Sift the flour, bicarbonate of soda, salt, cinnamon and ginger together into a bowl. Stir in the raisins, sugar and poppy seeds.

- Mix the almond milk, oil and vinegar together in a jug. Add to the dry ingredients and lightly stir together until just mixed. Quickly fold in the apple and carrot, then divide the mixture between the paper cases or the holes of the muffin tin.

- Bake straight away in a preheated oven, 190°C (375°F), Gas Mark 5, for 15–20 minutes until well risen and golden.

- Transfer to a wire rack to cool.

V

· LIGHT BITES ·

Nachos with Chipotle Sauce

SERVES 4 • PREP & COOKING TIME 30 minutes, plus cooling

- 200 g (7 oz) packet tortilla chips
- 200 g (7 oz) canned refried beans
- 200 g (7 oz) canned black beans, rinsed and drained
- 1 pickled jalapeño chilli, drained and sliced
- 150 g (5 oz) Cheddar cheese, grated

FOR THE
CHIPOTLE SAUCE
- 1 onion
- 3 tomatoes
- 2 garlic cloves, peeled and left whole
- 1 teaspoon chipotle paste
- salt and black pepper

TO SERVE
- 1 avocado, stoned, peeled and chopped
- handful of cherry tomatoes, halved
- handful of coriander leaves
- 4 tablespoons soured cream

For some, Super Bowl Sunday is the party of the year, so celebrate with these nachos that will be sure to make you a winner among your friends. Everybody loves them and it's easy to scale up the quantities to feed a crowd.

- Make the chipotle sauce. Heat a large, dry nonstick frying pan, add the onion and cook for 5 minutes, turning frequently. Add the tomatoes and cook for a further 5 minutes, then add the garlic and continue to cook for 3 minutes, or until the ingredients are softened and charred. Transfer to a food processor or blender and whizz to a coarse paste. Leave to cool, then add the chipotle paste and season to taste. Set aside.

- Place a layer of tortilla chips in a heatproof serving dish. Mix together the refried and black beans in a bowl, then spoon some of the beans over the chips and scatter with a layer of the chilli and cheese. Repeat the layers, finishing with a heavy layer of the cheese.

- Bake in a preheated oven, 200°C (400°F), Gas Mark 6, for 7 minutes, or until the cheese has melted.

- Scatter over the avocado, tomatoes and coriander, drizzle with the chipotle sauce and soured cream and serve.

VG

• BREAKFASTS •

Blackberry, Apple & Celeriac Juice

MAKES 200 ml (⅓ pint) • PREP TIME 5 minutes

- 100 g (3½ oz) celeriac
- 50 g (2 oz) apple
- 100 g (3½ oz) frozen blackberries, plus extra to decorate
- 2–3 ice cubes

Tart apple and juicy blackberries combine with the earthiness of celeriac in this richly purple-hued juice. This easy recipe uses frozen blackberries so you can make it year-round.

- Peel the celeriac and cut the flesh into cubes. Roughly chop the apple and add it with the celeriac to a juicer and juice.

- Transfer the juice to a food processor or blender, add the blackberries and a couple of ice cubes and process briefly.

- Pour the juice into a glass, decorate with extra blackberries and serve immediately.

v

· LIGHT BITES ·

Spring Onion Welsh Rarebit

SERVES 2 • PREP & COOKING TIME 10 minutes

- 15 g (½ oz) butter
- 4 spring onions, sliced
- 100 g (4 oz) Cheddar cheese, grated
- 1 egg yolk
- 1–2 tablespoons brown ale or milk
- ½ teaspoon English mustard
- 2 slices of granary bread, lightly toasted

Cheese on toast with attitude, this can be whipped up in just 10 minutes. For a tangy alternative, crumbly blue cheese, such as Stilton, could be used in place of the Cheddar cheese.

- Heat the butter in a small saucepan and fry the spring onions for 2–3 minutes until softened. Leave to cool, then mix with the cheese and egg yolk, adding enough milk or ale to make a spreadable mixture. Stir in the mustard.

- Spread the mixture over the toast and cook under a preheated hot grill for about 2 minutes until golden and bubbling.

• MAINS •

Five-Spice Salmon

SERVES 4 • PREP & COOKING TIME 20 minutes

- 2 teaspoons crushed pepper
- 2 teaspoons Chinese five-spice powder
- 1 teaspoon salt
- large pinch of cayenne pepper
- 4 salmon fillets, about 175 g (6 oz) each, skinned
- 3 tablespoons sunflower oil
- 500 g (1 lb) choi sum or pak choi, sliced
- 3 garlic cloves, sliced
- 3 tablespoons Chinese rice wine or dry sherry
- 75 ml (3 fl oz) vegetable stock
- 2 tablespoons light soy sauce
- 1 teaspoon sesame oil

This is one for when you need dinner on the table ASAP. Served with jasmine rice, it's a family-friendly recipe but fancy enough to make for guests too.

- Combine the pepper, five-spice powder, salt and cayenne pepper in a small bowl.

- Brush the salmon with a little of the oil and dust with the spice coating. Cook the fish in a preheated frying pan for 4 minutes, then turn and cook for a further 2–3 minutes until the fish is just cooked through. Transfer to a plate, cover with foil and leave to rest for 5 minutes.

- Meanwhile, heat the remaining oil in a wok, add the choi sum or pak choi and stir-fry for 2 minutes, then add the garlic and stir-fry for a further 1 minute. Add the rice wine or sherry, stock, soy sauce and sesame oil and cook for a further 2 minutes until the greens are tender.

- Serve the salmon and greens immediately.

V

• DESSERTS •

Orange & Caraway Seed Cake

SERVES 10 • PREP & COOKING TIME 1 hour 30 minutes

- 175 g (6 oz) butter, softened
- 175 g (6 oz) caster sugar
- 3 eggs, beaten
- 250 g (8 oz) self-raising flour
- 1 teaspoon baking powder
- 1½ teaspoons caraway seeds, roughly crushed
- grated zest of 1 orange plus 5–6 tablespoons orange juice
- 25 g (1 oz) sugar lumps, roughly crushed

Delicately flavoured with aromatic caraway seeds and orange, this simple cake is sure to become a family favourite, sliced thinly and enjoyed with a cup of tea. It will keep well in an airtight tin for up to a week.

- Beat the butter and sugar together in a mixing bowl until pale and creamy. Gradually mix in alternate spoonfuls of beaten egg and flour until all has been added and the mixture is smooth. Stir in the baking powder, caraway seeds, orange zest and juice to make a soft dropping consistency.

- Spoon the mixture into a greased 1 kg (2 lb) loaf tin, its base and 2 long sides also lined with oiled greaseproof paper. Spread the surface level and sprinkle over the crushed sugar lumps. Bake in a preheated oven, 160°C (325°F), Gas Mark 3, for 1 hour–1 hour 10 minutes until well risen, the top is cracked and golden and a skewer inserted into the centre comes out clean.

- Leave to cool in the tin for 10 minutes then loosen the edges and lift out of the tin using the lining paper. Transfer to a wire rack, peel off the lining paper and leave to cool.

v

• DESSERTS •

Red Velvet Cupcakes

MAKES 12 • PREP & COOKING TIME 45 minutes, plus cooling

- 150 g (5 oz) self-raising flour
- 2 tablespoons cocoa powder
- ½ teaspoon bicarbonate of soda
- 100 ml (3½ fl oz) buttermilk
- 1 teaspoon vinegar
- 50 g (2 oz) lightly salted butter, softened
- 100 g (3½ oz) caster sugar
- 1 egg
- 50 g (2 oz) raw beetroot, peeled and finely grated

FOR THE FROSTING
- 200 g (7 oz) full-fat cream cheese
- 2 teaspoons vanilla extract
- 300 g (10 oz) icing sugar
- 12 fresh cherries, to decorate

Say 'I love you' with a cupcake. Decorate with a swirl of creamy frosting and a simple fresh cherry, as here, or get creative with heart-shaped sparkles, edible glitter or rice paper roses. Look in the bakery aisle or online for inspiration.

- Line a 12-hole cupcake tin with paper cupcake cases. Combine the flour, cocoa powder and bicarbonate of soda in a bowl. Mix together the buttermilk and vinegar in a jug.

- Beat together the butter and caster sugar in a separate bowl until pale and creamy, then beat in the egg and beetroot.

- Sift half the flour mixture into the bowl and stir in gently with a large metal spoon. Stir in half the buttermilk mixture. Sift and stir in the remaining flour mixture, then the remaining liquid. Divide the cupcake mixture between the paper cases.

- Bake in a preheated oven, 180°C (350°F), Gas Mark 4, for 20–25 minutes or until risen and just firm to the touch. Transfer to a wire rack to cool.

- Beat the cream cheese with a wooden spoon in a bowl until softened. Beat in the vanilla extract and icing sugar until smooth. Swirl over the tops of the cakes and decorate each with a cherry.

V

• BREAKFASTS •

Parmesan French Toast with Tapenade Tomatoes

SERVES 6 • PREP & COOKING TIME 25 minutes

- 6 plum tomatoes
- 4 tablespoons ready-made olive tapenade
- extra virgin olive oil, for drizzling
- 150 ml (¼ pint) milk
- 3 eggs
- 3 tablespoons freshly grated Parmesan or vegetarian hard cheese*
- 50 g (2 oz) butter
- 6 slices of white bread
- handful of baby spinach leaves
- a few basil leaves, to serve
- salt and black pepper

A savoury twist on French toast and perfect for a weekend brunch, this is also great as a quick and comforting supper. It's delicious with a poached egg in place of the tomatoes too.

- Cut the tomatoes in half and scoop out the seeds. Arrange cut-side up in a baking dish. Spoon a little of the tapenade on to each tomato and drizzle over some oil. Cook under a preheated hot grill for 2–3 minutes until soft and golden. Keep warm.

- Beat the milk, eggs, Parmesan and a little salt and pepper together in a bowl. Pour into a shallow dish.

- Melt half the butter in a large frying pan. Dip 3 bread slices into the egg mixture, add to the pan and fry over a medium heat for 3–4 minutes, turning once, until golden on both sides. Remove and keep warm. Repeat with the remaining bread slices and egg mixture.

- Serve the French toast topped with the grilled tomatoes, baby spinach leaves and a few basil leaves.

*For guidance on vegetarian cheeses, see page 5.

• LIGHT BITES •

Mini Harissa Sausage Rolls

MAKES 30 • PREP & COOKING TIME 50 minutes

- 500 g (1 lb) good-quality pork sausagemeat
- 50 g (2 oz) walnut pieces, roughly chopped
- 5 cm (2 inch) fresh root ginger, peeled and coarsely grated
- 1 teaspoon black peppercorns, roughly crushed
- 500 g (1 lb) ready-made puff pastry, defrosted if frozen
- beaten egg, to glaze
- 3 teaspoons harissa paste
- salt

Who doesn't love a sausage roll? This recipe takes an old favourite and gives it some zing by adding fiery harissa paste and fresh ginger. They'll be gone in minutes!

- Add the sausagemeat, walnuts and ginger to a large bowl, sprinkle over the pepper and a little salt, then mix together with a wooden spoon or your hands.

- Roll the pastry out thinly on a lightly floured surface and trim to a 30 cm (12 inch) square. Cut the square into 3 strips, 10 cm (4 inches) wide, then brush lightly with beaten egg. Spread 1 teaspoon of harissa in a band down the centre of each pastry strip, then top each strip with one-third of the sausagemeat mixture, spooning into a narrow band.

- Fold the pastry over the filling and press the edges together well with the flattened tip of a small sharp knife. Trim the edge to neaten if needed, then slash the top of the strips.

- Brush the sausage rolls with beaten egg, then cut each strip into 10 pieces and arrange slightly spaced apart on 2 lightly oiled baking sheets. Cook in a preheated oven, 200°C (400°F), Gas Mark 6, for about 20 minutes until golden and the pastry is well risen. Transfer to a wire rack then leave to cool for 20 minutes. Serve warm or cold.

• MAINS •

Mediterranean Lamb Stew with Spring Onion Pesto

SERVES 4 • PREP & COOKING TIME 45 minutes

- 2 tablespoons olive oil
- 500 g (1 lb) lean lamb fillet, very thinly sliced
- 1 red onion, chopped
- 1 large aubergine, about 375 g (12 oz), cut into small chunks
- 2 garlic cloves, crushed
- 400 g (13 oz) can chopped tomatoes
- 2 tablespoons sun-dried tomato paste
- 1 teaspoon light muscovado sugar
- 150 ml (¼ pint) vegetable stock
- salt and black pepper

FOR THE SPRING ONION PESTO
- ½ bunch of spring onions, trimmed and roughly chopped
- 50 g (2 oz) Parmesan cheese, crumbled
- 2 teaspoons wine vinegar or fresh lemon juice
- 3 tablespoons olive oil

This looks and tastes like you've been cooking all day but comes together in under an hour. The oniony pesto adds such a punch of fresh flavour. Serve with chunks of sourdough.

- Heat 1 tablespoon of the oil in a large flameproof casserole. Add the lamb and fry gently for 5 minutes. Remove the lamb and set aside.

- Heat the remaining oil in the casserole, add the onion and aubergine and fry for about 5 minutes until beginning to colour. Add the garlic, tomatoes, tomato paste, sugar and stock and bring to the boil. Reduce the heat, cover the pan and simmer gently for 5 minutes.

- Return the lamb to the casserole and stir into the vegetables. Cook gently for 15 minutes. Check the seasoning.

- Put the spring onions, Parmesan, wine vinegar or lemon juice and the olive oil into a blender or food processor and whizz to a coarse paste. Transfer this pesto to a small bowl.

- Spoon the stew into bowls and top with spoonfuls of pesto.

V

• DESSERTS •

Deep Dish Puff Apple Pie

SERVES 6 • PREP & COOKING TIME 1 hour

- 1 kg (2 lb) or about 5 cooking apples, quartered, cored, peeled and thickly sliced
- 100 g (3½ oz) caster sugar, plus extra for sprinkling
- grated zest of 1 small orange
- ½ teaspoon ground mixed spice or ground cinnamon
- 3 whole cloves
- 400 g (13 oz) chilled ready-made puff pastry
- beaten egg, to glaze

Sweet, spiced apples combine with flaky puff pastry in this version of the traditional family favourite. Serve it warm with spoonfuls of crème fraîche or extra-thick cream, or a scoop of the **Cherry Almond Ice Cream** on page 267.

- Fill a 1.2 litre (2 pint) pie dish with the apples. Mix the sugar with the orange zest, mixed spice or cinnamon and cloves, then sprinkle over the apples.

- Roll the pastry out on a lightly floured surface until a little larger than the top of the dish. Cut 2 long strips from the edges, about 1 cm (½ inch) wide. Brush the dish rim with a little beaten egg, press the strips on top, then brush these with egg. Lift the remaining pastry over the dish and press the edges together well.

- Trim off the excess pastry, then flute the edges of the pastry (see page 289 for how to do this). Reroll the trimmings and cut out small heart shapes or circles with a small biscuit cutter. Brush the top of the pie with beaten egg, add the pastry shapes, then brush these with egg. Sprinkle with a little extra sugar.

- Bake in a preheated oven, 200°C (400°F), Gas Mark 6, for 20–25 minutes until the pastry is well risen and golden.

Buttermilk Pancakes with Bacon & Maple Syrup

SERVES 4 • PREP & COOKING TIME 30 minutes

- 1 egg, beaten
- 175 ml (6 fl oz) buttermilk
- 15 g (½ oz) butter, melted
- 50 g (2 oz) tapioca or rice flour
- 25 g (1 oz) fine cornmeal
- 1 teaspoon bicarbonate of soda
- 1 tablespoon sunflower oil
- 8 unsmoked streaky bacon rashers
- maple syrup, to serve

Thick, fluffy pancakes served with crispy bacon and sweetly sticky maple syrup are deservedly an American classic. No buttermilk? An easy substitute is to mix 1 tablespoon of lemon juice into 1 cup of milk and allow it to sit for 5 minutes.

- Whisk together the egg, buttermilk and melted butter. Sift in the flour, cornmeal and bicarbonate of soda and mix together gently – do not overmix.

- Heat the oil in a frying pan over a medium heat and pour in 3 large spoonfuls of the batter, to give 3 pancakes. Cook for 2–3 minutes, until bubbles start to appear. Flip the pancakes over gently and cook for a further 1–2 minutes. Remove from the pan and keep warm.

- Repeat with the remaining batter to make a total of 12 pancakes.

- Meanwhile, cook the bacon under a preheated hot grill for 3–4 minutes on each side until crisp.

- Serve the pancakes in stacks of 3 topped with the bacon rashers and drizzled with maple syrup.

• LIGHT BITES •

Crab Cakes

SERVES 4 • PREP & COOKING TIME 30 minutes, plus chilling

- 300 g (10 oz) potatoes, peeled and chopped
- 375 g (12 oz) fresh white crab meat
- 3 spring onions, sliced
- handful of coriander, leaves and stalks finely chopped
- good squeeze of lime juice
- ½ chilli, deseeded and finely chopped
- 1 egg yolk
- 3 tablespoons polenta
- 2 tablespoons vegetable oil
- salt and black pepper
- lime wedges, to serve

Golden and crispy on the outside, soft and sweet on the inside, these crab cakes make a lovely light meal with crisp salad leaves alongside plus some sweet chilli sauce or tartar sauce. Serve the crab cakes as soon as they're cooked.

- Cook the potatoes in a saucepan of salted boiling water for 15 minutes or until tender. Drain well, return to the pan and mash. Leave to cool. Stir in all the remaining ingredients except the polenta and oil.

- Put the polenta on a plate, shape the crab mixture into 8 cakes and coat in the polenta. Cover and chill for 20 minutes.

- Heat the oil in a large frying pan, add the cakes and fry for 2–3 minutes on each side until golden. Serve with lime wedges.

• MAINS •

Pork & Paprika Goulash

SERVES 4 • PREP & COOKING TIME 30 minutes

- 2 tablespoons vegetable oil
- 400 g (13 oz) pork loin, cubed
- 1 onion, sliced
- 2 teaspoons smoked paprika
- 400 g (13 oz) can chopped tomatoes
- 500 g (1 lb) potatoes, diced
- salt and black pepper
- 4 tablespoons soured cream, to serve
- handful of chopped parsley, to garnish

Paprika is the key ingredient in this Hungarian favourite, which is a great pick-me-up on a cold day. It freezes well and is easy to scale up so is a good choice for batch cooking. Serve it on its own or over brown rice or buttered noodles.

- Heat half the oil in a deep frying pan. Add the pork, season to taste and cook for 5 minutes until browned all over. Remove from the pan and set aside.

- Add the remaining oil to the pan with the onion and cook for 5 minutes until softened.

- Stir in the paprika, then add the tomatoes and potatoes. Season to taste, bring to the boil, then reduce the heat and simmer for 10 minutes.

- Return the pork to the pan and cook for a further 5 minutes until the pork and potatoes are cooked through. Divide between bowls, top with the soured cream and serve sprinkled with parsley.

VG

• DESSERTS •

Blood Orange Sorbet

SERVES 4–6 • PREP & COOKING TIME 45 minutes,
plus chilling and freezing

- 250 g (8 oz) caster sugar
- pared rind of 2 blood oranges
- 300 ml (½ pint) blood orange juice
- strips of orange rind, to decorate

Sorbets aren't just for summer. The distinctive, tangy flavour of blood oranges makes a refreshing, palate-cleansing end to a winter meal. Serve with a splash of chilled Campari, if you like.

- Heat the sugar over a low heat in a small saucepan with 250 ml (8 fl oz) water, stirring occasionally until completely dissolved.

- Add the orange rind and increase the heat. Without stirring, boil the syrup for about 12 minutes and then set aside to cool completely.

- When it is cold, strain the sugar syrup over the orange juice and stir together. Refrigerate for about 2 hours until really cold.

- Pour the chilled orange syrup into an ice-cream machine and churn for about 10 minutes. When the sorbet is almost frozen, scrape it into a plastic container and put it in the freezer compartment for a further hour until completely frozen.

- Alternatively, pour the chilled orange syrup into a shallow metal container and put it in the freezer for 2 hours. Remove and whisk with a hand-held electric whisk or balloon whisk, breaking up all the ice crystals. Return it to the freezer and repeat this process every hour or so until frozen.

- Serve scoops of sorbet decorated with thin strips of orange rind.

v

· BREAKFASTS ·

Berry, Honey & Yogurt Pots

SERVES 4 • PREP & COOKING TIME 10 minutes

- 400 g (13 oz) frozen mixed berries, defrosted
- juice of 1 orange
- 6 tablespoons honey
- 400 ml (14 fl oz) vanilla yogurt
- 50 g (2 oz) granola

Super-easy and super-fast, these pretty breakfast treats use frozen fruit for extra convenience, though you could use fresh if you have it. You could also add a little finely chopped mint for a refreshing burst of flavour.

- Whizz half the berries with the orange juice and honey in a blender until fairly smooth. Transfer to a bowl and stir in the remaining berries.

- Divide one-third of the berry mixture between 4 glasses or small bowls. Top with half the yogurt.

- Layer with half the remaining berry mixture and top with the remaining yogurt.

- Top with the remaining berry mixture and sprinkle over the granola just before serving.

• MAINS •

Chicken Cacciatore

SERVES 4 • PREP & COOKING TIME 30 minutes

- 4 boneless, skinless chicken breasts, each about 125 g (4 oz)
- 500 g (1 lb) cherry or mini plum tomatoes, halved
- 1 red onion, cut into wedges
- 2 garlic cloves, finely chopped
- 2–3 stems rosemary, torn into pieces
- 6 tablespoons red wine
- 2 tablespoons balsamic vinegar
- 250 g (8 oz) dried linguine or fettuccine
- 2 tablespoons grated mature Cheddar cheese (optional)
- black pepper

This Italian 'hunter's stew', rich with tomatoes and garlic, is a chuck-it-all-in recipe that makes life easy for a busy cook. Serve with your pasta of choice and dig in.

- Arrange the chicken in a large roasting tin or ovenproof dish so that it lies in a single layer. Add the tomatoes and onion, then sprinkle over the garlic and rosemary. Drizzle with the wine and vinegar and add a little pepper.

- Bake in a preheated oven, 220°C (425°F), Gas Mark 7, for 20 minutes or until the onions and chicken are browned and the juices run clear when the chicken is pierced with a skewer.

- Halfway through cooking, bring a large saucepan of water to the boil, add the pasta and cook for 8–10 minutes until al dente.

- Drain the pasta and return to the empty pan. Slice the chicken breasts and add to the pasta with the onions, tomatoes and pan juices. Toss together and spoon into bowls. Sprinkle with a little extra rosemary and top with grated cheese, if liked.

V

• DESSERTS •

Lemon Cheesecake Blondies

MAKES 12–16 • PREP & COOKING TIME 30 minutes

- 125 g (4 oz) unsalted butter
- 100 g (3½ oz) white chocolate, broken into small pieces
- 50 g (2 oz) cream cheese
- 2 large eggs
- 100 g (3½ oz) soft light brown sugar
- 1 teaspoon lemon extract
- ¼ teaspoon salt
- 150 g (5 oz) plain flour

FOR THE TOPPING
- 125 g (4 oz) cream cheese
- 1 large egg yolk
- 50 g (2 oz) caster sugar
- 1 teaspoon finely grated lemon zest

What's even better than a blondie? A blondie combined with cheesecake! Squidgy and delectable, these can be served warm or cold and, for an extra flourish, add a handful of sharply sweet raspberries alongside.

- Place the butter and white chocolate in a small saucepan over a low heat and warm until just melted.

- Meanwhile, make the topping. Beat together all the ingredients in a small bowl until smooth.

- Place the cream cheese, eggs, brown sugar, lemon extract and salt in a large bowl and beat together until smooth. Using a rubber spatula, stir in the melted chocolate and flour.

- Scrape the mixture into a greased 23 cm (9 inch) square brownie tin, lined with nonstick baking paper. Spoon over the topping and swirl the two mixtures together with the tip of a knife.

- Bake in a preheated oven, 200°C (400°F), Gas Mark 6, for 15–17 minutes until golden.

- Leave to cool in the tin for 1–2 minutes, then lift on to a board using the lining paper and cut into 12–16 squares.

V

• BREAKFASTS •

Sunflower Seed & Rye Bread

MAKES 1 loaf • PREP & COOKING TIME 1 hour

- 200 g (7 oz) plain flour, plus extra for dusting
- 200 g (7 oz) wholemeal spelt flour
- 100 g (3½ oz) rye flour
- 2 teaspoons baking powder
- 1 teaspoon salt
- 75 g (3 oz) sunflower seeds, plus 2 tablespoons
- 500 g (1 lb) natural yogurt
- milk, to glaze

Needing no proving time and no kneading, this sunflower seed-studded loaf is super-quick to rustle up for breakfast. Serve warm with butter and a dollop of your favourite jam or the **Dark Oxford Marmalade** on page 37.

- Mix together the flours, baking powder, salt and the 75 g (3 oz) sunflower seeds in a bowl. Stir in the yogurt and mix to a fairly soft dough.

- Shape the dough into a log on a floured surface, then drop into a greased 1.25 kg (2½ lb) or 1.5 litre (2½ pint) loaf tin. Brush with a little milk and sprinkle with the remaining sunflower seeds.

- Bake in a preheated oven, 220°C (425°F), Gas Mark 7, for 20 minutes. Reduce the oven temperature to 160°C (325°F), Gas Mark 3, and bake for a further 30 minutes. The base of the bread should sound hollow when tapped. If necessary, return to the oven for a little longer. Transfer to a wire rack to cool.

Make the most of your leftovers...
Don't throw away stale bread. Blitz in a food processor to make breadcrumbs and freeze. Use them to add a crunchy coating to fish and goujons before frying and as a topping for mac and cheese or cauliflower cheese. Or add to stuffing, burgers and meatballs.

Devilled Fillet Steaks

SERVES 4 • PREP & COOKING TIME 20 minutes

- 2 tablespoons olive oil
- 4 fillet steaks, about 175 g (6 oz) each
- 2 tablespoons balsamic vinegar
- 75 ml (3 fl oz) full-bodied red wine
- 4 tablespoons beef stock
- 2 garlic cloves, chopped
- 1 teaspoon crushed fennel seeds
- 1 tablespoon sun-dried tomato purée
- ½ teaspoon crushed dried chillies
- salt and black pepper

TO GARNISH
- chopped flat-leaf parsley
- rocket leaves (optional)

When you're after a quick meal, these succulent steaks with their chilli-spiked sauce are just the thing. All you need to accompany them is a crisp green salad, or if you fancy something a bit heartier, some sweet potato wedges or chips.

- Heat the oil in a nonstick frying pan until smoking hot. Add the steaks and cook over a very high heat for about 2 minutes on each side, if you want your steaks to be medium rare. Remove to a plate, season with salt and pepper and keep warm in a low oven.

- Pour the vinegar, wine and stock into the pan and boil for 30 seconds, scraping any sediment from the base of the pan. Add the garlic and fennel seeds and whisk in the sun-dried tomato purée and crushed chillies. Bring the sauce to the boil and boil fast to reduce until syrupy.

- Transfer the steaks to serving plates, pouring any collected meat juices into the sauce. Return the sauce to the boil, then season with salt and pepper.

- Pour the sauce over the steaks and serve immediately, garnished with chopped parsley and rocket leaves, if liked. Slice the steaks before serving, if you wish.

V

• DESSERTS •

Mini Orange Shortbreads

MAKES about 80 • PREP & COOKING TIME 25 minutes, plus cooling

- 250 g (8 oz) plain flour, sifted
- 175 g (6 oz) unsalted butter, cut into small pieces
- grated zest of 1 orange
- ½ teaspoon mixed spice
- 75 g (3 oz) caster sugar
- 2 teaspoons cold water

TO SERVE
- 2 teaspoons icing sugar
- 1 teaspoon cocoa powder

These mini orange shortbreads are perfect for a party. To make a lemony version, replace the orange zest with lemon zest and dust over 2 teaspoons of caster sugar mixed with finely grated zest of half a lemon to serve.

- Place the flour in a bowl, add the butter and rub in with the fingertips until the mixture resembles fine breadcrumbs. Stir in the remaining ingredients with the measured water and mix to form a dough.

- Roll out on a lightly floured surface to a thickness of 2.5 mm (⅛ inch). Using a 1.5 cm (¾ inch) plain cutter, cut out approximately 80 rounds.

- Place the rounds on nonstick baking sheets and bake in a preheated oven, 200°C (400°F), Gas Mark 6, for 10–12 minutes until golden. Carefully transfer to a wire rack to cool.

- Mix together the icing sugar and cocoa powder and dust a little over the shortbreads before serving.

And, for leap year luck ...

v

• LIGHT BITES •

Herby Stuffed Tomatoes

SERVES 4 • PREP & COOKING TIME 30 minutes

- 250 g (8 oz) ricotta or cream cheese
- 2 spring onions, finely chopped
- 4 tablespoons chopped mixed herbs, such as chervil, chives, parsley, basil, marjoram and tarragon
- finely grated zest of 1 lemon
- 1 tablespoon lemon juice
- 4 large beef tomatoes
- salt and black pepper

Filled with fresh herbs and soft cheese, these tomatoes are a great choice for brunch, served with crisp toast. They're very forgiving so won't mind being left to cook in the oven for longer if you forget about them.

- For the herby ricotta filling, mix together the ricotta or cream cheese with the spring onions, mixed herbs and lemon zest and juice. Season with salt and pepper and set aside.

- Cut the tops off the tomatoes and scoop out the seeds. Stuff the tomatoes with the ricotta filling and transfer the tomatoes to a baking sheet. Bake in a preheated oven, 190°C (375°F), Gas Mark 5, for 20–25 minutes or until the tomatoes are tender.

VG

Glühwein

SERVES 6 • PREP & COOKING TIME 15 minutes

- 2 lemons, sliced
- 1 orange, sliced
- 1 bottle red wine
- 125 g (4 oz) sugar
- 8 whole cloves
- 2 cinnamon sticks
- 150 ml (¼ pint) brandy

This recipe will fill the kitchen with the heady scent of cloves and cinnamon. The brandy added at the end gives it an extra kick but it's not essential. Take care not to let the mixture boil or you will boil off the alcohol!

- Place the slices of 1 lemon in a saucepan with the sliced orange, red wine, sugar, cloves and cinnamon sticks. Simmer gently for 10 minutes, then reduce the heat and add the brandy.

- Serve the glühwein in small cups or heatproof glasses with the remaining slices of lemon.

March

GOOD TO EAT THIS MONTH

beetroot * broccoli * carrots * cauliflower * kale * leeks
* parsnips * radishes * spinach * spring greens * spring
onions * swede * apples * pears * rhubarb * parsley *
rosemary * sage

DATES TO LOOK FORWARD TO THIS MONTH

St David's Day
Pancake Day (Shrove Tuesday)
Holi
St Patrick's Day
Mother's Day UK
Eid al-Fitr

There's not an abundance of new seasonal produce this month.
It's an in-between sort of month: too late for winter's root veg
to be at their best and too early for the cheering arrival of new
spring vegetables. But it's a time of transition when we head
out of the dark depths of winter and finally start to welcome
in spring. Days are lighter, cheery daffodils and very early tulips
brighten gardens and parks and there is the occasional busy buzz
of awakening bumblebees.

So this month draws inspiration from sunnier places with
recipes like **Aubergine Thai Green Curry** (page 86), **Bean Chilli**
(page 105), **Calcutta Beef Curry** (page 99) and **Seafood Paella**
(page 90) that have zest and heat and the promise of warmth
to come.

There's lots to celebrate this month: days for the patron saints
of Wales and Ireland, pancake flipping on Shrove Tuesday –
practice makes perfect and, don't worry, the first one is always
a dud! – Mothering Sunday, plus the festivals of Holi and Eid
al-Fitr. You'll find delicious recipes for all those special dates on
the following pages.

v

· DESSERTS ·

Blueberry, Cinnamon & Honey Welsh Cakes

MAKES 14–16 · PREP & COOKING TIME 20 minutes

- 225 g (7½ oz) self-raising flour, plus extra for dusting
- 1 teaspoon ground cinnamon
- 100 g (3½ oz) unsalted butter, softened, plus extra for frying
- pinch of salt
- 50 g (2 oz) caster sugar
- 75 g (3 oz) dried blueberries
- 1 large egg, lightly beaten
- 2 tablespoons runny honey, plus extra to serve

Celebrate St David's Day with this spin on the Welsh cake. They're traditionally made on a griddle but a large, heavy-based frying pan will do the job. They need to be served warm.

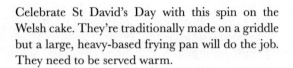

- Sift the flour and cinnamon into a large bowl. Add the butter and rub in with the fingertips until the mixture resembles fine breadcrumbs, then stir in the salt, sugar and blueberries. Add the egg and honey and mix to form a soft but not sticky dough.

- Turn the dough out on to a floured surface and roll out to 5 mm (¼ inch) thick, then stamp out 14–16 rounds using a 7 cm (3 inch) plain cutter.

- Heat a knob of butter in a large, heavy-based frying pan, add the rounds and cook over a low heat for 2–3 minutes, then flip over and cook for a further 2–3 minutes until risen and golden. Repeat with the remaining rounds, adding a little more butter to the pan if necessary.

- Serve warm, drizzled with extra honey.

VG

• BREAKFASTS •

Mushroom Tofu Scramble

SERVES 4 • PREP & COOKING TIME 15 minutes

- 2 tablespoons rapeseed or olive oil
- 200 g (7 oz) chestnut mushrooms, quartered
- 250 g (8 oz) firm tofu, drained, patted dry and crumbled
- 125 g (4 oz) baby plum tomatoes, halved
- 1 tablespoon mushroom ketchup
- 3 tablespoons chopped flat-leaf parsley
- salt and black pepper

For a healthy and satisfying vegan take on scrambled eggs, try this protein-packed tofu and mushroom scramble. The mushroom ketchup adds a deep umami flavour to the dish. Serve it with hash browns or hot toast.

- Heat the oil in a frying pan, add the mushrooms and cook over a high heat, stirring frequently, for 2 minutes until browned and softened. Add the tofu and cook, stirring, for 1 minute.

- Add the tomatoes to the pan and cook for 2 minutes until starting to soften. Stir in the mushroom ketchup and half the parsley and season with salt and pepper.

- Serve immediately, sprinkled with the remaining parsley.

VG

· LIGHT BITES ·

Miso Soup

SERVES 4 • PREP & COOKING TIME 25 minutes, plus soaking

FOR THE RICE
- 275g (9oz) glutinous rice

FOR THE SOUP
- 2 litres (3½ pints) vegetable stock
- 2 tablespoons miso paste
- 125g (4oz) shiitake mushrooms, sliced
- 200g (7oz) firm tofu, cubed

A staple of Japanese cuisine, ultra-savoury miso paste is made with fermented soya beans. It forms the basis of this vegan soup which, here, is served with delicious sticky rice for a more substantial meal.

- Wash the rice in several changes of water and drain. Put it in a large mixing bowl, cover with cold water and leave to soak for about 1 hour.

- Drain the rice and wash it again. Put in a saucepan with 275 ml (9 fl oz) water and bring to a simmer. Cover and cook very gently for 20 minutes, or until the water is absorbed and the rice is tender. Add a little more water if the pan dries out before the rice is cooked.

- Meanwhile, to make the soup, put the stock in a saucepan and heat until simmering.

- Add the miso paste, shiitake mushrooms and tofu to the stock and simmer gently for 5 minutes. Serve immediately with the rice.

V

• DESSERTS •

Toffee & Banana Pancakes

SERVES 4 • PREP & COOKING TIME 55 minutes, plus resting

- 100 g (3½ oz) plain flour
- pinch salt
- 1 egg
- 1 egg yolk
- 300 ml (½ pint) milk
- 2–3 tablespoons sunflower oil
- 2 bananas, sliced

FOR THE TOFFEE SAUCE
- 50 g (2 oz) unsalted butter
- 50 g (2 oz) light muscovado sugar
- 2 tablespoons golden syrup
- 150 ml (¼ pint) double cream

It's Pancake Day so get out the frying pan and start flipping! You could keep it simple by serving the pancakes with a squeeze of lemon and a scattering of sugar but it would be a shame to miss out on the toffee sauce, which is spectacular.

- Sift the flour into a bowl, add the salt, egg and egg yolk, then gradually whisk in the milk to make a smooth batter. Set aside for 30 minutes.

- Put the butter, sugar and syrup for the toffee sauce in a small saucepan and heat gently, stirring occasionally, until the butter has melted and the sugar dissolved. Bring to the boil and cook for 3–4 minutes until just beginning to darken around the edges.

- Take the pan off the heat, then gradually pour in the cream. Tilt the pan to mix and as bubbles subside stir with a wooden spoon. Set aside.

- Pour the oil for cooking the pancakes into an 18 cm (7 inch) frying pan, heat and then pour off the excess into a small bowl or jug. Pour a little pancake batter over the base of the pan, tilt the pan to coat the base evenly with batter, then cook for 2 minutes until the underside is golden. Loosen with a palette knife, turn over and cook the second side in the same way. When cooked, slide on to a plate and keep warm. Cook the remaining batter, oiling the pan as needed.

- Fold the pancakes and arrange on serving plates. Top with banana slices and drizzle with the toffee sauce.

· MAINS ·

Aubergine Thai Green Curry

SERVES 4 • PREP & COOKING TIME 20 minutes

- 300 ml (½ pint) coconut milk
- 40 g (1½ oz) Thai green curry paste
- 300 ml (½ pint) vegetable stock
- 4 small round aubergines, each cut into 8 pieces
- 40 g (1½ oz) palm sugar
- 1 teaspoon salt
- 4 teaspoons Thai fish sauce
- 25 g (1 oz) galangal or fresh root ginger, peeled
- 425 g (14 oz) canned straw mushrooms, drained
- 50 g (2 oz) green pepper, thinly sliced

TO GARNISH
- handful of Thai basil leaves
- 2 tablespoons coconut milk

To make this vegan- and vegetarian-friendly, use a vegan version of the Thai fish sauce. There are several available that use seaweed to replicate the salty, umami taste of fish sauce.

- Heat the coconut milk in a saucepan with the curry paste, stirring to mix well. Add the stock and then the aubergines, sugar, salt, fish sauce, galangal or ginger and mushrooms.

- Bring to the boil and cook, stirring, for 2 minutes. Add the green pepper, lower the heat and cook for 1 minute. Serve in bowls, garnished with the basil leaves and drizzled with coconut milk. Discard the piece of galangal or root ginger before serving.

V

· DESSERTS ·

Squidgy Apple Cake

SERVES 16 • PREP & COOKING TIME 1 hour

- 250 g (8 oz) slightly salted butter, softened
- 250 g (8 oz) golden caster sugar, plus extra for sprinkling
- 2 teaspoons ground mixed spice
- 4 eggs
- 300 g (10 oz) self-raising flour
- 1 teaspoon baking powder
- 4 tart dessert apples

You'll find sugar and spice and all things nice in this soft and delectable apple cake. Serve it cold with a big dollop of thick whipped cream or warm with steaming hot custard.

- Beat together the butter, sugar, mixed spice, eggs, half of the flour and the baking powder in a bowl until pale and creamy. Peel 3 of the apples and coarsely grate into the bowl, stirring after each one is grated. Stir in the remaining flour.

- Spoon the mixture into a greased and lined 32 × 22 cm (12½ × 8½ inch) shallow baking tin and level the surface. Peel and grate the remaining apple over the surface.

- Bake in a preheated oven, 180°C (350°F), Gas Mark 4, for 40–45 minutes until golden, just firm to the touch and a skewer inserted into the centre comes out clean.

- Sprinkle with caster sugar and leave to cool in the tin. Peel off the lining paper and cut into squares, then serve, warm or cold.

V

• BREAKFASTS •

Creamy Baked Egg & Mushroom Pots

SERVES 4 • PREP & COOKING TIME 20 minutes

- 75 g (3 oz) butter, plus extra for greasing
- 2 garlic cloves, chopped
- 1 tablespoon chopped parsley
- 250 g (8 oz) portobello mushrooms, chopped
- 150 ml (¼ pint) double cream
- 4 eggs
- salt and black pepper

These little ramekins of garlicky mushrooms paired with rich cream and eggs are ideal for an indulgent, special-occasion weekend breakfast, or as a light lunch or supper. Fingers of toasted sourdough for dipping are a must!

- Melt the butter in large frying pan with the garlic and parsley until just beginning to foam. Add the mushrooms and fry over a medium heat for 4–5 minutes, until soft and golden.

- Meanwhile, mix the cream in a bowl with a pinch of salt and pepper. Stir the mushrooms into the cream and divide between 4 buttered ramekins.

- Crack an egg into each ramekin and place the ramekins in a roasting tin. Pour hot water into the tin so that it comes about halfway up the sides of the ramekins. Cook in a preheated oven, 200°C (400°F), Gas Mark 7, for 7–8 minutes, or until the egg white is set but the yolk is still runny.

v

· LIGHT BITES ·

Onion & Mushroom Quesadillas

SERVES 4 • PREP & COOKING TIME 40 minutes

- 3 tablespoons olive oil
- 2 red onions, thinly sliced
- 1 teaspoon caster sugar
- 200 g (7 oz) button mushrooms, sliced
- 8 flour tortillas
- 150 g (5 oz) Cheddar cheese, grated
- a small handful of parsley, chopped
- salt and black pepper

Got some tortillas knocking around in your storecupboard? Use them to create these quesadillas, packed with oozy melted cheese and golden mushrooms, perfect as lunch or a snack.

- Heat 2 tablespoons of the oil in a large frying pan, add the onions and cook until soft. Add the sugar and cook for 3 minutes or until caramelized. Remove the onions with a slotted spoon and set aside. Heat the remaining oil in the pan, add the mushrooms and cook for 3 minutes or until golden brown. Set aside.

- Heat a nonstick frying pan and add 1 tortilla. Scatter over a quarter of the red onions, mushrooms, Cheddar and parsley. Season to taste with salt and pepper. Cover with another tortilla and cook until browned on the underside. Turn over and cook until browned on the other side. Remove from the pan and keep warm.

- Repeat with the remaining tortillas and ingredients. Cut into wedges and serve with a salad.

· MAINS ·

Seafood Paella

SERVES 4 · PREP & COOKING TIME 1 hour

- 2 tablespoons olive oil
- 1 large onion, finely diced
- 1 garlic clove, crushed
- 1 red pepper, deseeded and chopped into 5 mm (¼ inch) dice
- 300 g (10 oz) paella rice
- 1.5 litres (1¾ pints) hot fish stock or water
- pinch of saffron threads
- 2 large tomatoes, roughly chopped
- 300 g (10 oz) raw peeled king prawns
- 200 g (7 oz) clams, cleaned
- 200 g (7 oz) mussels, scrubbed and debearded
- 200 g (7 oz) squid, cleaned and cut into rings, tentacles discarded
- 150 g (5 oz) frozen peas, defrosted
- 2 tablespoons chopped parsley
- salt and black pepper

Spanish signature dish paella has any number of variations and can include chicken and chorizo. This recipe keeps it deliciously simple with seafood only.

- Heat the oil in a large frying pan. Add the onion, garlic and red pepper to the pan and fry for a few minutes until they have started to soften, then add the rice and fry for 1 minute.

- Pour enough hot stock over the rice to cover it by about 1 cm (½ inch). Add the saffron threads and stir well. Bring the rice up to the boil, then add the tomatoes and reduce the heat to a simmer. Stir well once again, then simmer for 10–12 minutes, stirring occasionally to prevent the rice catching on the bottom of the pan.

- Add the prawns, clams and mussels (first discarding any that don't shut when tapped) and squid to the pan, along with a little more water or stock if the rice is too dry. Cook until the clams and mussels open (discarding any that don't), the prawns are pink and the squid turns white and loses its transparency.

- Stir in the peas and parsley and cook for a few more minutes until the peas are hot, then season to taste with salt and pepper.

- Put the frying pan in the centre of the table so everyone can dig in and add a bowl of lemon wedges for squeezing over.

V

• DESSERTS •

Orange & Sultana Scones

MAKES 10 • PREP & COOKING TIME 30 minutes

- 375 g (12 oz) self-raising flour
- 50 g (2 oz) butter, diced
- 50 g (2 oz) caster sugar, plus extra for sprinkling
- 75 g (3 oz) sultanas
- grated zest of 1 orange
- 1 egg, beaten
- 150–200 ml (5–7 fl oz) semi-skimmed milk

Serve these fruity scones with a hint of citrus zest warm or just cold, split and topped with apricot jam and clotted or thick, whipped cream. They are best eaten on the day they are made.

- Put the flour in a mixing bowl or a food processor. Add the butter and rub in with your fingertips or process until the mixture resembles fine breadcrumbs. Stir in the sugar, sultanas and orange zest.

- Add all but 1 tablespoon of the egg then gradually mix in enough of the milk to mix to a soft but not sticky dough.

- Knead lightly then roll out on a lightly floured surface until 1.5 cm (¾ inch) thick. Stamp out 5.5 cm (2¼ inch) circles using a plain round biscuit cutter. Transfer to a lightly greased baking sheet. Re-knead the trimmings and continue rolling and stamping out until you have made 10 scones.

- Brush the tops with the reserved egg and sprinkle lightly with a little extra caster sugar. Bake in a preheated oven, 200°C (400°F), Gas Mark 6, for 10–12 minutes until well risen and the tops are golden. Leave to cool on the baking sheet.

v

· BREAKFASTS ·

Freeform Spinach, Egg & Feta Breakfast Tarts

SERVES 4 • PREP & COOKING TIME 30 minutes

- 250 g (8 oz) frozen leaf spinach, defrosted
- 125 g (4 oz) feta cheese, diced
- 2 tablespoons mascarpone cheese
- pinch of freshly grated nutmeg
- 4 sheets of filo pastry, defrosted if frozen
- 50 g (2 oz) butter, melted
- 4 eggs
- salt and black pepper

These are an elegant choice for a special brunch: spinach, feta and eggs beautifully presented in filo pastry cases. They use frozen spinach, for convenience, and you can get ahead by taking it out of the freezer to defrost overnight.

- Drain the spinach and squeeze out all the excess water, then chop finely. Put in a bowl and mix in the feta, mascarpone, nutmeg and salt and pepper to taste.

- Lay the sheets of filo pastry on top of one another, brushing each with a little melted butter. Cut out 4 × 15 cm (6 inch) rounds using a saucer as a template.

- Divide the spinach mixture between the pastry rounds, spreading the filling out but leaving a 2.5 cm (1 inch) border. Gather the edges up and over the filling to form a rim. Make a shallow well in the spinach mixture.

- Transfer the tarts to a baking sheet and bake in a preheated oven, 200°C (400°F), Gas Mark 6, for 8 minutes.

- Remove from the oven and carefully crack an egg into each hollow. Return to the oven and bake for a further 8–10 minutes until the eggs are set.

• LIGHT BITES •

Smoked Trout Bruschetta

SERVES 4 • PREP & COOKING TIME 10 minutes

- 12 thick slices of French bread
- 2 large garlic cloves, halved
- 2 tablespoons extra virgin olive oil, plus extra for drizzling
- 250 g (8 oz) tzatziki
- 250 g (8 oz) hot-smoked trout, flaked
- chopped dill, to garnish
- black pepper

You can use ready-made tzatziki for these or make your own, just coarsely grate 1 large cucumber and squeeze out all the liquid, then put the flesh in a bowl. Add 4–5 tablespoons thick Greek yogurt, season well with salt and pepper and mix.

- Toast the bread in a preheated griddle pan or under a preheated grill.

- While still hot, rub the toast all over with the garlic halves and sprinkle with the oil. Top each piece with a large spoonful of tzatziki and pile on the trout. Season to taste with pepper and serve garnished with chopped dill and drizzled with extra oil.

• MAINS •

Lobster Thermidor

SERVES 4 • PREP & COOKING TIME 20 minutes

- 15 g (½ oz) butter
- 1 tablespoon olive oil
- 1 shallot, finely chopped
- 3 tablespoons dry sherry
- 1 teaspoon Dijon mustard
- 100 ml (3½ fl oz) crème fraîche
- 2 small ready-cooked lobsters, about 675 g (1 lb 5 oz) each
- 50 g (2 oz) Gruyère or vegetarian hard cheese, grated*
- salt

This stunning-looking dish is surprisingly easy to make and a luxurious choice for a special occasion. Serve with a green salad dressed with a sharp lemony vinaigrette to cut through the rich flavours, and perhaps some crusty bread for soaking up the creamy sauce.

- Heat the butter and oil in a small saucepan. Add the shallot and cook for 5 minutes until softened. Pour over the sherry and cook for 2 minutes until nearly boiled away. Stir in the mustard and crème fraîche, heat through and season with salt.

- Meanwhile, using a large knife, cut the lobsters lengthways in half. Remove the meat from the tail and claws, reserving the main shell halves. Cut the lobster meat into large chunks.

- Add the lobster meat to the sauce and warm through. Carefully spoon into the tail cavities of the reserved lobster shell halves and scatter over the Gruyère. Cook under a preheated hot grill for 3–5 minutes until golden and bubbling.

*For guidance on vegetarian cheeses, see page 5.

V

• DESSERTS •

Falooda

SERVES 2 • PREP & COOKING TIME 20 minutes,
plus soaking and chilling

- 2 teaspoons sweet basil seeds
- 500 ml (17 fl oz) full-fat milk
- 1 tablespoon granulated sugar
- a handful of falooda sev
- 2 tablespoons rose syrup
- 2 scoops of vanilla ice cream

TO DECORATE
(OPTIONAL)
- a small handful of pistachios, roughly chopped
- a few edible dried rose petals

Celebrate Holi with falooda, a cross between a dessert and a drink. Sweet basil seeds are similar to chia seeds but swell up much faster when soaked. They're available online and at Indian grocery stores, as are falooda sev, the cornstarch vermicelli noodles.

- Add the basil seeds to a small bowl, cover with water and leave to soak for 30 minutes, then drain and set aside.

- Put the milk and sugar in saucepan over a medium heat and gently bring to a boil. Lower the heat and simmer for 5–7 minutes. Remove from the heat and chill in the refrigerator until cold and slightly thickened.

- Cook the falooda sev according to the packet instructions then drain, rinse with cold water and drain again. Using kitchen scissors, cut them into 2.5 cm (1 inch) pieces.

- Now assemble: add a teaspoonful of soaked basil seeds each to 2 glasses and top with the falooda sev. Add a tablespoon of rose syrup to each glass then pour in the chilled milk. Spoon over the remaining basil seeds and top with a scoop of ice cream.

- Serve immediately, decorated with chopped pistachios and rose petals, if you like.

V

• BREAKFASTS •

Banana & Peanut Butter Smoothie

SERVES 1 • PREP TIME 10 minutes, plus freezing

- 1 ripe banana
- 300 ml (½ pint) semi-skimmed milk
- 1 tablespoon smooth peanut butter

Breakfast time, lunchtime or snack time – any time's a good time to enjoy this lovely smoothie. You could use tahini or almond butter in place of the peanut butter.

- Peel and slice the banana, put it in a freezerproof container and freeze for at least 2 hours or overnight.

- Put the banana, milk and peanut butter in a food processor or blender and process until smooth.

- Pour the smoothie into a tall glass and serve immediately.

V

• LIGHT BITES •

Beetroot, Orange & Goats' Cheese Salad

SERVES 2–4 • PREP & COOKING TIME 45 minutes

- 7 small beetroot
- 1 teaspoon cumin seeds
- 1 tablespoon red wine vinegar
- 2 oranges
- 65 g (2½ oz) watercress
- 75 g (3 oz) soft goats' cheese
- cracked black pepper

FOR THE DRESSING
- 1 tablespoon honey
- 1 teaspoon wholegrain mustard
- 1½ tablespoons white wine vinegar
- 3 tablespoons olive oil
- salt and black pepper

If you're short on time, you could substitute ready-cooked chilled beetroot instead of cooking your own. If you do cook the beetroot, don't forget to wear rubber or food-handling gloves to peel it, unless you want bright pink palms!

- Scrub and trim the beetroot and put them in a foil-lined roasting tin with the cumin seeds and vinegar and bake in a preheated oven, 190°C (375°F), Gas Mark 5, for 30 minutes or until cooked. Check by piercing one with a knife. Allow the beetroot to cool slightly and then, wearing food-handling gloves, rub off the skin and slice the globes into halves, or quarters if large.

- Meanwhile, peel and segment the oranges. Make the dressing by whisking the honey, mustard, vinegar and oil. Season to taste with salt and pepper.

- Put the watercress in a bowl with the beetroot and add the dressing. Mix gently to combine. Arrange the oranges on a plate, top with the salad and crumble over the cheese. Season with cracked black pepper and serve.

V

• DESSERTS •

Chocolate Guinness Cake

SERVES 10 • PREP & COOKING TIME 1 hour 30 minutes,
plus standing and chilling

- 125 g (4 oz) butter, softened
- 250 g (8 oz) light muscovado sugar
- 175 g (6 oz) plain flour
- 50 g (2 oz) cocoa powder
- ½ teaspoon baking powder
- 1 teaspoon bicarbonate of soda
- 3 eggs, beaten
- 200 ml (7 fl oz) Guinness or other stout
- 25 g (1 oz) white chocolate curls, to decorate
- sifted cocoa powder, for dusting

FOR THE WHITE
CHOCOLATE
FROSTING
- 200 ml (7 fl oz) double cream
- 200 g (7 oz) white chocolate, broken into pieces

It's St Patrick's Day so there has to be Guinness and what better than combining it with chocolate? Just like the white head that sits atop a perfectly poured glass of stout, this has a white topping that contrasts beautifully with the dark, moist cake beneath.

- Cream the butter and sugar together in a mixing bowl until pale and creamy. Sift the flour, cocoa, baking powder and bicarbonate of soda into a bowl. Gradually beat in alternate spoonfuls of egg, flour mixture and Guinness until all have been added and the mixture is smooth.

- Spoon into a 20 cm (8 inch) spring-form tin, greased and base-lined with oiled greaseproof paper, and spread the surface level. Bake in a preheated oven, 160°C (325°F), Gas Mark 3, for 45–55 minutes until well risen, the top is slightly cracked and a skewer inserted into the centre comes out clean.

- Leave to cool in the tin for 10 minutes then loosen the edges, turn out on to a wire rack and peel off the lining paper.

- Make the white chocolate frosting. Bring half the cream just to the boil in a small saucepan, then remove from the heat. Add the chocolate, set aside for 10 minutes until melted. Stir then chill for 15 minutes. Whip the remaining cream then whisk in the chocolate cream until thick. Chill for another 15 minutes.

- Transfer the cake to a serving plate and spoon the chocolate cream over the top. Decorate with chocolate curls and dust with sifted cocoa powder.

• MAINS •

Calcutta Beef Curry

SERVES 4 • PREP & COOKING TIME 1 hour 40 minutes,
plus marinating

- 400 g (14 oz) stewing beef, cut into bite-sized pieces
- 5 tablespoons natural yogurt
- 1 tablespoon medium curry powder
- 2 tablespoons mustard oil
- 1 bay leaf
- 1 cinnamon stick
- 3 cloves
- 3 green cardamom pods, lightly crushed
- 1 large onion, halved and thinly sliced
- 3 garlic cloves, crushed
- 1 teaspoon peeled and finely grated fresh root ginger
- 1 teaspoon ground turmeric
- 1 teaspoon hot chilli powder
- 2 teaspoons ground cumin
- 400 ml (14 fl oz) beef stock
- salt
- rice, to serve

You'll need to start this the day before as the beef needs to marinate for 24 hours. But then it's just a bit of stir-frying before leaving the curry to blip away gently on the hob for an hour. To make it with chicken, swap the beef for 4 chicken thighs and 4 drumsticks and replace the beef stock with chicken stock.

- Place the meat in a non-metallic bowl. Mix together the yogurt and curry powder and pour over the meat. Season with salt, cover and marinate in the refrigerator for 24 hours.

- Heat the oil in a large nonstick wok or frying pan and add the bay leaf, cinnamon stick, cloves and cardamom pods. Stir-fry for 1 minute and then add the onion. Stir-fry over a medium heat for 4–5 minutes, then add the garlic, ginger, turmeric, chilli powder and cumin. Add the marinated meat and stir-fry for 10–15 minutes over a low heat.

- Pour in the beef stock and bring to the boil. Reduce the heat to low, cover tightly and simmer gently, stirring occasionally, for 1 hour or until the meat is tender. Check the seasoning and then serve immediately with rice.

V

· DESSERTS ·

Triple Choc Cookies

MAKES 20 • PREP & COOKING TIME 25 minutes

- 75 g (3 oz) butter, softened
- 175 g (6 oz) light muscovado sugar
- 1 egg
- 150 g (5 oz) self-raising flour
- 2 tablespoons cocoa powder
- 100 g (3½ oz) white chocolate, chopped
- 100 g (3½ oz) milk chocolate, chopped

The only thing better than chocolate is lots of it. Enjoy some chocolatey goodness with these easy-to-make triple chocolate. They're best eaten on the day they're made.

- Beat the butter and sugar together in a mixing bowl until pale and creamy. Stir in the egg, flour and cocoa powder and mix until smooth.

- Stir in the chopped chocolate then spoon 20 mounds of the mixture on to 2 greased baking sheets, leaving space between for them to spread during cooking.

- Bake in a preheated oven, 180°C (350°F), Gas Mark 4, for 8–10 minutes until lightly browned. Leave to harden for 1–2 minutes then loosen and transfer to a wire rack to cool completely.

v

• BREAKFASTS •

Breakfast Banana Split

SERVES 4 • PREP & COOKING TIME 10 minutes

- 50 g (2 oz) unsalted butter
- 2 tablespoons honey
- 4 bananas, cut in half lengthways
- 2 dessert apples, grated
- 300 g (10 oz) Greek yogurt
- finely grated zest of 1 orange
- 50 g (2 oz) walnuts, toasted
- 2 tablespoons flaked almonds, toasted
- 2–3 tablespoons maple syrup

A retro dessert favourite becomes a breakfast favourite with this recipe – fried bananas combine with thick Greek yogurt, honey, apples and toasted nuts. Delicious!

- Melt the butter in a frying pan with the honey until it sizzles. Place the bananas in the frying pan, cut-side down, and cook for 3–4 minutes, until golden.

- Meanwhile, mix together the grated apple, yogurt and orange zest.

- Spoon the bananas on to 4 serving plates and top with a large dollop of the yogurt mixture. Sprinkle over the nuts, then drizzle with the maple syrup and any juices from the pan to serve.

V

• LIGHT BITES •

Cheese, Tomato & Basil Muffins

MAKES 8 • PREP & COOKING TIME 35 minutes

- 150 g (5 oz) self-raising flour
- ½ teaspoon salt
- 100 g (3½ oz) fine cornmeal
- 65 g (2½ oz) Cheddar cheese, grated
- 50 g (2 oz) drained sun-dried tomatoes in oil, chopped
- 2 tablespoons chopped basil
- 1 egg, lightly beaten
- 300 ml (½ pint) milk
- 2 tablespoons extra virgin olive oil

Warm from the oven and slathered with butter, these are a great lunch and also make a good lunchbox filler. Swapping in chopped black olives for the sundried tomatoes works well too.

- Sift the flour and salt into a bowl and stir in the cornmeal, 50 g (2 oz) of the cheese, the tomatoes and basil. Make a well in the centre.

- Beat the egg, milk and oil together in a separate bowl or jug, pour into the well and stir together until just combined. The batter should remain a little lumpy.

- Spoon the batter into a lightly oiled 8-hole muffin tray and scatter over the remaining cheese. Bake in a preheated oven, 180°C (350°F), Gas Mark 4, for 20–25 minutes until risen and golden.

- Leave to cool in the tin for 5 minutes, then transfer to a wire rack to cool. Serve warm with butter.

V

• MAINS •

Baked Brie with Maple Syrup

SERVES 4 • PREP & COOKING TIME 20 minutes

- 300 g (10 oz) whole baby Brie or Camembert*
- 25 g (1 oz) pecans
- 3 tablespoons maple syrup
- 3 tablespoons soft brown sugar
- thyme sprigs

You'll keep coming back to this indulgent and delicious recipe. Creamy, oozy, gooey melted cheese, served with a sweet maple sauce and crunchy toasted pecans – what's not to love? Serve it with plenty of crusty bread.

- Remove any plastic packaging from the cheese and return it to its wooden box.

- Place on a baking sheet and cook in a preheated oven, 200°C (400°F), Gas Mark 6, for 15 minutes.

- Meanwhile, toast the pecans in a small dry frying pan for 3–5 minutes until lightly browned, then set aside. Put the maple syrup and sugar in a small saucepan and bring to the boil. Cook for 1 minute until foamy.

- Take the cheese from the oven and cut a small cross in the centre. Drizzle over the maple syrup, scatter with the pecans and thyme and serve.

*For guidance on vegetarian cheeses, see page 5.

VG

• BREAKFASTS •

Tomato, Carrot & Ginger Juice

SERVES 1 • PREP TIME 5 minutes

- 2.5 cm (1 inch) cube fresh root ginger
- 100 g (3½ oz) celery, plus extra to serve (optional)
- 300 g (10 oz) tomatoes
- 175 g (6 oz) carrot
- 1 garlic clove
- 2.5 cm (1 inch) piece fresh horseradish
- 2–3 ice cubes

This juice recipe includes both fresh ginger and horseradish to add punchy flavour. Add less of the horseradish if you like things less spicy as a little goes a long way.

- Peel and roughly chop the ginger. Trim the celery and cut it into 5 cm (2 inch) lengths. Add both to a juicer with the tomatoes, carrot, garlic and horseradish and juice.

- Transfer the juice to a food processor or blender, add a couple of ice cubes and process briefly.

- Pour the juice into a small glass, garnish with celery slivers, if liked, and serve immediately.

V

• MAINS •

Bean Chilli
with Avocado Salsa

SERVES 4–6 • PREP & COOKING TIME 45 minutes

- 3 tablespoons olive oil
- 2 teaspoons cumin seeds, crushed
- 1 teaspoon dried oregano
- 1 red onion, chopped
- 1 celery stick, chopped
- 1 red chilli, deseeded and sliced
- 2 × 400 g (13 oz) cans chopped tomatoes
- 50 g (2 oz) sun-dried tomatoes, thinly sliced
- 2 teaspoons sugar
- 300 ml (½ pint) vegetable stock
- 2 × 400 g (13 oz) cans red kidney beans, drained
- handful of coriander, chopped
- 100 g (3½ oz) soured cream
- salt and black pepper

FOR THE
AVOCADO SALSA
- 1 small avocado
- 2 tomatoes
- 2 tablespoons sweet chilli sauce
- 2 teaspoons lime juice

A flavour-packed and colourful vegetarian chilli that is perked up even more with a fresh salsa and dollops of soured cream. Serve this one-pot winner with toasted pitta or flatbreads.

- Heat the oil in a large saucepan over a medium-low heat, add the cumin seeds, oregano, onion, celery and chilli and cook gently, stirring frequently, for about 6–8 minutes or until the vegetables are beginning to colour.

- Add the canned tomatoes, sun-dried tomatoes, sugar, stock, beans and coriander and bring to the boil. Reduce the heat and simmer for about 20 minutes or until the juices are thickened and pulpy.

- Make the salsa. Peel, stone and finely dice the avocado and put it in a small bowl. Halve the tomatoes, scoop out the seeds and finely dice the flesh. Add to the bowl along with the chilli sauce and lime juice. Mix well.

- Season the bean mixture with salt and pepper and spoon into bowls. Top with spoonfuls of soured cream and the avocado salsa.

· MAINS ·

Lemon Chilli Chicken

SERVES 4 • PREP & COOKING TIME 1 hour 15 minutes,
plus marinating

- 1.75 kg (3½ lb) chicken, cut into 8 pieces
- 8 garlic cloves
- 4 juicy lemons, squeezed, skins reserved
- 1 small red chilli, deseeded and chopped
- 2 tablespoons orange flower honey
- 4 tablespoons chopped parsley, plus sprigs to garnish
- salt and black pepper

Spice up supper with this citrussy dish. Leave the chicken to soak up the flavours in the marinade for as long as you can spare but at least 2 hours. Serve with rice and sweet green peas.

- Arrange the chicken pieces in a shallow flameproof dish. Peel and crush 2 of the garlic cloves and add them to the lemon juice with the chilli and honey. Stir well, then pour this mixture over the chicken. Tuck the lemon skins around the meat, cover and leave to marinate in the refrigerator for at least 2 hours or overnight, turning once or twice.

- Turn the chicken pieces so they are skin-side up, scatter over the remaining whole garlic cloves and put the lemon skins, cut-sides down, on top.

- Cook the chicken in a preheated oven, 200°C (400°F), Gas Mark 6, for 45 minutes or until golden brown and tender. Stir in the parsley, season to taste and serve garnished with parsley sprigs.

V

• BREAKFASTS •

Tomato, Pepper & Egg Tortillas

SERVES 4 • PREP & COOKING TIME 45 minutes

- 1 tablespoon olive oil
- 1 small onion, finely chopped
- 1 garlic clove, crushed
- 1 mild green chilli, deseeded and finely chopped
- 1 small green pepper, deseeded and thinly sliced
- 1 small red pepper, deseeded and thinly sliced
- 400 g (13 oz) can chopped tomatoes
- 2 tablespoons tomato ketchup
- 4 eggs
- 4 corn tortillas
- smoked paprika, for sprinkling
- salt and black pepper

Colourful and packed with veg, these tortillas will get your five-a-day off to a flying start. If you like things spicier, add more chilli or drizzle over a little hot sauce to taste.

- Heat the oil in a large frying pan with a lid, add the onion, garlic, chilli and peppers and cook over a medium heat, stirring frequently, for about 10–15 minutes until the peppers are soft. Stir in the tomatoes and ketchup and season with salt and pepper. Bring to the boil, then simmer for 5 minutes until thickened.

- Make 4 shallow hollows in the tomato mixture with the back of a spoon and break an egg into each hollow. Cover the pan and cook over a low heat for about 5 minutes until just set.

- Meanwhile, warm the tortillas according to the packet instructions. Place a tortilla on each serving plate and carefully transfer the egg and tomato mixture on to each tortilla. Serve immediately, sprinkled with a little smoked paprika.

· LIGHT BITES ·

Basque Fish Soup

SERVES 6 • PREP & COOKING TIME 1 hour

- 2 tablespoons olive oil
- 1 onion, finely chopped
- ½ green pepper, deseeded and diced
- ½ red pepper, deseeded and diced
- 1 courgette, diced
- 2 garlic cloves, finely chopped
- 250 g (8 oz) potatoes, cut into chunks
- ½ teaspoon smoked paprika
- 150 ml (¼ pint) red wine
- 1 litre (1¾ pints) fish stock
- 400 g (13 oz) can chopped tomatoes
- 1 tablespoon tomato purée
- 2 whole mackerel, gutted, rinsed with cold water inside and out
- salt and cayenne pepper

Enjoy the flavours of Spain in this soup that simmers heart-healthy mackerel in a heavenly wine, tomato and paprika broth. Serve with lemon wedges for squeezing over and plenty of crusty bread for mopping up every last drop.

- Heat the oil in a large saucepan, add the onion and fry gently for 5 minutes until softened. Add the peppers, courgette, garlic and potato and fry for 5 minutes, stirring. Mix in the paprika and cook for 1 minute.

- Pour in the red wine, fish stock, tomatoes, tomato purée, salt and cayenne pepper. Bring to the boil, stirring, then add the whole mackerel. Cover and simmer gently for 20 minutes until the fish flakes easily when pressed with a knife.

- Lift the fish out with a slotted spoon and put on a plate. Simmer the soup uncovered for a further 15 minutes. Peel the skin off the fish then lift the flesh away from the backbone. Flake into pieces, checking carefully for any bones.

- Return the mackerel flakes to the pan. Reheat and ladle into shallow bowls.

V

· LIGHT BITES ·

Potted Cheese

SERVES 8-10 • PREP & COOKING TIME 15 minutes

- 500 g (1 lb) hard cheese, such as Cheddar, grated
- 1 teaspoon English mustard powder
- ½ teaspoon powdered mace
- ¼ teaspoon cayenne pepper
- 175 g (6 oz) butter
- 150 ml (¼ pint) sweet sherry or white wine
- 50 g (2 oz) butter, melted

This classic is a wonderful way to use up all those scraps of cheese from a cheeseboard, turning leftovers into something to wow dinner guests. Serve it as you would pâté, with hot toast, crackers or crusty bread for a dinner party starter or snack.

- Place the grated cheese, mustard powder, mace, cayenne pepper and butter in a food processor or blender and blitz to a smooth paste

- Add the sherry or wine gradually, blending each time until it is quite absorbed before adding more.

- When the cheese mixture is creamy and smooth, put it into one large pot or several individual ramekins, pressing it down firmly to avoid air bubbles.

- Pour the melted butter gently over the top. Leave undisturbed until it has set.

- Refrigerate until needed and take out of the fridge about 10 minutes before you want to serve.

· MAINS ·

Chorizo Carbonara

SERVES 4 • PREP & COOKING TIME 25 minutes

- 125 g (4 oz) chorizo sausage, sliced
- 1 tablespoon olive oil
- 375 g (12 oz) dried penne
- 4 eggs
- 50 g (2 oz) Parmesan cheese, freshly grated, plus extra to serve
- salt and black pepper

Spicy, smoky chorizo really fires up the pasta in this easy Spain-meets-Italy dish. Made with just five ingredients (plus a touch of salt and pepper), it will be on the table in under half an hour.

- Put the chorizo and oil in a frying pan over a very low heat and cook, turning occasionally, until crisp. The melted fat released by the chorizo will be an essential part of your sauce.

- Cook the pasta in a large saucepan of salted boiling water according to the packet instructions until it is al dente.

- Meanwhile, crack the eggs into a bowl, add the Parmesan and season with salt and a generous grinding of pepper. Mix together with a fork.

- Just before the pasta is ready, increase the heat under the frying pan so that the oil and melted chorizo fat start to sizzle.

- Drain the pasta thoroughly, return to the pan and immediately stir in the egg mixture and the sizzling-hot contents of the frying pan. Stir vigorously so that the eggs cook evenly. Serve immediately with a scattering of grated Parmesan.

V

• DESSERTS •

Turkish Delight Cakes with Rosewater Cream

MAKES 18 • PREP & COOKING TIME 20 minutes

- 3 large egg whites
- pinch of salt
- 100 g (3½ oz) ground almonds
- 100 g (3½ oz) plain flour, sifted
- 150 g (5 oz) caster sugar
- 150 g (5 oz) unsalted butter, melted and cooled
- 1 teaspoon rosewater
- 75 g (3 oz) rose-flavoured Turkish delight, chopped
- edible rose petals, to decorate

FOR THE ROSEWATER CREAM
- 200 ml (7 fl oz) double cream
- 1 teaspoon rosewater
- ½ teaspoon vanilla bean paste or extract
- 4 tablespoons icing sugar, sifted

Make Mother's Day special with these little rosewater-infused cakes studded with chunks of Turkish delight. If you can't find edible rose petals to decorate, chopped pistachios are a pretty topping too.

- Whisk the egg whites and salt in a large, clean bowl with a hand-held electric whisk until they form soft peaks, then gently fold in the ground almonds, flour and sugar. Fold in the melted butter, rosewater and Turkish delight.

- Spoon the mixture into 18 holes of 2 × 12-hole silicone friand trays, madeleine trays or mini muffin tins lightly brushed with melted butter.

- Bake in a preheated oven, 220°C (425°F), Gas Mark 7, for 8–10 minutes until risen and golden.

- Meanwhile, make the rosewater cream. Whip all the ingredients in a bowl with a hand-held electric whisk until soft peaks form, then place in a serving bowl.

- Remove the cakes from the oven and transfer to a wire rack to cool slightly. Serve with dollops of the rosewater cream and decorated with edible rose petals.

V

• DESSERTS •

Citrus Baklava

MAKES 24 • PREP & COOKING TIME 1 hour 10 minutes, plus chilling

- 400 g (13 oz) filo pastry, defrosted if frozen
- 125 g (4 oz) butter, melted

FOR THE FILLING
- 100 g (3½ oz) walnut pieces
- 100 g (3½ oz) shelled pistachio nuts, plus extra slivers to decorate
- 100 g (3½ oz) blanched almonds
- 75 g (3 oz) caster sugar
- ½ teaspoon ground cinnamon

FOR THE SYRUP
- 1 lemon
- 1 small orange
- 250 g (8 oz) caster sugar
- pinch of ground cinnamon
- 150 ml (¼ pint) water

Sweet, sticky and so moreish, this baklava is a heavenly blend of crispy pastry, nuts and cinnamon with an added citrus pep, so make a tray to share with friends and family this Eid al-Fitr. It will keep in the fridge for up to 2 days.

- Make the filling. Dry-fry the nuts in a nonstick pan for 3–4 minutes, stirring, until lightly browned. Leave to cool slightly, then roughly chop and mix with the sugar and cinnamon.

- Unfold the pastry and cut into rectangles the same size as the base of an 18 × 28 cm (7 × 11 inch) small roasting tin. Wrap half of the pastry in clingfilm so it doesn't dry out.

- Brush each unwrapped sheet of pastry with melted butter, then layer up in the roasting tin. Spoon in the filling, then unwrap and cover with the remaining pastry, brushing with melted butter as you go.

- Cut the pastry into 6 squares, then cut each square into 4 triangles. Bake in a preheated oven, 180°C (350°F), Gas Mark 4, for 30–35 minutes, covering with foil after 20 minutes to prevent it overbrowning.

- Meanwhile, make the syrup. Pare the rind off the lemon and orange with a zester or vegetable peeler, then cut into strips. Squeeze the juice. Put the rind and juice in a saucepan with the sugar, cinnamon and measured water. Heat gently until the sugar dissolves then simmer for 5 minutes without stirring.

- Pour the hot syrup over the pastry as soon as it comes out of the oven. Leave to cool, then chill for 3 hours. Remove from the tin and arrange the pieces on a serving plate, sprinkled with slivers of pistachio.

• DRINKS •

Fresh Lemonade

MAKES 1.8 litres (3 pints) • PREP & COOKING TIME 10 minutes, plus cooling

- 75 g (3 oz) caster sugar
- 1.8 litres (3 pints) water
- 4 lemons, sliced, plus extra slices to serve
- ice cubes

For fresh limeade, follow the recipe below and simply use 6 limes in place of the 4 lemons, or you could use a mixture. Try adding chopped mint while the limeade cools for a refreshing mint zing.

- Place the sugar in a pan with 600 ml (1 pint) of the measured water and all the sliced lemons. Bring to the boil, stirring well until all the sugar has dissolved.

- Remove from the heat and add all the remaining water. Stir, then set aside to cool completely.

- Once cold, roughly crush the lemons, to release all the juice. Strain through a sieve, add the ice cubes, and serve in glasses decorated with slices of lemon.

Make the most of your leftovers...
Too many lemons? Slice and freeze a few for adding straight from the freezer to drinks. Place the lemon slices in a single layer on a baking sheet and place in the freezer for a few hours. This way they won't all clump together. Once they are solid, store in a ziplock bag or airtight container.

April

GOOD TO EAT THIS MONTH

asparagus * beetroot * broccoli * carrots * cucumber
* kale * lettuce * morel mushrooms * new potatoes *
parsnips * radishes * rocket * samphire * spinach *
spring greens * watercress *
rhubarb * chives * dill

DATES TO LOOK FORWARD TO THIS MONTH

Passover
Good Friday
Easter Sunday
St George's Day

Shakespeare may have called it the cruellest month, but there's
a softness in the air and warmth in the sun, if we're lucky. There
are lambs in the fields, the trees are covered with a fuzz of green
and all about we can see signs that spring is here.

And, when it comes to celebrations, it's a wonderful month.
You'll find **Chocolate Walnut Brownie**s for Passover (page 127),
delectable **Double Chocolate Truffles** for Easter Sunday (page
135), **Hot Cross Buns** for Good Friday (page 133) and **Steak &
Ale Casserole** for St George's Day (page 138).

Asparagus, with it's all too brief season, arrives this month.
Eat the slender green spears as often as you can simply steamed,
with a little melted butter and salt, or go one better and try
the **Asparagus with Frazzled Eggs** on page 120 and the **Pea &
Asparagus Risotto** on page 130.

Watercress is in season from now until October. It adds peppery
flavour to soups, salads and stir-fries. Try it in the delicious
Spaghetti with Watercress Pesto & Blue Cheese dish on page 118.

Gorgeous new potatoes are here also, to serve in buttery, mint-
flecked piles with just about any main dish. They're lovely in the
north Italian pasta speciality on page 145.

V

• BREAKFASTS •

Banana Muffins

MAKES 12 • PREP & COOKING TIME 30 minutes

- 200 g (7 oz) plain flour
- 35 g (1½ oz) bran
- 75 g (3 oz) soft dark brown sugar
- 1 teaspoon baking powder
- ¾ teaspoon bicarbonate of soda
- ½ teaspoon ground mixed spice (optional)
- 200 ml (7 fl oz) buttermilk
- 2½ tablespoons groundnut oil
- 2 large eggs, beaten
- 1 teaspoon vanilla extract
- 2 small, very ripe bananas, mashed

Guaranteed to be a hit with all the family, these super easy muffins are delicious eaten still warm and also make a great grab-and-go breakfast or snack.

- Mix together the dry ingredients in a large bowl. Stir together the remaining ingredients in a separate bowl, then pour the wet ingredients on to the dry mixture and stir with a large metal spoon until just combined.

- Spoon the mixture into a lightly greased large, 12-hole nonstick muffin tray, and bake in a preheated oven, 180°C (350°F), Gas Mark 4, for 20–22 minutes or until risen and golden and a skewer inserted into the centres comes out clean.

- Transfer to a wire rack to cool slightly.

• LIGHT BITES •

Chicken Club Sandwich

SERVES 4 • PREP & COOKING TIME 25 minutes

- 4 small boneless, skinless chicken breasts, thinly sliced
- 8 rashers of smoked streaky bacon
- 1 tablespoon sunflower oil
- 12 slices of bread
- 4 tablespoons mayonnaise
- 125 g (4 oz) dolcelatte or other blue cheese, thinly sliced
- 4 tomatoes, thinly sliced
- 40 g (1½ oz) watercress

This version of everyone's favourite stacked sandwich uses blue cheese and chicken, but be as creative as you like with the ingredients you have to hand: maybe use hard-boiled eggs in place of the chicken, mix a little mustard with the mayo or add a few slices of ripe avocado.

- Fry the chicken and bacon in the oil for 6–8 minutes, turning once or twice until golden and the chicken is cooked through.

- Toast the bread on both sides, then spread with the mayonnaise. Divide the chicken and bacon between 4 slices of toast, then top with the sliced cheese. Cover the cheese with 4 more slices of toast, then add the tomato slices and watercress. Complete the sandwich stacks with the final slices of toast.

- Press the sandwiches together, then cut each stack into 4 small triangles. Secure with cocktail sticks, if needed, and serve immediately.

v

• MAINS •

Spaghetti with Watercress Pesto & Blue Cheese

SERVES 2 • PREP & COOKING TIME 15 minutes

- 200 g (7 oz) wholewheat spaghetti
- 50 g (2 oz) blue cheese, thickly sliced*
- salt and black pepper

FOR THE
WATERCRESS PESTO
- 50 g (2 oz) walnuts
- 75 g (3 oz) watercress, plus extra sprigs to garnish
- 1 tablespoon crème fraîche

The peppery leaves of watercress combine with toasted walnuts in this fresh-tasting spin on pesto. It's delicious with pasta and also works well as a dip with crudités or spread in a wrap.

- Cook the pasta in a large saucepan of salted boiling water according to the packet instructions until al dente.

- Meanwhile, make the watercress pesto. Tip the walnuts into a small frying pan and dry-fry over a medium heat for 3 minutes, giving the pan a shake every now and again, until they start to turn brown. Leave to cool for a minute or two.

- Place the nuts, watercress and crème fraîche in a small food processor or blender and whizz together to form a pesto. Season well.

- Drain the pasta, then spoon into serving bowls and arrange slices of the cheese on top. Serve with dollops of the pesto and garnished with watercress sprigs.

*For guidance on vegetarian cheeses, see page 5.

V

• DESSERTS •

Thumbprint Cookies

MAKES 14 • PREP & COOKING TIME 40 minutes

- 125 g (4 oz) unsalted butter, softened
- 50 g (2 oz) light brown sugar
- 1 egg, separated
- ½ teaspoon ground mixed spice
- 100 g (3½ oz) plain flour
- 75 g (3 oz) slivered almonds, crushed
- 5 tablespoons strawberry or raspberry jam
- icing sugar, for dusting (optional)

They're called thumbprint cookies because you use your thumb to make a dent in the middle to fill with jam. Kids will love helping you make these – a great way to keep them entertained on a wet afternoon! The cookies will keep in an airtight container in a cool place for a few days.

- Beat the butter and brown sugar until creamy. Add the egg yolk, ground mixed spice and flour and mix to form a soft dough. Lightly beat the egg white to break it up and tip it on to a plate. Scatter the almonds on a separate plate.

- Shape the dough into small balls, 3 cm (1¼ inches) in diameter, and roll them first in the egg white and then in the almonds until well coated.

- Place the balls on a greased baking sheet, spaced slightly apart, and flatten slightly. Bake in a preheated oven, 180°C (350°F), Gas Mark 4, for 10 minutes, then remove from the oven.

- Allow to cool a little, then lightly flour your thumb and make a thumbprint in the centre of each cookie. Spoon a little jam into each cavity and return the cookies to the oven for an extra 10 minutes or until pale golden.

- Transfer to a wire rack to cool. Dust the edges of the cookies with icing sugar, if liked.

V

• BREAKFASTS •

Asparagus with Frazzled Eggs

SERVES 4 • PREP & COOKING TIME 20 minutes

- 500 g (1 lb) asparagus spears, trimmed
- olive oil, for coating and shallow-frying
- 4 eggs, chilled
- salt and black pepper
- Parmesan shavings or vegetarian hard cheese, to serve*

Make the most of asparagus season by enjoying it for breakfast too – here with crispy frazzled eggs to provide contrast and that all-important soft yolk to ooze softly over the asparagus.

- Blanch the asparagus in a saucepan of salted boiling water for 2 minutes. Drain and refresh under cold water. Drain again, pat dry and toss in a little oil to coat.

- Cook the asparagus in a preheated griddle pan for 2–3 minutes on each side until tender but still with a bite. Set aside to cool slightly.

- Pour enough oil into a large frying pan to coat the base generously and heat until almost smoking. Crack each egg into a cup and carefully slide into the pan (watch out as the oil will splutter). Once the edges of the eggs have bubbled up and browned, reduce the heat to low, cover and cook for a further 1 minute. Remove from the pan with a slotted spoon and drain on kitchen paper. The yolks should have formed a skin, but should remain runny underneath.

- Divide the asparagus between 4 serving plates and top each pile with an egg. Scatter with pepper and Parmesan shavings.

*For guidance on vegetarian cheeses, see page 5.

• LIGHT BITES •

Rocket & Garlic Crumbed Mussels

SERVES 4 • PREP & COOKING TIME 25 minutes

- 25 g (1 oz) wild rocket leaves
- 1 garlic clove
- 50 g (2 oz) fresh white breadcrumbs
- 4 tablespoons extra virgin olive oil
- 1 kg (2 lb) mussels, scrubbed and debearded
- salt and black pepper
- lemon wedges, to serve

The rule to remember for cooking mussels safely is that if they stay open when tapped before cooking or stay closed once they've been cooked, they should be discarded.

- Blitz the rocket and garlic in a food processor until roughly chopped. Add the breadcrumbs and pulse until combined, then stir in the oil. Season with salt and pepper. Cover and chill until needed.

- Put the mussels in a large saucepan with a tight-fitting lid and add water to a depth of 2.5 cm (1 inch). Cover and bring to the boil over a high heat. Cook the mussels, shaking the pan frequently, for 2–3 minutes, or until the shells have opened. Drain, discarding any that remain closed. Pull away and discard the empty shell halves, reserving only the halves with the mussels attached.

- Place the mussels, flesh-side up, on a baking sheet. Divide the breadcrumb topping between the mussels and cook on the top shelf of a preheated high grill for 1–2 minutes until the breadcrumbs are golden. Serve immediately with lemon wedges on the side.

· MAINS ·

Spiced Chicken Tagine

SERVES 4 • PREP & COOKING TIME 1 hour 15 minutes

- 1 tablespoon olive oil
- 8 chicken thighs, skinned
- 1 onion, sliced
- 2 garlic cloves, finely chopped
- 500 g (1 lb) plum tomatoes, skinned (optional), cut into chunks
- 1 teaspoon turmeric
- 1 cinnamon stick, halved
- 2.5 cm (1 inch) piece fresh root ginger, peeled and grated
- 2 teaspoons honey
- 100 g (3½ oz) ready-to-eat dried apricots, quartered
- 200 g (7 oz) couscous
- 450 ml (¾ pint) boiling water
- grated zest and juice of 1 lemon
- small bunch coriander, roughly chopped
- salt and black pepper

This mouth-watering Moroccan-inspired dish is a great make-ahead choice and a good one to freeze. Serve it with a bowl of thick yogurt swirled with spicy, aromatic harissa paste if you fancy a kick of added heat.

- Heat the oil in a large frying pan, add the chicken and fry until browned on both sides. Lift out and transfer to a tagine or casserole dish. Add the onion to the pan and fry until golden.

- Stir in the garlic, tomatoes, spices and honey. Add the apricots and a little salt and pepper and heat through. Spoon over the chicken, cover the dish and bake in a preheated oven, 180°C (350°F), Gas Mark 4, for 45 minutes or until the chicken is cooked through.

- When the chicken is almost ready, soak the couscous in the boiling water for 5 minutes. Stir in the lemon zest and juice, coriander and seasoning. Spoon on to serving plates and top with the chicken and tomatoes, discarding the cinnamon stick just before eating.

V

• LIGHT BITES •

Portuguese Custard Tarts

MAKES 12 • PREP & COOKING TIME 1 hour plus cooling

- 1 tablespoon vanilla sugar
- ½ teaspoon ground cinnamon
- 450 g (14½ oz) chilled ready-made sweet shortcrust pastry
- a little flour, for dusting
- 3 eggs
- 2 egg yolks
- 2 tablespoons caster sugar
- 1 teaspoon vanilla extract
- 300 ml (½ pint) double cream
- 150 ml (¼ pint) milk
- icing sugar, for dusting

Who can resist one of these little beauties? Portuguese custard tarts, or pastéis de nata, with their flaky pastry and sweet custard filling, are justifiably famous around the world.

- Mix the vanilla sugar with the cinnamon. Cut the pastry in half and roll out each piece on a lightly floured surface to a 20 cm (8 inch) square. Sprinkle 1 square with the spiced sugar and position the second square on top. Reroll the pastry to a 40 × 30 cm (16 × 12 inch) rectangle and cut out 12 circles, each 10 cm (4 inch) across, using a large cutter or small bowl as a guide.

- Press the pastry circles into the sections of a 12-hole nonstick muffin tray, pressing them firmly into the bottom and around the sides. Prick each pastry base, line with a square of foil, add macaroni or beans and bake in a preheated oven, 190°C (375°F), Gas Mark 5, for 10 minutes.

- Remove the foil and macaroni or beans and bake for an additional 5 minutes. Reduce the oven temperature to 160°C (325°F), Gas Mark 3.

- Beat together the eggs, egg yolks, caster sugar and vanilla extract. Heat the cream and milk in a pan until bubbling around the edges and pour it over the egg mixture, stirring. Strain the custard into a jug and pour into the pastry shells.

Make the most of your leftovers...

Don't bin the egg whites left over from this recipe. Use them to bake **Florentines** (page 101), **Turkish Delight Cakes** (page 111) or **Fruited Friands** (page 297).

- Bake for about 20 minutes or until the custard is only just set. Let the tarts cool in the tin, then remove and serve dusted with icing sugar.

BREAKFASTS •

Hot-Smoked Salmon Kedgeree with Quails' Eggs

SERVES 4 • PREP & COOKING TIME 30 minutes

- 3 tablespoons boiling water
- pinch of saffron threads
- 1 tablespoon vegetable oil
- 25 g (1 oz) butter
- 1 onion, finely chopped
- 1 garlic clove, finely chopped
- 1 teaspoon peeled and finely grated fresh root ginger
- 1 teaspoon mild curry powder
- 250 g (8 oz) basmati rice
- 750 ml (1¼ pints) fish or vegetable stock
- 6 quails' eggs
- 300 g (10 oz) hot-smoked salmon fillets, skinned
- 5 tablespoons crème fraîche
- salt and black pepper
- chopped flat-leaf parsley, to garnish

Kedgeree is traditionally served for breakfast but you can tuck into this soothing fish, egg and rice dish, with its mildly spicy curry flavour, any time of day. It makes a great winter brunch or supper dish.

- Pour the measured water over the saffron in a jug and leave to infuse. Meanwhile, heat the oil and butter in a large saucepan. Add the onion and gently cook for 5 minutes until softened. Stir in the garlic and ginger and cook for a further 1 minute. Add the curry powder followed by the rice and stir until well coated.

- Pour over the stock and saffron with its soaking liquid. Bring to the boil, then leave to simmer for 15 minutes.

- Meanwhile, boil the quails' eggs in a saucepan of boiling water for 3 minutes. Drain and cool under the cold tap, then shell and halve.

- Break the salmon into flakes and add to the rice with the egg halves. Take off the heat, cover and leave to stand for 5 minutes to warm through. Gently stir in the crème fraîche and season.

- Spoon on to serving plates and scatter with chopped parsley to serve.

• LIGHT BITES •

Vietnamese-Style Noodle Salad

SERVES 4 • PREP & COOKING TIME 25 minutes

- 200 g (7 oz) fine rice noodles
- ½ cucumber, deseeded and cut into matchsticks
- 1 carrot, peeled and cut into matchsticks
- 150 g (5 oz) bean sprouts
- 125 g (4 oz) mangetout, cut into thin strips
- 2 tablespoons chopped coriander
- 2 tablespoons chopped mint
- 1 red chilli, deseeded and finely sliced
- 2 tablespoons chopped unsalted peanuts, to garnish

FOR THE DRESSING
- 1 tablespoon sunflower or groundnut oil
- ½ teaspoon caster sugar
- 1 tablespoon Thai fish sauce
- 2 tablespoons lime juice

Low in calories and packed with crunchy veg and fresh herbs in a tangy dressing, this refreshing salad is a meal in itself or can be served as a side with grilled chicken or fish.

- Bring a large saucepan of water to the boil, then turn off the heat and add the rice noodles. Cover and leave to cook for 4 minutes, or according to the packet instructions, until just tender. Drain the noodles and cool immediately in a bowl of ice-cold water.

- Meanwhile, make the dressing by placing the ingredients in a screw-top jar, adding the lid and shaking until the sugar has dissolved.

- Drain the noodles and return to the bowl. Pour over half of the dressing, then tip in the vegetables, herbs and chilli. Toss until well combined.

- Heap the noodle salad on serving plates and drizzle with the remaining dressing. Serve scattered with chopped peanuts.

• MAINS •

Creamy Oysters & Mushrooms in Brioche Pots

SERVES 4 • PREP & COOKING TIME 20 minutes

- 150 ml (¼ pint) dry white wine or Champagne
- 2 shallots, finely chopped
- 100 ml (3½ fl oz) double cream
- 25 g (1 oz) butter
- 2 pancetta rashers, sliced into thin matchsticks
- 75 g (3 oz) oyster mushrooms, halved if large
- 8 oysters, shucked, reserving the liquor
- 4 individual brioche rolls
- a handful of chives, finely chopped, plus extra to garnish (optional)

Impress your guests with these little bread 'bowls' for a special meal. Scoop out the creamy contents with a small spoon then eat the bread, steeped in all the lovely flavours, last.

- Boil the wine or Champagne with the shallots in a saucepan until reduced by half. Add the cream and cook until you have a rich, creamy sauce.

- Heat 15 g (½ oz) of the butter in a frying pan. Add the pancetta and cook for 2 minutes until turning golden, then add the mushrooms and cook for 3 minutes until browned all over. Add to the sauce with the oysters and their liquor and cook for 2 minutes.

- Meanwhile, slice the lid off each brioche and pull out most of the bread inside. Melt the remaining butter in a small saucepan and brush all over the inside of the brioche. Place on a baking sheet in a preheated oven, 200°C (400°F), Gas Mark 6, for 5–10 minutes until crisp.

- Stir the chives into the sauce, then spoon into the brioche pots, scatter with more chives, if you like, and serve.

V

• DESSERTS •

Chocolate Walnut Brownies

SERVES 4 • PREP & COOKING TIME 30 minutes

- 225 g (7½ oz) unsalted butter
- 225 g (7½ oz) plain dark chocolate, chopped
- 200 g (7 oz) golden caster sugar
- 3 eggs, beaten
- 150 g (5 oz) ground almonds
- 100 g (3½ oz) walnuts, chopped

Celebrate Passover with these rich flourless brownies. They are so simple to make: just melt, mix and bake, and all done in half an hour. Serve them warm with a dollop of vanilla ice cream.

- Melt the butter and chocolate together in a small saucepan over a low heat. Stir in the sugar.

- Beat the eggs into the pan, then stir in the almonds and walnuts.

- Pour into a 23 cm (9 inch) square cake tin and bake in a preheated oven, 180°C (350°F), Gas Mark 4, for 25 minutes, until the top is set but the middle is still gooey.

V

• BREAKFASTS •

Nutty Clementine Yogurts

SERVES 2 • PREP TIME 5 minutes, plus chilling

- 2 passion fruit
- 250 ml (8 fl oz) natural yogurt
- 4 tablespoons honey
- 50 g (2 oz) hazelnuts, toasted and roughly chopped
- 4 clementines, peeled and chopped into small pieces

Layers of sunshine flavour from juicy clementines and passion fruit combine with creamy yogurt in this low-cal and delicious breakfast recipe. You could sprinkle over toasted pumpkin seeds in place of the hazelnuts.

- Halve the passion fruit and scoop the pulp into a large bowl. Add the yogurt and mix them together gently.

- Put 2 tablespoonfuls of the honey in the bases of two narrow glasses and scatter with half of the hazelnuts. Spoon half of the yogurt over the nuts and arrange half of the clementine pieces on top of the yogurt.

- Repeat the layering, reserving a few of the nuts for decoration. Scatter the nuts over the top and chill the yogurts until you are ready to serve them.

V

• LIGHT BITES •

Spinach & Feta Filo Parcels

SERVES 2 • PREP & COOKING TIME 30 minutes

- 250 g (8 oz) spinach leaves, rinsed
- 125 g (4 oz) feta cheese, crumbled
- large pinch of freshly grated nutmeg
- 2 tablespoons chopped parsley
- 4 sheets of filo pastry
- 4 tablespoons olive oil
- salt and black pepper

With flavours that evoke sunshine on a Greek island, these feta and spinach pockets can be served straight from the oven or at room temperature and are perfect with a simple tomato and red onion salad or with a dollop of tzatziki.

- Place the spinach in a large saucepan without any extra water, cover and cook for 2 minutes until wilted. Drain and squeeze out as much excess water as possible.

- Chop the spinach and mix with the feta, nutmeg and parsley in a bowl. Season with pepper (the feta is salty so check before adding salt).

- Place 2 sheets of filo pastry on top of one another and brush lightly with oil. Place half the filling at the end of the sheet, then fold over to make a triangle and continue folding until the filling is enclosed. Brush with oil. Repeat to make 1 more parcel.

- Place the parcels on a baking sheet and bake in a preheated oven, 200°C (400°F), Gas Mark 6, for 15 minutes until crisp and golden.

v

· MAINS ·

Pea & Asparagus Risotto

SERVES 4 • PREP & COOKING TIME 30 minutes

- 1 tablespoon olive oil
- 1 onion, finely chopped
- 1 garlic clove, crushed
- 300 g (10 oz) risotto rice
- 125 ml (4 fl oz) dry white wine
- 1 litre (1¾ pints) hot vegetable stock
- 125 g (4 oz) fine asparagus spears, halved
- 75 g (3 oz) frozen peas
- 25 g (1 oz) butter
- salt and black pepper

TO SERVE
- 50 g (2 oz) rocket
- Parmesan or vegetarian hard cheese shavings*

With deliciously sweet peas and delicate asparagus, this is a dish that sings of spring. Creamy without being too rich, it's sure to become a firm favourite. For a special treat, you could serve it with juicy seared scallops.

- Heat the oil in a large, heavy-based saucepan. Add the onion and cook for 5 minutes until softened. Add the garlic and rice and cook for 30 seconds until coated in the oil. Pour in the wine and bubble until boiled away.

- Gradually add the stock, a ladleful at a time, stirring continuously and allowing each ladleful to be absorbed before adding the next. After 10 minutes, add the asparagus, then cook for a further 5 minutes until the rice is tender.

- Stir in the peas and butter, cover and leave to stand for 1–2 minutes. Season the risotto to taste, then spoon into warmed bowls and top each portion with a handful of rocket and some Parmesan shavings.

*For guidance on vegetarian cheeses, see page 5.

V

· DESSERTS ·

Lemon & Orange Mousse

SERVES 4 • PREP TIME 15 minutes, plus chilling

- 300 ml (½ pint) double cream
- grated zest and juice of 1 lemon, plus extra finely pared strips of rind to decorate
- grated zest and juice of ½ orange, plus extra finely pared strips of rind to decorate
- 65 g (2½ oz) caster sugar
- 2 egg whites

Make these simple but elegant citrussy desserts ahead of time for a relaxed weekend supper with friends. They need just 15 minutes of prep and a few hours of hands-off chilling time.

- Whip together the cream, grated lemon and orange zest and sugar in a large bowl until the mixture starts to thicken. Add the lemon and orange juices and whisk again until the mixture thickens.

- Whip, in a separate large, perfectly clean bowl, the egg whites until soft peaks form, then fold into the citrus mixture. Spoon the mousse into 4 glasses and chill in the refrigerator. Decorate with lemon and orange rind strips.

V

· BREAKFASTS ·

Garlic Mushrooms with Potato Rösti

SERVES 4 • PREP & COOKING TIME 40 minutes

- 3 potatoes, scrubbed but unpeeled, about 625 g (1¼ lb) total weight
- ½ onion, very thinly sliced
- 4 tablespoons vegetable oil
- 50 g (2 oz) butter
- 1 garlic clove, chopped
- 250 g (8 oz) button mushrooms, thinly sliced
- 2 tablespoons finely chopped parsley (optional)
- salt and black pepper
- 1 large bunch of watercress, to serve

Originating in Switzerland as a simple two-ingredient peasant dish, a rösti is essentially a giant hash brown or potato fritter. Golden and crispy, it is great served with garlicky mushrooms, as here, or topped with a poached egg or smoked salmon and soured cream.

- Cook the potatoes whole in a large saucepan of lightly salted boiling water for 8–10 minutes. Drain and set aside until cool enough to handle.

- Coarsely grate the potatoes and mix in a bowl with the sliced onion, 2 tablespoons of the oil and plenty of salt and pepper.

- Heat the remaining oil in a large nonstick frying pan and add the rösti mixture, pushing down to flatten it so that it covers the base of the pan. Cook for 7–8 minutes, then slide on to an oiled plate or board. Flip the rösti back into the pan to cook the other side for 7–8 minutes until crisp and golden.

- Meanwhile, melt the butter in a frying pan and cook the garlic and mushrooms gently for 6–7 minutes, until softened and golden. Season to taste with salt and pepper, then stir in the chopped parsley, if using.

- Cut the rösti into wedges, then arrange on serving plates, scatter over the watercress and spoon over the mushrooms with their juices. Serve immediately.

v

• DESSERTS •

Hot Cross Buns

MAKES 12 • PREP & COOKING TIME 1 hour 20 minutes, plus standing and rising

- 2 tablespoons active dried yeast
- 1 teaspoon sugar
- 150 ml (¼ pint) milk, warmed
- 4 tablespoons warm water
- 500 g (1 lb) strong bread flour
- 1 teaspoon salt
- ½ teaspoon ground mixed spice
- ½ teaspoon ground cinnamon
- ½ teaspoon grated nutmeg
- 50 g (2 oz) caster sugar
- 50 g (2 oz) butter, melted and cooled
- 1 egg, beaten
- 125 g (4 oz) currants
- 40 g (1½ oz) chopped mixed peel
- 75 g (3 oz) ready-made shortcrust pastry

FOR THE GLAZE
- 3 tablespoons caster sugar
- 4 tablespoons milk and water

Fluffy and fragrant, these delicately spiced fruity treats are a must-have on Good Friday, preferably toasted and slathered with butter. Making your own is definitely worth the effort!

- Blend the yeast and sugar into the warmed milk and water. Stir into 125 g (4 oz) of the flour and leave in a warm place for about 20 minutes. Sift the remaining flour into a bowl, add the salt, spices and caster sugar.

- Add the butter and egg to the yeast mixture. Stir this into the flour and mix well. Add the dried fruit and mix to a fairly soft dough. Add a little water if necessary.

- Turn out the dough on to a lightly floured surface and knead well. Place in an oiled plastic bag and allow to rise for 1–1½ hours at room temperature until doubled in size.

- Turn out on to a floured surface and knead with your knuckles to knock out the air bubbles.

- Divide the dough and shape into 12 round buns. Flatten each slightly then space well apart on floured baking sheets. Cover and put in a warm place again to rise for 20–30 minutes until doubled in size. Meanwhile, thinly roll out the pastry and cut it into 24 thin strips about 8 cm (3½ inches) long.

- Dampen the strips and lay 2, damp side down, in a cross over each bun. Bake in a preheated oven, 190°C (375°F), Gas Mark 5, for 20 minutes or until golden brown and firm.

- Make the glaze. Dissolve the sugar in the milk and water mixture over a low heat. Brush the cooked buns twice with the glaze, then serve hot, split and buttered.

v

· LIGHT BITES ·

Potato Skins & Soured Cream Dip

SERVES 6 • Prep + cook 15 minutes, plus potato baking

- 6 large potatoes, baked and left to go cold
- 1 tablespoon olive oil
- 150 g (5 oz) grated Cheddar cheese

FOR THE SOURED CREAM DIP
- 200 g (7 oz) soured cream
- 1 garlic clove, crushed
- 1 tablespoon chopped chives
- salt and black pepper

Hot, crunchy, cheesy potato skins and a creamy, chive-flecked dip – everyone will love this. Serve with pre-dinner drinks and watch it disappear in a flash! If you're pushed for time, then use ready-made tzatziki or salsa for dipping instead.

- To make the dip, combine the ingredients in a bowl and season to taste.

- Take the cooled potatoes and cut into quarters. Scoop out and put the flesh to one side for another recipe (see the box below).

- Transfer the skins to a bowl, pour over the olive oil and carefully mix with your hands.

- Place the skins cut-side down on a baking sheet and cook under a preheated hot grill for 2 minutes. Turn the skins over and carefully sprinkle a little cheese on to each skin. Cook for a further 2 minutes until the cheese is melted.

- Serve immediately with the dip.

Make the most of your leftovers...
Use up the potato flesh in the **Crab Cakes** on page 69, **Potato Drop Scones** on page 156 or the **Potato Cakes** on page 401.

V

• DESSERTS •

Double Chocolate Truffles

MAKES 24 • PREP TIME 45 minutes, plus chilling

- 250ml (8fl oz) double cream
- 400g (13oz) dark chocolate
- 3–4 tablespoons brandy or rum
- 2 tablespoons cocoa powder, sifted
- crystallized violets, to decorate

These make a lovely Easter gift – once they are completely set, place the truffles in mini cupcakes cases and pack into a gift box lined with pretty tissue paper. For a minty version, add 3–4 tablespoons of mint liqueur to the chocolate truffle mix instead of the brandy or rum.

- Pour the cream into a small pan and bring to the boil. Take the pan off the heat and break in half the chocolate. Leave to stand until it has melted, then stir in the brandy or rum and mix until smooth. Chill for 4 hours until the truffle mixture is firm.

- Line a baking sheet with greaseproof paper and dust with cocoa powder. Scoop a little truffle mixture on to a teaspoon, then transfer it to a second spoon and back to the first again, making a well-rounded egg shape (or use a melon baller). Slide the truffle on to the cocoa-dusted paper. Repeat until all the mixture is used up. Chill again for 2 hours, or overnight if possible, until firm.

- Melt the remaining chocolate in a bowl over a pan of simmering water, making sure the bottom of the bowl does not touch the water. Stir well, then, holding one truffle at a time on a fork over the bowl, spoon melted chocolate over the top to coat it.

- Place the truffles on a piece of greaseproof paper on a nonstick baking sheet. Swirl a little chocolate over the top of each with a spoon and finish with a crystallized violet.

- Chill for at least 1 hour.

· MAINS ·

Chilli Beef Parcels with Polenta Pastry

MAKES 6 • PREP & COOKING TIME 1 hour 40 minutes

- 2 teaspoons sunflower oil
- 250 g (8 oz) minced beef
- 1 small onion, chopped
- 1 garlic clove, finely chopped
- ½ teaspoon dried crushed chillies
- ¼ teaspoon ground cinnamon
- 2 teaspoons light muscovado sugar
- 1 bay leaf
- 200 g (7 oz) can chopped tomatoes
- 200 g (7 oz) can red kidney beans, drained
- 150 ml (¼ pint) beef stock
- beaten egg, to glaze
- salt and black pepper

FOR THE POLENTA PASTRY
- 300 g (10 oz) plain flour
- 50 g (2 oz) polenta
- 75 g (3 oz) butter, diced
- 75 g (3 oz) white vegetable fat, diced
- 4–4½ tablespoons cold water

Crispy polenta pastry encasing a mildly spiced minced beef and kidney bean filling makes these pastries a dinner not to be missed. Serve them hot with soured cream and a chunky tomatoey salsa – try the one on page 207.

- Heat the oil in a saucepan, add the mince and onion and fry, stirring, until the mince is browned. Stir in the garlic, chillies, cinnamon, sugar and bay leaf. Mix in the tomatoes, kidney beans and stock, then add plenty of salt and pepper. Bring to the boil, stirring, then cover and simmer gently for 45 minutes. Leave to cool.

- Make the pastry. Add the flour, polenta, fats and a little salt and pepper to a bowl. Rub in the fats with your fingertips or an electric mixer until you have fine crumbs. Add enough water to form a smooth dough, then knead lightly on a surface dusted with flour.

- Cut the pastry in half, roll out one half and trim to a 12 × 36 cm (5 × 15 inch) rectangle, then cut into 3 × 12 cm (5 inch) squares.

- Spoon half the filling into the centre of the pastry squares. Brush the edges with beaten egg, then bring the points of the pastry up to the centre, pressing the straight edges of the pastry together.

- Transfer to an oiled baking sheet and repeat with the remaining pastry and filling to make 6 pies. Brush the pies with beaten egg, then bake in a preheated oven, 190°C (375°F), Gas Mark 5, for 20 minutes.

V

• DESSERTS •

Rhubarb & Raspberry Crumble

SERVES 4 • PREP & COOKING TIME 35 minutes

- 200 g (7 oz) plain flour
- pinch of salt
- 150 g (5 oz) unsalted butter
- 200 g (7 oz) soft brown sugar
- 500 g (1 lb) fresh or frozen rhubarb (defrosted if frozen), sliced
- 125 g (4 oz) fresh or frozen raspberries
- 3 tablespoons orange juice

You can use fresh or frozen fruit for this easy-to-make crumble so you can enjoy it all year round. Serve with cream or, for a double hit of raspberry, raspberry ripple ice cream.

- Put the flour and salt in a bowl, add the butter and rub in with the fingertips until the mixture resembles breadcrumbs. Stir in 150 g (5 oz) of the sugar.

- Mix together the fruits, the remaining sugar and orange juice and tip into a greased dish. Sprinkle over the topping and cook in a preheated oven, 200°C (400°F), Gas Mark 6, for about 25 minutes or until golden brown and bubbling.

· MAINS ·

Steak & Ale Casserole

SERVES 5–6 • PREP & COOKING TIME 2 hours

- 2 tablespoons plain flour
- 1 kg (2 lb) braising steak, cut into chunks
- 25 g (1 oz) butter
- 1 tablespoon oil
- 2 onions, chopped
- 2 celery sticks, sliced
- several thyme sprigs
- 2 bay leaves
- 400 ml (14 fl oz) strong ale
- 300 ml (½ pint) beef stock
- 2 tablespoons black treacle
- 500 g (1 lb) parsnips, peeled and cut into wedges
- salt and black pepper

Celebrate St George, the patron saint of England, with this classic English casserole. It improves with keeping, so tastes even better the day after it is made. Serve it with creamy mashed potato for mopping up the delicious gravy.

- Season the flour with salt and pepper and use to coat the beef. Melt the butter with the oil in a large, flameproof casserole and fry the beef in batches until deep brown. Drain with a slotted spoon while cooking the remainder.

- Add the onions and celery and fry gently for 5 minutes. Return the beef to the pan and add the herbs, ale, stock and treacle. Bring just to the boil, then reduce the heat and cover with a lid.

- Bake in a preheated oven, 160°C (325°F), Gas Mark 3, for 1 hour.

- Add the parsnips to the dish and return to the oven for a further 30 minutes or until the beef and parsnips are tender. Check the seasoning and serve.

V

• BREAKFASTS •

Rocket & Goats' Cheese Omelette

SERVES 4 • PREP & COOKING TIME 20 minutes

- 12 eggs
- 4 tablespoons milk
- 4 tablespoons chopped mixed herbs, such as chervil, chives, marjoram, parsley and tarragon
- 50 g (2 oz) butter
- 125 g (4 oz) soft goats' cheese, diced
- small handful of baby rocket leaves
- salt and black pepper

This is a great recipe for a leisurely breakfast or light supper. For the best results, serve each omelette as soon as it is ready. Alternatively, keep the omelettes warm in a low oven and serve all together.

- Beat the eggs, milk, herbs and salt and pepper together in a large bowl. Melt a quarter of the butter in an omelette pan. As soon as it stops foaming, swirl in a quarter of the egg mixture and cook over a medium heat, forking over the omelette so that it cooks evenly.

- As soon as it is set on the underside, but still a little runny in the centre, scatter a quarter of the cheese and a quarter of the rocket leaves over one half of the omelette. Carefully slide the omelette on to a serving plate, folding it in half as you go. Serve immediately and repeat to make the other 3 omelettes.

· LIGHT BITES ·

Prawn, Pea Shoot & Quinoa Salad

SERVES 4 • PREP & COOKING TIME 20 minutes

- 300 g (10 oz) quinoa
- 75 g (3 oz) mangetout, blanched and halved
- 200 g (7 oz) asparagus spears, cooked, cooled and cut into bite-sized pieces
- 50 g (2 oz) pea shoots
- 400 g (13 oz) cooked tiger prawns, shells removed

FOR THE DRESSING
- 2 tablespoons olive oil
- 2 tablespoons lemon juice
- 20 g (¾ oz) dried cranberries
- 50 g (2 oz) hazelnuts, chopped and toasted

You could use any grain in place of the quinoa – bulgur wheat or spelt would work well, or you could use couscous if that's what you have in the storecupboard. Serve the salad soon after dressing, to keep the hazelnuts crunchy.

- Cook the quinoa according to the instructions on the packet. Set aside to cool.

- Stir the mangetout and asparagus through the quinoa.

- Make the dressing by mixing together the oil, lemon juice, cranberries and hazelnuts.

- Spoon the pea shoots and prawns over the quinoa, drizzle over the dressing and serve.

• MAINS •

Asian Braised Belly of Pork

SERVES 6 • PREP & COOKING TIME 2 hours, plus cooling
and marinating

- 1.25 kg (2½ lb) piece of boned pork belly, skin removed and trimmed of excess fat
- 2 bay leaves
- 100 ml (3½ fl oz) rice vinegar
- 100 g (3½ oz) palm or light muscovado sugar
- 2 tablespoons salted black beans
- 2 tablespoons hoisin sauce
- 4 tablespoons dark soy sauce
- 1 teaspoon black pepper
- 2 garlic cloves, crushed

A little bit sweet, a little bit salty and totally delicious, this succulent pork makes an excellent main course for a dinner party as you can do most of the prep the night before, then put it in the oven and get on with other things. Pair it with steamed rice and crunchy Asian greens.

- Put the piece of pork in a large saucepan and cover with water. Bring to the boil, reduce the heat and cook for 10 minutes. Leave to cool in the liquid, then drain, reserving the liquid. Score a crisscross pattern over the fatty side of the meat and cut into 6 portions. Place in a shallow glass or ceramic dish.

- Mix together all the remaining ingredients and pour over the pork. Cover and leave to marinate in the refrigerator overnight.

- Transfer the pork and its marinade to a casserole dish. Lift the fat off the reserved broth and pour enough over the pork to just cover it.

- Place in a preheated oven, 200°C (400°F), Gas Mark 6, and cook for 30 minutes. Reduce the temperature to 180°C (350°F), Gas Mark 4, and cook for about 2 hours until the pork is completely tender. Drain the pork and keep warm while finishing the sauce.

- Pour the sauce into a saucepan and bring to the boil. Cook until reduced by about two-thirds, then serve alongside the pork.

V

· BREAKFASTS ·

Honey & Granola Pancakes

SERVES 4 • PREP & COOKING TIME 20 minutes

- 150 g (5 oz) plain flour
- 2 teaspoons baking powder
- 2 eggs
- 275 ml (9 fl oz) milk
- 3 tablespoons honey
- 200 g (7 oz) crunchy, granola-style cereal, lightly crushed
- 50 g (2 oz) butter

TO SERVE
- honey
- Greek yogurt

Granola adds a lovely crunch to these honey-sweet pancakes. You can use any shop-bought granola or, for homemade, try the **Honey-roasted Granola** on page 318.

- Sift the flour and baking powder together into a large bowl, then make a well in the centre of the mixture.

- Whisk together the eggs, milk and honey and pour into the well. Whisk the wet ingredients in the well as you gradually incorporate the flour into the mixture. Stir in the granola.

- Melt a knob of butter in a large nonstick frying pan and pour small amounts of the batter into the pan to form small, thick pancakes that are about 8 cm (3¼ inches) in diameter.

- Cook over a medium-low heat for 2–3 minutes until bubbles start appearing on the surface of the pancakes. Flip over and cook the other side for a further minute, until golden.

- Repeat with the remaining mixture until you have made all the pancakes. This quantity of batter should yield about 16 pancakes.

• MAINS •

Roast Lamb Stuffed with Rice & Peppers

SERVES 4 • PREP & COOKING TIME 1¾ hours

- 2 red peppers, deseeded and halved
- 50 g (2 oz) wild rice, cooked
- 5 garlic cloves, chopped
- 5 semi-dried tomatoes, chopped
- 2 tablespoons chopped flat-leaf parsley
- 625 g (1¼ lb) boneless leg of lamb, butterflied
- 4 artichoke halves
- salt and black pepper

Roast lamb gets an Italian twist here with rice, succulent semi-dried tomatoes, roasted peppers and plenty of garlic combining for a flavour sensation.

- Put the pepper halves in a roasting tin and cook in a preheated oven, 180°C (350°F), Gas Mark 4, for 20 minutes, until the skin has blackened and blistered. Cover with damp kitchen paper and set aside. When the peppers are cool enough to handle, peel off the skin and chop the flesh. (Leave the oven on.)

- Mix together one of the chopped peppers, the rice, garlic, tomatoes and parsley. Season to taste.

- Put the lamb on a board and make a horizontal incision, almost all the way along, to make a cavity for stuffing. Fold back the top half, spoon in the stuffing and fold back the top. Secure with skewers.

- Cook the lamb for 1 hour, basting frequently, and adding the artichokes and other pepper for the last 15 minutes of cooking time. Slice the lamb and serve immediately.

• MAINS •

Smoked Haddock Fish Cakes

SERVES 4 • PREP & COOKING TIME 1 hour

- 625 g (1¼ lb) potatoes, cut into chunks
- 500 g (1 lb) smoked haddock
- 4 eggs
- 25 g (1 oz) butter
- 2–3 tablespoons milk
- 3 tablespoons chopped chives or parsley
- 2 tablespoons water
- 125 g (4 oz) fresh breadcrumbs
- 4 tablespoons sunflower oil
- salt and black pepper

FOR THE TARTAR SAUCE
- 200 ml (7 fl oz) crème fraîche
- finely grated zest of 1 lemon
- 2 tablespoons chopped chives or parsley
- 3 teaspoons capers, roughly chopped
- 50 g (2 oz) gherkins, finely chopped

Golden and crunchy on the outside, packed with soft fish and hard-boiled eggs on the inside, this recipe gives you everything you want in a fish cake. The key is to keep the fish in big chunks rather than flaking to a mush. Add a green salad and some lemon wedges for squeezing over.

- Half-fill the base of a steamer with water and bring to the boil. Cook the potatoes in the water in the base for 15 minutes or until tender, and the fish in the top for 8–10 minutes until it flakes when pressed with a knife. Hard-boil 2 of the eggs for 8 minutes.

- Skin and flake the fish, discarding any bones. Shell and roughly chop the hard-boiled eggs. Drain and mash the potatoes with the butter, milk and seasoning. Stir the fish, chopped egg and chopped herbs into the mash. Divide into 8 portions and pat into thick rounds.

- Beat the remaining eggs in a shallow dish with the measured water. Put the breadcrumbs in a second shallow dish. Coat the fishcakes in egg on both sides, then coat in the breadcrumbs. Place on a baking tray.

- Mix all the sauce ingredients with a little seasoning. Spoon into a serving dish, cover and chill until required.

- Heat half the oil in a frying pan, add 4 fishcakes, cover and fry over a medium heat for 8–10 minutes, turning once, until golden on both sides and hot through. Keep hot in the oven while cooking the remaining cakes in the remaining oil. Serve with spoonfuls of sauce.

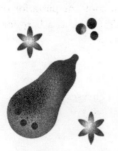

V

• MAINS •

New Potato & Green Bean Pasta with Pesto

SERVES 4 • PREP & COOKING TIME 20 minutes

- 300 g (10 oz) trofie pasta
- 6 new potatoes, scrubbed and halved
- 125 g (4 oz) green beans, trimmed
- salt and black pepper

FOR THE PESTO
- 75 g (3 oz) basil leaves
- 25 g (1 oz) toasted pine nuts, plus extra to serve
- 1 garlic clove, crushed
- 100 ml (3½ fl oz) extra-virgin olive oil
- 3 tablespoons grated Parmesan or vegetarian hard cheese, plus extra to serve*

This recipe is a traditional one from Liguria, in northern Italy. Trofie is a Ligurian pasta but you could use any pasta shape. You can use shop-bought pesto if you're in a hurry but this homemade fresh one is lovely.

- Cook the pasta in a large pan of salted boiling water according to the packet instructions until al dente.

- Meanwhile, cook the potatoes in a large pan of salted boiling water for 7 minutes. Add the beans and cook for a further 5 minutes.

- To make the pesto, pound all the ingredients together in a mortar with a pestle to form a chunky pesto and season. Alternatively, place all the ingredients in a food processor and whizz together.

- Drain the pasta and vegetables and return to a pan. Toss together with the pesto and season.

- Spoon into serving bowls and serve scattered with extra Parmesan and toasted pine nuts.

Make the most of your leftovers...
Add a little extra when you cook the pasta for this dish, then put it to one side to use as a base for a pasta salad for lunch tomorrow.

*For guidance on vegetarian cheeses, see page 5.

May

GOOD TO EAT THIS MONTH

asparagus * beetroot * broad beans * broccoli *
cabbage * carrots * garlic * Jersey Royal potatoes *
lettuce * peas * spinach * spring greens * spring onions
* watercress * elderflowers * gooseberries * rhubarb *
chives * dill * mint * oregano * tarragon

DATES TO LOOK FORWARD TO THIS MONTH

Mother's Day (US and other countries)

This month is the cusp between summer and spring. In the
countryside the hedgerows are green with rows of pretty cow
parsley frothing beneath them. The danger of frost has passed
in most places so summer flowers are being planted in gardens
and parks.

We've made the transition from hearty soups and stews to
lighter, brighter meals like **Broad Bean Crostini** (page 157) and
Cod Cheek Tacos (page 175).

Fabulous Jersey Royals, with their creamy texture and wonderful
flavour, only make an appearance for a short period every year so
make the most of them with the recipes on pages 150 and 174.
And don't peel or scrape them when you cook them, a lot of the
flavour is in the skin.

In-season beetroot is the star of the show in two unusual, but
wonderful, recipes: the **Chocolate & Beetroot Fudge Cake** on
page 155 and the **Chilled Beetroot & Apple Soup** on page 170.

Elderflowers are ready to pick around late May to mid-June.
See the recipe on page 179 for a delicious homemade cordial.

V

· BREAKFASTS ·

Sugarless Fruit Granola Bars

MAKES 9 • PREP & COOKING TIME 1 hour, plus cooling

- 225 g (7½ oz) peeled, cored and roughly chopped dessert apple
- 1 tablespoon lemon juice
- 1 tablespoon agave syrup
- ½ teaspoon ground cinnamon
- sunflower oil, for oiling

FOR THE GRANOLA
- 125 g (4 oz) rolled oats
- 125 g (4 oz) ready-to-eat dried apricots
- 125 g (4 oz) fresh Medjool dates, stoned and roughly chopped
- 2 tablespoons ground flaxseed (linseed)
- 2 tablespoons smooth peanut butter
- 55 ml (2 fl oz) agave syrup

These vegan granola bars are sweetened the natural way with apricots, dates, roasted apple and agave syrup, which is similar in consistency to honey. They are chewy and delicious and you won't miss the sugar at all!

- Line a baking sheet with baking parchment. Toss the apple with the lemon juice, agave syrup and cinnamon in a bowl, then spread out on the lined baking sheet and roast in a preheated oven, 160°C (325°F), Gas Mark 3, for 20 minutes. Remove from the oven and leave to cool.

- Increase the oven temperature to 180°C (350°F), Gas Mark 4. Pulse all the ingredients for the granola together in a food processor a few times until mixed and mashed.

- Fold in the cooled roasted apple, then spoon into a lightly oiled 20 cm (8 inch) square shallow cake tin and level with the back of a spoon. Bake in the oven for 20 minutes.

- Leave to cool for 15 minutes before cutting into 9 squares.

v

• LIGHT BITES •

Spring Green Pea Soup

SERVES 4 • PREP & COOKING TIME 25 minutes

- 1 tablespoon butter
- bunch of spring onions, chopped
- 1.25 kg (2½ lb) fresh peas, shelled, or 500 g (1 lb) frozen peas
- 750 ml (1¼ pints) vegetable stock
- 2 tablespoons thick natural yogurt or single cream
- fresh nutmeg, for grating
- 1 tablespoon chopped and 2 whole chives, to garnish

This vibrant and versatile soup is equally delicious warm or chilled. You can change it up by adding 2 tablespoons of chopped mint before you purée it and serving each bowl garnished with a mint sprig.

- Melt the butter in a large pan and soften the onions, but do not allow them to colour. Add the peas to the pan with the stock. Bring to the boil and simmer for about 5 minutes for frozen peas, but for up to 15 minutes for fresh peas, until they are cooked. Be careful not to overcook fresh peas or they will lose their flavour.

- Remove from the heat and purée in a blender or food processor. Add the yogurt or cream and grate in a little nutmeg.

- Reheat gently if necessary, and serve sprinkled with chives.

· MAINS ·

Spring Braised Duck

SERVES 4 • PREP & COOKING TIME 2 hours

- 4 duck legs
- 2 teaspoons plain flour
- 25 g (1 oz) butter
- 1 tablespoon olive oil
- 2 onions, sliced
- 2 streaky bacon rashers, finely chopped
- 2 garlic cloves, crushed
- 1 glass white wine, about 150 ml (¼ pint)
- 300 ml (½ pint) chicken stock
- 3 bay leaves
- 500 g (1 lb) small new potatoes
- 200 g (7 oz) fresh peas
- 150 g (5 oz) asparagus tips
- 2 tablespoons chopped mint
- salt and black pepper

Showcase this month's finest produce – use Jersey Royals if you can – with this one-pot recipe that is perfect for a relaxed meal with friends. You can do the first three steps before they arrive.

- Halve the duck legs through the joints. Mix the flour with a little seasoning and use to coat the duck pieces.

- Melt the butter with the oil in a sturdy roasting pan or flameproof casserole and gently fry the duck pieces for about 10 minutes until browned. Drain to a plate and pour off all but 1 tablespoon of the fat left in the pan.

- Add the onions and bacon to the pan and fry gently for 5 minutes. Add the garlic and fry for a further 1 minute. Add the wine, stock and bay leaves and bring to the boil, stirring. Return the duck pieces and cover with a lid or foil.

- Place in a preheated oven, 160°C (325°F), Gas Mark 3, for 45 minutes.

- Add the potatoes to the pan, stirring them into the juices. Sprinkle with salt and return to the oven for 30 minutes.

- Add the peas, asparagus and mint to the pan and return to the oven for a further 15 minutes or until all the vegetables are tender. Check the seasoning and serve.

• DESSERTS •

Gooseberry & Elderflower Pies

MAKES 4 • PREP & COOKING TIME 1 hour, plus chilling

- 125 g (4 oz) caster sugar, plus extra for sprinkling
- 2 teaspoons cornflour
- 400 g (13 oz) gooseberries, topped and tailed
- 1 tablespoon elderflower cordial (see page 179), undiluted
- milk or beaten egg, to glaze

FOR THE PASTRY
- 175 g (6 oz) plain flour
- 40 g (1½ oz) icing sugar
- 100 g (3½ oz) butter, diced
- 2 egg yolks
- grated zest of 1 lemon

For elderflower cream, to serve as an accompaniment to these lovely pies, whip 200 ml (7 fl oz) double cream, then fold in 2 tablespoons undiluted elderflower cordial and the grated zest of ½ lemon.

- To make the pastry, add the flour, icing sugar and butter to a mixing bowl and mix until you have fine crumbs.

- Add the egg yolks and lemon zest and mix together until you have a soft ball. Wrap in clingfilm and chill for 15 minutes.

- Mix the sugar, cornflour and gooseberries together in a bowl.

- Cut the chilled pastry into 4 pieces, then roll each piece out to a rough-shaped 18 cm (7 inch) circle. Grease 4 pie tins, each 10 cm (4 inches) in diameter and 2.5 cm (1 inch) deep. Drape the pastry into each tin, leaving the excess pastry overhanging the edges of the tins.

- Spoon in the gooseberry mixture and mound up in the centre, then drizzle over the elderflower cordial. Fold the overhanging pastry up and over the filling, pleating where needed and leaving the centres of the pies open.

- Brush the pastry with milk or beaten egg, sprinkle with a little sugar and bake in a preheated oven, 190°C (375°F), Gas Mark 5, for 20–25 minutes until golden. Leave to stand for 15 minutes, then loosen the edges and lift the pies out of the tins. Serve with whipped cream or elderflower cream (see above).

V

• BREAKFASTS •

Sunshine Breakfast Muffins

MAKES 10 • PREP & COOKING TIME 30 minutes

- 250 g (8 oz) plain flour
- 1 tablespoon baking powder
- 100 g (3½ oz) rolled oats
- 125 g (4 oz) ready-to-eat dried apricots, chopped
- 50 g (2 oz) dried cranberries
- 2 tablespoons mixed seeds, such as sunflower, linseed, pumpkin and hemp
- 50 g (2 oz) soft light brown sugar
- ½ teaspoon salt
- 2 eggs, lightly beaten
- 175 ml (6 fl oz) milk
- 75 ml (3 fl oz) sunflower oil
- 4 tablespoons clear honey

Start the day the sunshine way with these muffins. Packed with plenty of the nourishing stuff – eggs, oats, seeds and dried fruit – these are also a feel-good snack for any time of day.

- Line a 12-hole muffin tin with 10 paper muffin cases.

- Sift the flour and baking powder together into a large bowl. Stir in the oats, dried fruits, seeds, sugar and salt with a metal spoon.

- Beat the eggs, milk, oil and honey together in a jug. Pour over the dry ingredients and stir until only just combined – the batter should be lumpy and fairly runny.

- Spoon the mixture into the muffin cases so that they are two-thirds full and bake on the top shelf of a preheated oven, 190°C (375°F), Gas Mark 5, for 20–25 minutes until risen and golden.

- Leave to cool in the tin for 5 minutes, then transfer to a wire rack to cool completely.

• LIGHT BITES •

Pork, Apple & Chicken Pie

SERVES 6–8 • PREP & COOKING TIME 2 hours

- 175 g (6 oz) lard
- 175 ml (6 fl oz) milk and water mixed
- 2 teaspoons English mustard
- 375 g (12 oz) plain flour
- ½ teaspoon salt

FOR THE FILLING
- 500 g (1 lb) lean pork and leek or Cumberland sausages, skinned
- 500 g (1 lb) skinless boneless chicken thighs, chopped
- 125 g (4 oz) smoked bacon, diced
- 5 cloves, roughly crushed
- ¼ teaspoon ground allspice
- small bunch of sage
- 1 Braeburn apple, cored and sliced
- 1 egg yolk mixed with 1 tablespoon water
- salt and black pepper

Everybody loves a pie. This hearty pork and chicken pie takes a little effort but is a real crowd-pleaser for a summer lunch or picnic. Serve with a fruity chutney, sharp mustard or pickles, and a green salad.

- First make the pastry. Heat the lard in the milk and water in a small saucepan until melted then stir in the mustard.

- Mix the flour and salt in a bowl, stir in the melted lard mixture and mix to a soft ball. Cool for 10 minutes. Mix the sausagemeat, chicken, bacon, cloves, allspice and plenty of salt and pepper together in a bowl. Remove one-third of the pastry and set aside. Press the remaining warm pastry over the base and sides of a deep 18 cm (7 inch) loose-bottomed cake tin.

- Spoon in half the filling and level. Cover with half the sage leaves, then the apple slices, then spoon over the rest of the filling. Level and top with the remaining sage. Brush the edges of the pastry with the egg glaze.

- Roll the reserved pastry to a circle a little larger than the tin, arrange on the pie and press the edges together. Trim off the excess then crimp the edge. Make a slit in the top of the pie, then brush with egg glaze.

- Cook in a preheated oven, 180°C (350°F), Gas Mark 4, for 1½ hours, covering with foil after 40 minutes, when golden. Leave to cool, remove the tin then put the pie, still on the tin base, in the refrigerator for 3–4 hours or overnight. When ready to serve, remove the base and cut the pie into wedges.

VG

• MAINS •

Vegetable Paella with Almonds

SERVES 4 • PREP & COOKING TIME 45 minutes

- 4 tablespoons olive oil
- 1 onion, chopped
- pinch of saffron threads
- 225 g (7½ oz) arborio rice
- 1.2 litres (2 pints) vegetable stock
- 175 g (6 oz) fine asparagus spears, trimmed and cut into 5 cm (2 inch) lengths
- bunch of spring onions, cut into strips
- 175 g (6 oz) midi plum tomatoes on the vine, halved
- 125 g (4 oz) frozen peas
- 3 tablespoons flaked almonds, toasted
- 3 tablespoons chopped flat-leaf parsley
- salt

A vegan take on the classic Spanish paella, this is a great meal to share with friends. Pile it up on a large platter, place it in the centre of the table, add a big green salad and let everyone dig in.

- Heat 1 tablespoon of the oil in a large, heavy-based frying pan, add the onion and saffron and cook over a medium heat, stirring frequently, for 5 minutes, until the onion is softened and golden. Add the rice and stir well, then season with some salt. Add the stock and bring to the boil, then cover and simmer, stirring occasionally, for 20 minutes until the stock is almost all absorbed and the rice is tender and cooked through.

- Meanwhile, heat the remaining oil in a separate frying pan, add the asparagus and spring onions and cook over a medium heat for 5 minutes until softened and lightly charred in places. Remove from the pan with a slotted spoon. Add the vine tomatoes to the pan and cook for 2–3 minutes on each side until softened.

- Add the peas to the rice and cook for a further 2 minutes, then add the asparagus, spring onions and tomatoes and gently toss through. Scatter with the almonds and parsley and serve.

VG

• DESSERTS •

Chocolate & Beetroot Fudge Cake

SERVES 12 • PREP & COOKING TIME 1 hour 10 minutes, plus cooling and chilling

- 250 g (8 oz) plain flour
- 75 g (3 oz) cocoa powder
- 1 teaspoon bicarbonate of soda
- 300 g (10½ oz) light muscovado sugar
- 250 g (8 oz) ready-cooked fresh beetroot (not pickled), chopped
- 300 ml (½ pint) almond milk
- 100 ml (3½ fl oz) sunflower oil, plus extra for oiling
- 2 teaspoons vanilla extract
- 1 tablespoon cider vinegar
- pink edible sprinkles or fresh unsprayed rose petals, washed and patted dry, to decorate

FOR THE FROSTING
- 150 g (5 oz) vegan spread
- 225 g (8 oz) icing sugar
- 1 teaspoon vanilla extract
- 150 g (5 oz) dairy-free plain dark chocolate, melted and cooled

It might seem a surprising combination, but naturally sweet beetroot makes this vegan centrepiece chocolate cake beautifully moist. Cooked beetroot – it's important it's not pickled – can be found in the vegetable section of most supermarkets.

- Sift the flour, cocoa powder and bicarbonate of soda together into a large bowl. Stir in the muscovado sugar.

- Blend the beetroot in a blender or food processor until smooth. With the motor running, pour in the almond milk, oil, vanilla and vinegar.

- Pour the beetroot mixture on to the dry ingredients and stir until mixed. Pour into an oiled and base-lined 20 cm (8 inch) springform cake tin and bake in a preheated oven, 180°C (350°F), Gas Mark 4, for 45–50 minutes until just firm to the touch. Leave to cool in the tin.

- Meanwhile, beat the spread, icing sugar and vanilla together for the frosting in an electric mixer until soft, then gradually beat in the melted chocolate until well combined and smooth. Refrigerate for 1 hour.

- Release the cooled cake from the tin, spread with the chilled icing and decorate with sprinkles or rose petals.

V

• BREAKFASTS •

Potato Drop Scones

SERVES 4 • PREP & COOKING TIME 30 minutes

- 550 g (1 lb 2 oz) large potatoes, peeled and cut into small chunks
- 1½ teaspoons baking powder
- 2 eggs
- 75 ml (3 fl oz) milk
- vegetable oil, for frying
- salt and black pepper

Serve these potato cakes instead of toast with your favourite cooked breakfast. They're a great way of using up any leftover mashed potato and, if you've got some, you could add a tablespoon or two of snipped chives or a few sliced spring onions to the potato mixture.

- Cook the potatoes in a saucepan of salted boiling water for 15 minutes or until tender. Drain well, return to the pan and mash until smooth. Leave to cool slightly.

- Beat in the baking powder, then the eggs, milk and a little seasoning, and continue to beat until everything is evenly combined.

- Heat a little oil in a heavy-based frying pan. Drop heaped dessertspoonfuls of the mixture into the pan, spacing them slightly apart, and fry for 3–4 minutes, turning once, until golden.

- Transfer to a serving plate and keep warm while frying the remainder of the potato mixture. Serve immediately.

VG

• LIGHT BITES •

Broad Bean & Herb Crostini

MAKES 12 • PREP & COOKING TIME 20 minutes

- 250 g (8 oz) podded broad beans (you will need about double this quantity if buying in the pod)
- 2 tablespoons chopped mint
- 1 tablespoon chopped flat-leaf parsley
- finely grated zest of 1 lemon
- 2 spring onions, finely chopped
- 1 garlic clove, crushed
- 12 slices of French bread
- 2 tablespoons chilli oil
- salt and black pepper
- rocket, to garnish
- lemon wedges, to serve

These look so appetizing with the vibrant green broad bean mix atop little golden toasts. Popping the grey outer skins of the broad beans to reveal the green insides takes a while but it's definitely worth it. Little kids love doing it so you can always recruit some help!

- Cook the broad beans in a saucepan of boiling water for 3 minutes. Drain, rinse under cold water and drain again. Pop the beans out of the outer skins and put in a bowl.

- Crush the beans lightly with a potato masher, then stir in the mint, parsley, lemon zest, spring onions and garlic. Season with salt and pepper.

- Heat a griddle pan or frying pan until hot. Brush the bread slices with the chilli oil, add to the hot pan, in batches, and cook for 1 minute until toasted and crisp. Turn and cook on the other side for 1 minute.

- Spoon the broad bean mixture on to the toasts, garnish with rocket and serve with lemon wedges for squeezing over.

V

• DESSERTS •

Strawberry & Lavender Shortcakes

MAKES 8 • PREP & COOKING TIME 50 minutes

- 150 g (5 oz) plain flour
- 25 g (1 oz) ground rice
- 125 g (4 oz) butter, diced
- 50 g (2 oz) caster sugar
- 1 tablespoon lavender petals

TO DECORATE
- 250 g (8 oz) strawberries (or a mixture of strawberries and raspberries)
- 150 ml (¼ pint) double cream
- 16 small lavender flowers (optional)
- sifted icing sugar, for dusting

It's Mother's Day in the United States and other parts of the world so spoil her with these delectable shortcakes. They are best eaten on the day they are filled, but the plain biscuits can be stored in an airtight container for up to 3 days.

- Put the flour and ground rice in a mixing bowl or a food processor. Add the butter and rub in with your fingertips or process until the mixture resembles fine breadcrumbs.

- Stir in the sugar and lavender petals and squeeze the crumbs together with your hands to form a smooth ball. Knead lightly then roll out on a lightly floured surface until 5 mm (¼ inch) thick.

- Stamp out 7.5 cm (3 inch) circles using a fluted round biscuit cutter. Transfer to an ungreased baking sheet. Re-knead the trimmings and continue rolling and stamping out until you have made 16 biscuits.

- Prick with a fork, bake in a preheated oven, 160°C (325°F), Gas Mark 3, for 10–12 minutes until pale golden. Leave to cool on the baking tray.

- To serve, halve 4 of the smallest strawberries, hull and slice the rest. Whip the cream and spoon over 8 of the biscuits. Top with the sliced strawberries then the remaining biscuits. Spoon the remaining cream on top and decorate with the reserved halved strawberries and tiny sprigs of lavender, if liked. Dust lightly with sifted icing sugar.

• MAINS •

Ginger Pork Chops

SERVES 4 • PREP & COOKING TIME 30 minutes

- 4 lean pork chops, about 150 g (5 oz) each
- 3.5 cm (1½ inch) piece of fresh root ginger, peeled and grated
- 1 teaspoon sesame oil
- 1 tablespoon dark soy sauce
- 2 teaspoons stem ginger syrup or runny honey

FOR THE DRESSING
- 1½ tablespoons light soy sauce
- juice of 1 blood orange
- 2 pieces of stem ginger, finely chopped

FOR THE SALAD
- 2 large carrots, peeled and coarsely grated
- 150 g (5 oz) mangetout, shredded
- 100 g (3½ oz) bean sprouts
- 2 spring onions, thinly sliced
- 2 tablespoons unsalted peanuts, roughly chopped (optional)

A brief stint marinating in the fridge gives these Asian-style pork chops a boost of flavour and tenderizes the meat. All this dish needs to go with it is a bowl of steamed white or brown rice.

- Place the pork in a shallow ovenproof dish and rub with the ginger, sesame oil, soy sauce and stem ginger syrup or honey until well covered. Leave to marinate for 10 minutes.

- Make the dressing. Mix together all the ingredients in a bowl and set aside for the flavours to develop.

- Cook the pork in a preheated oven, 180°C (350°F), Gas Mark 4, for 18–20 minutes or until cooked through but still juicy.

- Meanwhile, mix the carrots, mangetout, bean sprouts and spring onions in a large bowl. Just before serving, toss with the dressing and pile into serving dishes.

- Sprinkle with the peanuts, if using, and top with the pork chops, drizzled with cooking juices. Serve immediately.

V

• DESSERTS •

Creamy Lemon & Almond Rice Pudding

SERVES 4 • PREP & COOKING TIME 30 minutes

- 100 g (3½ oz) short-grain pudding rice, rinsed
- 50 g (2 oz) caster sugar
- grated zest and juice of 2 lemons, plus extra zest to decorate
- 100 g (3½ oz) sultanas
- 450 ml (¾ pint) boiling water
- 410 g (13 oz) can evaporated milk
- 25 g (1 oz) flaked almonds

The tang of lemon cuts through the richness of this classic, while sultanas add little bursts of sweetness. Toasting the almonds to scatter over the top takes hardly any time and makes all the difference.

- Place the rice, sugar, lemon zest and juice, sultanas and measured water in a saucepan and simmer, uncovered, for 20–25 minutes. Stir in the evaporated milk and simmer for a further 5 minutes until the rice is tender.

- Meanwhile, place the almonds in a hot frying pan and dry-fry for 1–2 minutes until toasted.

- Pour the rice pudding into serving dishes and sprinkle with the flaked almonds and extra lemon zest. Serve immediately.

• BREAKFASTS •

Omelette Arnold Bennett

SERVES 2 • PREP & COOKING TIME 20 minutes

- 150 ml (5 fl oz) single cream
- 250 g (8 oz) smoked haddock
- 4 eggs, separated, plus 2 egg whites
- 10g (¼ oz) butter
- 10g (¼ oz) Gruyère or vegetarian hard cheese, grated*
- black pepper

The story goes that this omelette was invented for writer Arnold Bennett when he was staying at London's Savoy Hotel in the 1920s. It's an indulgent mixture of smoked haddock, fluffy egg and rich cheese.

- Place the cream and pepper to taste in a medium frying pan and add the smoked haddock skin-side up. Bring to a simmer.

- Remove the fish with a slotted spoon and skin and flake it. Return the fish to the pan and stir into the cream.

- Whisk together the egg yolks in a bowl. In a separate, grease-free bowl, whisk the egg whites until stiff. Gently fold the egg yolks into the egg whites.

- Melt a little butter in each of 2 omelette pans or small frying pans, then pour half the egg mixture into each. Move it around a little until it starts to cook.

- When the bottom of each omelette is cooked, pour over the creamy haddock mixture and sprinkle with the grated Gruyère. Place under a preheated hot grill and grill for 2–3 minutes until starting to turn golden. Serve immediately.

*For guidance on vegetarian cheeses, see page 5.

• LIGHT BITES •

Seared Chicken
& Vegetable Wraps

SERVES 4 • PREP & COOKING TIME 20 minutes

- 4 boneless, skinless chicken breasts, cut into long thin slices
- 4 courgettes, cut into long thin slices
- 1 red pepper, deseeded, quartered
- 1 yellow pepper, deseeded, quartered
- 4 tablespoons olive oil
- 2 garlic cloves, finely chopped
- 4 teaspoons sun-dried tomato paste
- 4 large soft flour tortillas
- 200 g (7 oz) cream cheese with garlic and herbs
- salt and black pepper

Warm chicken, colourful veg and garlicky cream cheese all wrapped up in soft tortillas make this delicious lunch. Try swapping the cream cheese for mayo mixed with a little sriracha for a spicy take on these.

- Arrange the chicken breasts, courgettes and peppers in a single layer on a foil-lined grill rack or baking sheet.

- Mix the oil, garlic, tomato paste and seasoning together and spoon over the chicken and vegetables. Grill for 12–15 minutes, turning once, until browned and the chicken is cooked through.

- Warm the tortillas according to the instructions on the packet, then spread with the cream cheese. Cut the peppers into strips. Divide the chicken and vegetables between the tortillas, then roll up tightly and cut in half. Serve warm.

V

• MAINS •

Nasi Goreng

SERVES 4 • PREP & COOKING TIME 30 minutes

- 2 large eggs
- 3 tablespoons sunflower oil
- 1 tablespoon tomato purée
- 1 tablespoon ketjap manis
- 625 g (1¼ lb) cooked rice
- 1 tablespoon light soy sauce
- 5 cm (2 in) piece cucumber, quartered lengthways and sliced
- salt and black pepper
- 8 spring onions, trimmed and thinly sliced on the diagonal, to garnish

FOR THE SPICE PASTE
- 2 tablespoons vegetable oil
- 4 garlic cloves, roughly chopped
- 50 g (2 oz) shallots, roughly chopped
- 25 g (1 oz) roasted salted peanuts
- 6 medium-hot red chillies, deseeded and roughly chopped
- 1 teaspoon salt

There are so many variations on this comforting Indonesian fried rice dish but this vegetarian version really delivers on taste. Ketjap (or kecap) manis – a syrupy and sweeter version of soy sauce – is a must. If you can't find ketjap manis, then replace with a tablespoon of dark soy sauce and a teaspoon of maple syrup.

- To make the spice paste, place all of the ingredients into a small food processor and whizz into a smooth paste, or grind using a pestle and mortar.

- Beat the eggs and season.

- Heat a little sunflower oil in a small frying pan over a medium-high heat, pour in one-third of the beaten egg and cook until set on top. Flip, cook for a few more seconds then turn out and roll up tightly. Repeat twice more with the remaining egg. Slice the omelettes across into thin strips.

- Heat a wok over a high heat until smoking. Add 2 tablespoons of the oil and the spice paste and stir-fry for 1–2 minutes.

- Add the tomato purée and ketjap manis and cook for a few seconds, then tip in the cooked rice and stir-fry over a high heat for 2 minutes until heated through.

- Add the strips of omelette and stir-fry for another minute before adding the soy sauce, cucumber and most of the spring onions and tossing together well.

- Spoon the nasi goreng on to a large plate, scatter over the remaining spring onions and serve.

V

• DESSERTS •

Traditional Rockcakes

MAKES 10–12 • PREP & COOKING TIME 30 minutes

- 250 g (8 oz) self-raising flour
- 1 ½ teaspoons baking powder
- 1 teaspoon ground cinnamon
- ½ teaspoon ground ginger
- 125 g (4 oz) unsalted butter, softened
- 100 g (3 ½ oz) demerara sugar, plus extra for sprinkling (optional)
- 1 teaspoon grated orange zest
- 100 g (3 ½ oz) sultanas
- 75 g (3 oz) currants
- 50 g (2 oz) mixed peel or chopped glacé cherries
- 1 large egg, lightly beaten
- 3–4 tablespoons milk

These are great for children to make – and eat! – as they are so quick and simple. Best eaten on the day they are made and especially good still warm from the oven. Don't be tempted to add too much milk: the dough should thick and lumpy.

- Sift the flour, baking powder and spices into a large bowl. Add the butter and rub in with the fingertips until the mixture resembles fine breadcrumbs, then stir in the sugar, orange zest, sultanas, currants and mixed peel or cherries. Pour in the egg, adding enough of the milk to form a soft, slightly sticky dough.

- Drop 10–12 mounds of the mixture on to a large baking sheet lined with nonstick baking paper so that they resemble rocks and sprinkle with a little extra sugar, if using.

- Bake in a preheated oven, 200°C (400°F), Gas Mark 6, for 18–20 minutes until golden. Transfer to a wire rack to cool slightly, then serve warm or cold.

V

• BREAKFASTS •

Baked Eggs with Blue Cheese

SERVES 4 • PREP & COOKING TIME 15 minutes

- 75 g (3 oz) blue cheese, such as Stilton, Roquefort or Gorgonzola*
- 150 ml (¼ pint) double cream
- 2 tablespoons chopped chives
- ½ teaspoon cracked black pepper
- butter, for greasing and spreading
- 4 large eggs
- 4 slices of granary bread

Aah, the bliss of dipping a finger of crunchy toast into a runny yolk. For an indulgent start to the day, treat yourself to this luxurious dish made with sharp, salty blue cheese and rich cream.

- In a small bowl, mash the blue cheese into the cream using the back of a fork. Stir in the chives and black pepper and divide between 4 buttered ramekins.

- Crack an egg into each ramekin and place them in a roasting tin. Pour hot water into the tin so that it comes about halfway up the sides of the ramekins. Cook in a preheated oven, 200°C (400°F), Gas Mark 7, for 7–8 minutes, or until the egg white is set but the yolk is still runny.

- Meanwhile, toast the bread until golden and butter lightly. Cut into strips for dipping. Remove the baked eggs from the oven and serve immediately with the toast.

*For guidance on vegetarian cheeses, see page 5.

· LIGHT BITES ·

Sardine & Lentil Salad

SERVES 4 • PREP & COOKING TIME 20 minutes

- 100 g (3½ oz) frozen peas
- 2 × 120 g (3¾ oz) cans boneless, skinless sardines in tomato sauce
- 410 g (13½ oz) can green lentils
- 5 cm (2 inches) cucumber
- 1 small red onion
- small bunch of mint, roughly chopped
- grated zest and juice of 1 lemon
- 1 cos lettuce
- black pepper

We should all eat oily fish for its incredible health-enhancing benefits and this quick-to-prepare salad is an excellent way to add it to your diet. Fibre-rich lentils also feature, along with a hint of red onion and mint to bring together the flavours.

- Cook the peas in a saucepan of boiling water for 3 minutes. Alternatively, cook them in the microwave for 1½ minutes on full power.

- Flake the sardines into chunks and put them in a large salad bowl with their sauce.

- Rinse and drain the lentils, dice the cucumber and chop the onion. Add the lentils, peas, cucumber and onion to the sardines. Add the mint to the salad with the lemon zest and juice and a little pepper and toss together.

- Separate the lettuce into leaves and arrange them on serving plates. Spoon the sardine salad on top and serve.

• MAINS •

Five-Spice Beef Stir-Fry

SERVES 4 • PREP & COOKING TIME 30 minutes, plus marinating

- 3 lean sirloin steaks, about 200 g (7 oz) each
- 100 g (3½ oz) sugar snap peas
- 1 carrot
- 100 g (3½ oz) baby corn
- spray olive oil
- 1 red chilli, thinly sliced
- 1 small onion, sliced
- 100 g (3½ oz) broccoli florets
- 300 ml (½ pint) boiling hot vegetable stock
- 2 tablespoons light soy sauce
- 1 tablespoon cornflour, mixed to a paste with 2 tablespoons cold water
- salt and white pepper
- spring onions, shredded, to garnish

FOR THE MARINADE
- 2 teaspoons Chinese five-spice powder
- 2 garlic cloves, crushed
- 2 teaspoons ground Szechuan peppercorns
- 1 tablespoon dark soy sauce
- ½ teaspoon dried chilli flakes
- 2 tablespoons Chinese rice wine

Prep is key when it comes to a stir-fry – get all of your ingredients chopped and ready to go before you turn on the heat. You'll need to marinate the beef for this recipe for at least 3 hours and overnight if possible.

- Slice the beef into thin strips and place in a glass or ceramic bowl with all the ingredients for the marinade. Toss to coat evenly, cover and leave to marinate in the refrigerator for 3–4 hours, or overnight if time permits.

- Trim the sugar snap peas, cut the carrots into thin matchsticks and halve the baby corn lengthways.

- Spray a large nonstick wok or frying pan with oil and heat to a high heat. Add the beef mixture and stir-fry for 2–3 minutes until browned and sealed.

- Add the chilli and onion to the pan and stir-fry for 1 minute, then add the remaining vegetables and stir-fry for a further 1–2 minutes. Add the stock and soy sauce and stir well.

- Bring to the boil, add the cornflour paste and stir to mix thoroughly. Cook, stirring constantly, for 2–3 minutes until the mixture has thickened.

- Remove the pan from the heat and season to taste with salt and white pepper. Ladle into bowls and serve with shredded spring onions.

V

• DESSERTS •

Churros

MAKES 12 • PREP & COOKING TIME 30 minutes

- 200 g (7 oz) plain flour
- ¼ teaspoon salt
- 5 tablespoons caster sugar
- 275 ml (9 fl oz) water
- 1 egg, beaten
- 1 egg yolk
- 1 teaspoon vanilla extract
- 1 litre (1¾ pints) sunflower oil
- 1 teaspoon ground cinnamon

These are best eaten on the day they are made. For an extra-indulgent treat, serve them with a homemade chocolate-maple dipping sauce: just melt ¾ cup chopped bittersweet chocolate, 3½ tablespoons unsalted butter and 1 tablespoon maple syrup together, stirring well.

- Mix the flour, salt and 1 tablespoon of the sugar in a bowl. Pour the water into a saucepan and bring to the boil. Take off the heat, add the flour mixture and beat well. Then return to the heat and stir until it forms a smooth ball that leaves the sides of the pan almost clean. Remove from the heat and leave to cool for 10 minutes.

- Gradually beat the whole egg, egg yolk, then the vanilla into the flour mixture until smooth. Spoon into a large nylon piping bag fitted with a 1 cm (½ inch) wide plain tip.

- Pour the oil into a medium saucepan to a depth of 2.5 cm (1 inch). Heat to 170°C (340°F) on a sugar thermometer, or pipe a tiny amount of the mixture into the oil. If the oil bubbles instantly, it is ready to use.

- Pipe coils, S-shapes and squiggly lines into the oil, in small batches, cutting the ends off with kitchen scissors. Cook the churros for 2–3 minutes until they float and are golden, turning over if needed to brown evenly.

- Lift the churros out of the oil, drain well on kitchen paper, then sprinkle with the remaining sugar mixed with the cinnamon. Continue piping and frying until all the mixture has been used. Serve warm or cold.

• BREAKFASTS •

Sausage, Bacon & Tomato Frittata

SERVES 4 • PREP & COOKING TIME 20 minutes

- flour, for dusting
- 175 g (6 oz) sausagemeat
- 2 tablespoons olive oil
- 6 streaky bacon rashers, snipped into pieces
- 4 vine tomatoes, cut into wedges
- 6 eggs
- 4 tablespoons chopped parsley
- black pepper

All the very best bits of a fry-up are crammed into this filling frittata. Serve it hot with buttered toast for breakfast or chill and pack it up for picnics and packed lunches.

- Using lightly floured hands, divide the sausagemeat into 8 pieces. Shape into very rough balls, then lightly flatten.

- Heat the oil in a nonstick frying pan with an ovenproof handle. Add the sausagemeat patties and cook over a medium heat for 5 minutes, turning once, until golden and cooked through. Add the bacon and cook for a further 3 minutes until cooked.

- Add the tomatoes, remove from the heat and evenly spread the ingredients around the pan.

- Beat the eggs with the parsley, then season with pepper and pour into the pan. Return to the heat and cook over a medium heat for 3–4 minutes until the base is set.

- Place the pan under a preheated hot grill (keeping the handle away from the heat) and cook for 3–4 minutes until it is set.

- Divide into wedges and serve.

V

• LIGHT BITES •

Chilled Beetroot & Apple Soup

SERVES 6 • PREP & COOKING TIME 1 hour 15 minutes, plus chilling

- 1 tablespoon olive oil
- 1 onion, roughly chopped
- 500 g (1 lb) bunch of uncooked beetroot, peeled and diced
- 1 large cooking apple, about 375 g (12 oz), cored, peeled and diced
- 1.5 litres (2½ pints) vegetable or chicken stock
- salt and black pepper

TO SERVE
- 6 tablespoons soured cream
- 1 red dessert apple, cored and diced
- handful of pomegranate seeds
- 4 tablespoons maple syrup

So pretty to look at with its vibrant scarlet colour and full of sweet, earthy flavours, this soup is perfect for entertaining as it needs to be made well ahead of eating.

- Heat the oil in a saucepan, add the onion and fry gently for 5 minutes until softened. Add the beetroot and apple, pour in the stock, season with salt and pepper and bring to the boil. Cover and simmer for 45 minutes, stirring occasionally, until the beetroot is tender.

- Cool slightly, then purée in batches in a blender or food processor until smooth. Pour into a large jug, taste and adjust the seasoning if needed. Chill in the refrigerator for 3–4 hours or overnight.

- Pour the soup into bowls and top each one with a spoonful of soured cream, sprinkle over the apple and pomegranate seeds and drizzle with a little maple syrup.

• MAINS •

Sri Lankan-Style Lamb Curry

SERVES 4 • PREP & COOKING TIME 45 minutes

- 500 g (1 lb) shoulder or leg of lamb, diced
- 2 potatoes, peeled and cut into large chunks
- 4 tablespoons olive oil
- 400 g (13 oz) can chopped tomatoes
- salt and black pepper

FOR THE CURRY PASTE
- 1 onion, grated
- 1 tablespoon peeled and finely chopped fresh root ginger
- 1 teaspoon finely chopped garlic
- ½ teaspoon ground turmeric
- 1 teaspoon ground coriander
- ½ teaspoon ground cumin
- ½ teaspoon fennel seeds
- ½ teaspoon cumin seeds
- 3 cardamom pods, lightly crushed
- 2 green chillies, deseeded if liked, finely chopped
- 5 cm (2 inch) cinnamon stick
- 2 lemon grass stalks, finely sliced

Ready in under an hour, this curry – full of soft chunks of tender meat – is a great standby recipe. If you like your spicing on the milder side, remove the seeds from the chillies before chopping them.

- Make the curry paste by mixing together all the ingredients in a large bowl. Add the lamb and potatoes and combine well.

- Heat the oil in a heavy-based pan or casserole and tip in the meat and potatoes. Use a wooden spoon to stir-fry for 6–8 minutes.

- Pour in the chopped tomatoes and 150 ml (¼ pint) water, bring to the boil and season well then allow to bubble gently for 20–25 minutes until the potatoes are cooked and the lamb is tender.

V

• DESSERTS •

Caramel Chocolate Fondants

SERVES 6 • PREP & COOKING TIME 30 minutes

- 200 g (7 oz) unsalted butter
- 225 g (7½ oz) plain dark chocolate, broken into small pieces
- 3 large eggs, plus 2 large egg yolks
- 75 g (3 oz) soft light brown sugar
- 50 g (2 oz) plain flour
- 6 dessertspoons ready-made dulce de leche or thick caramel sauce

Oh, the joy of dipping your spoon into one of these fondants, and the gooey caramel centre oozing out – melt-in-the-mouth decadence. It's all in the timing for that perfectly baked outside and molten centre so keep an eye on them.

- Place the butter and chocolate in a small saucepan over a low heat and warm until just melted. Stir gently, then set aside.

- Place the eggs plus egg yolks and sugar in a large bowl and beat with a hand-held electric whisk until thick and creamy. Fold in the flour and melted chocolate.

- Spoon the mixture into 6 greased 200 ml (7 fl oz) freezer-proof and heatproof ramekins or metal moulds, lightly dusted with flour. Dollop 1 spoonful of the dulce de leche or caramel sauce into the centre of each one, then cover with a little of the chocolate mixture. Place in the freezer for 8–10 minutes.

- Remove from the freezer, place on a baking tray and bake in a preheated oven, 200°C (400°F), Gas Mark 6, for 12–14 minutes until almost firm but still with a slight wobble in the centre. Leave to cool in the dishes for 2 minutes, then invert on to serving dishes.

• BREAKFASTS •

Corn Cakes with Smoked Salmon

SERVES 4 • PREP & COOKING TIME 20 minutes

- 2 eggs, beaten
- 4 tablespoons milk
- 300 g (10 oz) canned sweetcorn kernels, drained
- 75 g (3 oz) self-raising flour
- 2 spring onions, sliced
- 2 tablespoons vegetable oil
- 150 g (5 oz) smoked salmon
- 4 tablespoons mascarpone cheese
- salt and black pepper
- chopped chives, to garnish

This is the recipe to have up your sleeve if friends are coming round for brunch. You could also dress these corn cakes up with a tangy salsa and a dollop of soured cream as a light lunch or dinner-party starter.

- Beat together the eggs, milk, sweetcorn, flour and spring onions until you have a smooth batter. Season well.

- Heat 1 tablespoon of the oil in a large, nonstick frying pan. Add half the batter to the pan in separate spoonfuls to make 6 small pancakes. Cook for 2–3 minutes on each side until golden and cooked through. Set aside on kitchen paper while you cook the remaining batter.

- Pile the pancakes on to serving plates and arrange the smoked salmon and mascarpone on top. Scatter with the chives and serve.

V

· LIGHT BITES ·

New Potato & Avocado Salad

SERVES 4 • PREP & COOKING TIME 25 minutes

- 600 g (1¼ lb) small new potatoes
- 1 ripe avocado
- 1 punnet mustard and cress
- grated zest of ½ lemon
- 75 g (3 oz) rocket leaves
- salt and black pepper

FOR THE DRESSING
- 1 tablespoon wholegrain mustard
- juice of ½ lemon
- 2 tablespoons mayonnaise

The humble potato salad gets a makeover here. This warm salad showcases in-season new potatoes – use Jersey Royals if you can. Makes a great springtime lunch.

- Cook the potatoes in a saucepan of salted boiling water for 12–15 minutes or until just tender. Drain well and put in a large salad bowl.

- Halve the avocado and remove the stone. Cut the flesh into pieces.

- Whisk the dressing ingredients together in a small bowl, then add to the warm potatoes. Mix in the avocado pieces, mustard and cress, lemon zest and rocket. Season well.

- Divide between 4 serving plates and serve.

• MAINS •

Cod Cheek Tacos with Lime & Coriander

SERVES 4 • PREP & COOKING TIME 15 minutes

- 625 g (1¼ lb) cod cheeks, cut into 2.5cm (1 inch) cubes
- 2 tablespoons Cajun seasoning
- 8 taco shells
- 1 tablespoon groundnut oil
- 2 tablespoons lime juice
- 1 small cos lettuce, shredded
- 4 tablespoons chopped coriander
- 200 g (7 oz) ready-made fresh tomato salsa
- 200 g (7 oz) ready-made guacamole

Some days it seems there is simply not enough time to get everything done. That's when you need a super-speedy recipe like this one, which transforms a few store-bought ingredients and some fresh fish into a delicious meal in just 15 minutes.

- Preheat the oven to 180°C (350°F), Gas Mark 4. Place the fish in a large bowl and sprinkle over the Cajun seasoning. Gently shake the bowl to coat the fish pieces in the seasoning.

- Arrange the taco shells upright in an ovenproof dish and warm in the preheated oven for 5 minutes.

- Meanwhile, heat the oil in a large frying pan and cook the fish pieces for 2–3 minutes on each side until cooked through. Carefully transfer the fish to a bowl and drizzle with the lime juice.

- Fill the taco shells with the lettuce and top with the fish. Scatter the coriander on top and serve immediately with the tomato salsa and guacamole.

V

• LIGHT BITES •

Aïoli with Vegetable Dippers

SERVES 4 • PREP TIME 20 minutes

- 3 garlic cloves
- 2 egg yolks
- 1 teaspoon Dijon mustard
- 250 ml (8 fl oz) olive oil
- 2 tablespoons lemon juice
- salt and black pepper

FOR THE DIPPERS
- 125 g (4 oz) baby carrots, scrubbed, halved
- 125 g (4 oz) asparagus tips
- 75 g (3 oz) sugar snap peas
- 1 little gem lettuce, leaves separated

Creamy, garlicky aïoli meets crunchy vegetables – heaven. If the aïoli 'splits' or separates while you are making it, don't panic. Put 1 egg yolk into a separate bowl and then very gradually whisk the split mixture into the new egg yolk until smooth once more.

- Crush the garlic in a pestle and mortar with a little salt and pepper. Transfer to a large mixing bowl and add the egg yolks and mustard.

- Whisk the ingredients together with a balloon whisk or electric whisk until just mixed, then gradually trickle in the oil, drop by drop to begin with, until the mixture begins to thicken. Then continue with the oil in a very thin steady stream until about half has been added.

- Thin the mayonnaise with a little lemon juice, then continue whisking in the oil very gradually until very thick. Taste and add a little more lemon juice if you like. Cover and chill until required.

- Blanche the asparagus and sugar snaps in a saucepan of boiling water for 2 minutes. Drain and allow to cool.

- To serve, spoon the aïoli into a bowl and set on to a large platter. Arrange the vegetables around the bowl and serve.

• MAINS •

Lemon Griddled Fish with Cheesy Mashed Potato

SERVES 4 • PREP & COOKING TIME 30 minutes

- 3 tablespoons chopped mixed herbs (such as chives, parsley, rosemary and oregano)
- 4 tablespoons olive oil
- 1 garlic clove, crushed
- finely grated zest of 1 lemon
- 4 thick fish fillets, such as cod, haddock, pollack or coley, about 150 g (5 oz) each
- 1 kg (2 lb) floury potatoes, peeled and cut into chunks
- 2 tablespoons lemon juice
- 50 g (2 oz) Parmesan cheese, grated
- salt and black pepper

The most common mistake with fish is overcooking it – these fish fillets will take only minutes to cook. Starting with the skin side, and cooking that side for longer, protects the flesh and allows it to cook without drying out.

- Mix 1 tablespoon of the chopped herbs and 1 tablespoon of the oil with the garlic, lemon zest and a little seasoning, then massage over the fish fillets. Set aside for 10–15 minutes to marinate.

- Meanwhile, cook the potatoes in a large saucepan of lightly salted boiling water for 12–15 minutes, or until tender.

- Heat a ridged griddle pan and cook the fish fillets, skin side down, for 4–5 minutes, until the skin is crispy. Turn the fish over, turn off the heat and set aside for 3–4 minutes until the fish is cooked. Keep warm.

- Drain the potatoes, return to the pan and place over a gentle heat for 1–2 minutes to dry them out. Add the lemon juice, cheese, remaining herbs and remaining olive oil. Season to taste and mash until smooth, then spoon on to plates. Serve the cheesy mash with the grilled fish.

V

• DESSERTS •

White Chocolate & Macadamia Cookies

MAKES 14–16 • PREP & COOKING TIME 30 minutes

- 150 g (5 oz) unsalted butter, softened
- 225 g (7½ oz) caster sugar
- 1 large egg, lightly beaten
- 2 tablespoons milk
- 1 teaspoon vanilla bean paste or extract (optional)
- 75 g (3 oz) white chocolate chips
- 75 g (3 oz) macadamia nuts, roughly chopped
- 250 g (8 oz) plain flour
- 1 teaspoon bicarbonate of soda

Crispy on the outside, soft and chewy in the middle, these buttery cookies are a luxurious blend of white chocolate and nuts. So simple to make, this is a recipe you'll come back to time and again.

- Place the butter and sugar in a bowl and beat together using a hand-held electric whisk until light and fluffy. Add the egg, milk and vanilla bean paste or extract, if using, and beat well.

- Stir in the chocolate chips and macadamia nuts, then sift in the flour and bicarbonate of soda and mix gently to form a soft dough.

- Drop 14–16 small spoonfuls of the dough, well-spaced apart, on 2 baking sheets lined with nonstick baking paper.

- Bake in a preheated oven, 200°C (400°F), Gas Mark 6, for 12–15 minutes until pale golden. Leave to cool on the sheets for 2–3 minutes, then transfer to wire racks to cool completely.

• DRINKS •

Elderflower Cordial

MAKES about 1 litre (1¾ pints) • PREP TIME 15 minutes, plus standing

- 20 elderflower heads
- 3 lemons, sliced
- 25 g (1 oz) citric acid
- 1 kg (2 lb) granulated or caster sugar
- 1 litre (1 ¾ pints) boiling water

The creamy white flowers of the elder tree make a great cordial. Gather them on a dry day and, before you add them to the cordial, fill a large bowl with cold water and gently swish the elderflower heads in it to get rid of any dirt or insects. You can buy citric acid at chemists, some supermarkets and online.

- Put the elderflower heads, sliced lemons and citric acid in a large heatproof bowl.

- Dissolve the sugar in the measured boiling water, stirring frequently until dissolved. Add to the bowl of elderflowers. Cover and leave to stand overnight. Strain through a muslin-lined sieve and pour into sterilized bottles. Store in a cool place and use within 6 months.

June

GOOD TO EAT THIS MONTH

aubergines * beetroot * broad beans * broccoli *
carrots * cauliflower * courgettes * cucumber * fennel
* French beans * garlic * globe artichokes * lettuce
* mangetout * new potatoes * peppers * radishes *
rocket * runner beans * spinach * summer squash
* sweetheart cabbage * Swiss chard * tomatoes *
watercress * blackcurrants * blueberries * raspberries
* redcurrants * strawberries * basil * chillies * chives *
mint * oregano * parsley

DATES TO LOOK FORWARD TO THIS MONTH

Shavuot
Eid Al-Adha
Father's Day
Summer Solstice
Midsummer's Day
Start of Wimbledon Fortnight

This month is the tipping point of the year – we have the longest
day of the year in June – and summer is finally here. Roses are
blossoming, picnic season has arrived (you must try the amazing
Picnic Loaf on page 193 for super-stylish picnic feasting) and it's
time to enjoy the fresh, vibrant food of summer.

Fruit is superb in summer: beautifully coloured, plentiful and
sweetly perfumed. This month sees the arrival of blueberries,
blackcurrants, raspberries and redcurrants.

There's lots to celebrate in June so we have recipes for everything
from **Baked Ricotta Cheesecake** for Shavuot (page 182) to a
colourful, flavour-packed salad to mark the summer solstice
(page 202).

Two weeks of tennis begin at Wimbledon – synonymous with
strawberries and cream – at the end of the month, which is all the
excuse you need to make that unbeatable summer classic, **Eton
Mess** (page 211).

v

· DESSERTS ·

Baked Ricotta Cheesecake

SERVES 4 • PREP & COOKING TIME 20 minutes

- 480 g (17 oz) ricotta cheese
- 425 g (15 oz) cream cheese
- 2 eggs
- 1 teaspoon vanilla extract
- 125 g (4 oz) caster sugar

To celebrate Shavuot, the Jewish holiday that marks the giving of the Torah on Mount Sinai, it is traditional to eat dairy dishes. This creamy baked cheesecake is sure to be popular with friends and family. Serve it with a variety of jewel-coloured summer berries.

- Blend the ricotta and cream cheese with the eggs, vanilla extract and caster sugar until smooth. Turn the mixture into a greased 500 g (1 lb) loaf tin, the base and sides lined, and place in a small roasting tin.

- Pour hot water into the tin to a depth of 2.5 cm (1 inch) and bake in a preheated oven, 160°C (325°F), Gas Mark 3, for about 40 minutes or until lightly set.

- Lift the loaf tin out of the water and allow to cool in the tin. Remove the cheesecake from the tin, peel off the paper and cut into slices to serve.

V

· BREAKFASTS ·

Ricotta & Blueberry Pancakes

SERVES 4 • PREP & COOKING TIME 25 minutes

- 250 g (8 oz) ricotta cheese
- 125 ml (4 fl oz) milk
- 3 large eggs, separated
- 100 g (3½ oz) plain flour
- 3 tablespoons caster sugar
- 1 teaspoon baking powder
- finely grated zest of 1 lemon
- 125 g (4 oz) fresh blueberries
- unsalted butter, for frying
- lemon juice or maple syrup, to serve

The ricotta makes these pancakes delicately light and fluffy. Keep it simple and serve them with maple syrup or a squeeze of lemon juice and perhaps some thick, cool yogurt.

- Beat the ricotta with the milk and egg yolks in a large bowl. Stir in the flour, sugar, baking powder, lemon zest and blueberries until well combined.

- Whisk the egg whites with a hand-held electric whisk in a separate large, grease-free bowl until they form soft peaks, then gently fold into the ricotta mixture with a large metal spoon.

- Heat a little butter in a heavy-based frying pan over a medium heat. Add about one-quarter of the batter to the pan to make 3–4 pancakes about 7 cm (3 inches) in diameter and cook for 1–2 minutes on each side until golden and cooked through.

- Transfer the pancakes to a baking sheet and keep warm while you repeat with the remaining batter, adding a little more butter to the pan as necessary.

- Serve 3–4 pancakes per person, with lemon juice or maple syrup.

V

• LIGHT BITES •

Falafels with Beetroot Salad & Mint Yogurt

SERVES 2 • PREP & COOKING TIME 30 minutes

- 400 g (13 oz) can chickpeas, rinsed and drained
- ½ small red onion, roughly chopped
- 1 garlic clove, chopped
- ½ red chilli, deseeded
- 1 teaspoon ground cumin
- 1 teaspoon ground coriander
- a handful of flat-leaf parsley
- 2 tablespoons olive oil
- salt and black pepper

FOR THE BEETROOT SALAD
- 1 carrot, coarsely grated
- 1 raw beetroot, coarsely grated
- 50 g (2 oz) baby spinach leaves
- 1 tablespoon lemon juice
- 2 tablespoons olive oil

FOR THE MINT YOGURT
- 150 g (5 oz) Greek yogurt
- 1 tablespoon chopped mint leaves
- ½ garlic clove, crushed

Light, healthy and full of colour, this is a meal which will add sunshine to a your day. You could also serve it with some warm pitta breads. To make it vegan-friendly, replace the yogurt with a non-dairy option.

- To make the falafels, place the chickpeas, onion, garlic, chilli, cumin, coriander and parsley in a food processor. Season, then blend to make a coarse paste. Shape the mixture into 8 patties and set aside.

- To make the salad, place the carrot, beetroot and spinach in a bowl. Season, add the lemon juice and oil and stir well.

- To make the mint yogurt, mix all the ingredients together and season with a little salt.

- Heat the oil in a frying pan, add the falafels and fry for 4–5 minutes on each side until golden. Serve with the beetroot salad and mint yogurt.

• MAINS •

Chicken Tikka Masala

SERVES 4 • PREP & COOKING TIME 40 minutes

- 25 g (1 oz) butter
- 4 boneless, skinless chicken breasts, cubed
- 1 onion, quartered
- 3.5 cm (1½ inch) piece fresh root ginger, peeled and sliced
- 3 garlic cloves, sliced
- 1 hot red chilli, sliced, including seeds
- 1 teaspoon cumin seeds, roughly crushed
- 1 teaspoon coriander seeds, roughly crushed
- 1 teaspoon ground turmeric
- 1 teaspoon paprika
- 2 teaspoons garam masala
- 300 ml (½ pint) chicken stock
- 150 ml (¼ pint) double cream
- 4 tablespoons coriander, chopped, plus extra to garnish
- juice of ½–1 lemon

Way better than any takeaway, serve this family favourite with rice or flatbread so none of that delicious sauce goes to waste. It's freezer-friendly too so you could double up on the quantities and make enough for another meal.

- Heat the butter in a saucepan, add the chicken and fry for 3 minutes. Finely chop the onion, ginger, garlic and chilli in a food processor or with a knife. Add to the chicken and fry for 5 minutes, stirring until lightly browned.

- Mix in the spices and cook for 3–4 minutes until well coloured. Stir in the stock and cream, then simmer for 10 minutes, stirring occasionally until the chicken is tender.

- Stir in the chopped coriander and lemon juice to taste. Cook for 1 minute, then garnish with extra coriander.

• DESSERTS •

Chilled Blackcurrant & Mint Soufflé

SERVES 6 • PREP TIME 1 hour, plus chilling

- 250 g (8 oz) blackcurrants, defrosted if frozen
- 6 tablespoons water
- 4 teaspoons powdered gelatine
- 4 eggs, separated
- 200 g (7 oz) caster sugar
- 250 ml (8 fl oz) double cream
- 5 tablespoons finely chopped fresh mint
- icing sugar, for dusting

What a showstopper! This beautiful purple-blue soufflé is easier to make than it looks, but you don't have to tell your dinner guests that.

- Wrap a double thickness strip of nonstick baking paper around a 13 cm (5½ inch) diameter soufflé dish so the paper stands 6 cm (2½ inches) above the dish top.

- Put the blackcurrants and 2 tablespoons of the water in a saucepan, cover and cook gently for 5 minutes until softened. Blend until smooth, then press through a sieve.

- Put the remaining water in a small heatproof bowl and sprinkle over the gelatine, making sure the water absorbs all the powder. Set aside for 5 minutes, then stand the bowl in a pan half-filled with boiling water and simmer for 3–4 minutes, stirring occasionally, until the gelatine dissolves to a clear liquid.

- Put the yolks and sugar in a large heatproof bowl and place over a pan of simmering water so the bowl's base is not touching the water. Whisk for 10 minutes or until the eggs are very thick and pale. Remove from the heat and continue whisking until cool. Fold in the dissolved gelatine in a thin, steady stream, then fold in the purée.

- Whip the cream softly, then fold into the soufflé mix with the mint. Whisk the whites into stiff, moist-looking peaks. Fold a large spoonful into the soufflé mixture to loosen it, then gently fold in the remaining whites. Pour the mixture into the soufflé dish so that it stands above the rim of the dish. Chill for 4 hours or until set.

- Remove the paper and sift over some icing sugar. Serve immediately.

V

• BREAKFASTS •

Mango, Coconut & Lime Lassi

MAKES 600 ml (1 pint) • PREP TIME 5 minutes

- 1 large ripe mango
- juice of 1 orange
- juice of 1 lime
- 1 tablespoon honey
- 300 g (10 oz) natural yogurt
- 4 tablespoons coconut milk
- ice cubes (optional)

Sweet from the mango and honey and oh so refreshing, this is a deliciously healthy drink to enjoy any time of day. To make it vegan and dairy-free, swap the honey for maple syrup and the natural yogurt for coconut yogurt.

- Peel the mango, remove the stone and dice the flesh. Put the mango in a food processor or blender with the orange and lime juices, honey, yogurt and coconut milk. Process until smooth.

- Transfer the mixture to a jug then pour into tall glasses over ice, if using, and serve immediately.

• MAINS •

Royal Lamb Biryani

SERVES 4 • PREP & COOKING TIME 2 hours, plus marinating
and standing

- 4 garlic cloves, crushed
- 1 teaspoon peeled and finely grated fresh root ginger
- 150 ml (¼ pint) natural yogurt
- 6 tablespoons finely chopped coriander
- 500 g (1 lb) boneless lamb, cut into bite-sized pieces
- 8 tablespoons sunflower oil
- 2 onions, finely chopped
- 2 tablespoons medium curry powder
- 200 g (7 oz) canned chopped tomatoes
- 2 teaspoons cumin seeds
- 6 cloves
- 10 black peppercorns
- 4 green cardamom pods
- 1 cinnamon stick
- 200 g (7 oz) basmati rice
- 400 ml (14 fl oz) water
- 1 teaspoon saffron threads
- 3 tablespoons warm milk
- salt and black pepper

Make this spectacular dish to share with family and friends to mark Eid al-Adha, the Festival of Sacrifice, and one of the most important dates in the Muslim calendar.

- Mix together the garlic, ginger, yogurt and coriander and rub into the lamb. Marinate in the refrigerator for 4–6 hours.

- Heat half the oil in a heavy-based pan, add half the onions and cook for 12–15 minutes until golden. Add the meat and cook over a high heat for 15 minutes, stirring often.

- Stir in the curry powder and tomatoes, season and bring to the boil. Reduce the heat and simmer for 30 minutes or until the lamb is tender. Set aside.

- Meanwhile, heat the remaining oil in a separate pan. Add the cumin seeds, the remaining onion, cloves, peppercorns, cardamoms and cinnamon and stir-fry for 6–8 minutes. Add the rice and stir-fry for 2 minutes. Pour in the measured water, bring to the boil, cover and simmer for 6–7 minutes. Remove from the heat. Mix the saffron with the milk and set aside.

- Spread a thin layer of the meat mixture over the base of a lightly creased ovenproof casserole dish and cover evenly with half the rice. Drizzle over half the saffron mixture. Top with the remaining lamb then the remaining rice. Drizzle over the remaining saffron mixture and cover with foil and then the lid.

- Cook in a preheated oven at 180°C (350°F), Gas Mark 4, for 30 minutes. Remove from the oven and allow to rest, still covered, for 30 minutes before serving.

V

· LIGHT BITES ·

Olive Tapenade Toasts

SERVES 4 • PREP & COOKING TIME 20 minutes

- 12 thin slices of French bread
- 1 garlic clove, halved
- 200 g (7 oz) marinated, pitted mixed olives
- 2 tablespoons olive oil
- small bunch of basil
- 25 g (1 oz) pecorino or Parmesan or vegetarian hard cheese, grated*

Salty and garlicky, these are great as canapés with drinks, as a snack or to serve with a bowl of soup to make it more special. Any leftover tapenade is also lovely dotted on to scrambled eggs.

- Toast the bread lightly on both sides then rub one side with the garlic. Transfer to a baking sheet.

- Finely chop the olives in a blender or food processor, then add the oil and most of the basil and blend again to make a coarse paste. Spread over the garlic toasts.

- Cook the toasts in a preheated oven, 190°C (375°F), Gas Mark 5, for 10 minutes. Arrange on a serving plate and sprinkle with the pecorino or Parmesan and the remaining basil leaves.

*For guidance on vegetarian cheeses, see page 5.

• MAINS •

Dover Sole with Bulgur Wheat Salad

SERVES 4 • PREP & COOKING TIME 2 hours 15 minutes, plus standing

- 2 red peppers, deseeded and sliced
- 16 cherry tomatoes, halved
- 2 garlic cloves, thinly sliced
- 4 tablespoons olive oil, plus extra for greasing
- 200 g (7 oz) bulgur wheat
- 2 tablespoons lemon juice
- 1 baby gem lettuce
- 10 black kalamata olives, pitted
- 2 tablespoons finely chopped chives
- 2 large Dover soles, filleted and pin-boned
- salt and black pepper

The delicate flavour and texture of the Dover sole work really well with the punchy flavours of the grain and roasted tomato salad. You could double up on the salad quantities as it keeps well for a day or two in the refrigerator and makes a great packed lunch.

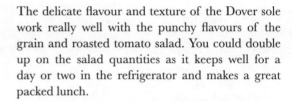

- Cover the base of a small ovenproof dish with the red peppers and place the tomatoes on top. Season the tomatoes with salt and pepper and stud with the slices of garlic. Drizzle with about 2 tablespoons of the oil and place in a preheated oven, 150°C (300°F), Gas Mark 2, for 2 hours.

- Place the bulgur wheat in a heatproof bowl and just cover with boiling water. Cover the bowl with clingfilm and leave to steam for 15 minutes. Drain the bulgur wheat, squeezing out any excess water. Add the lemon juice and some salt and pepper. Keep warm.

- Break up the leaves of the baby gem lettuce and mix with the roasted red peppers, bulgur wheat, olives, chives and remaining oil. Carefully stir in the roasted tomatoes, taking care not to break them up too much.

- Line a baking sheet with foil. Season the Dover sole fillets and place them on the foil, flesh-side down. Cook under a preheated grill for 4–5 minutes, then turn the fish over and grill for a further 2 minutes.

- Serve the fish with the warm bulgur wheat salad and a drizzle of olive oil.

V

• DESSERTS •

Chocolate & Raspberry Soufflés

SERVES 4 • PREP & COOKING TIME 30 minutes

- 100 g (3½ oz) plain dark chocolate, broken into squares
- 3 eggs, separated
- 50 g (2 oz) self-raising flour, sifted
- 40 g (1½ oz) caster sugar
- 150 g (5 oz) raspberries
- icing sugar, for dusting

Soufflés wait for no one! The heat of the oven expands the air in the egg white, creating beautifully puffy and high soufflés, and contracts when cooled. So serve them immediately, hot from the oven.

- Put the chocolate in a heatproof bowl and melt over a saucepan of gently simmering water.

- Place the melted chocolate in a large bowl and whisk in the egg yolks. Fold in the flour.

- Whisk the egg whites and caster sugar in a medium clean bowl until they form soft peaks. Beat a spoonful of the egg whites into the chocolate mixture to loosen it up before gently folding in the rest.

- Divide the raspberries between 4 lightly greased ramekins, pour over the chocolate mixture, then bake in a preheated oven, 190°C (375°F), Gas Mark 5, for 12–15 minutes until the soufflés have risen.

- Dust with icing sugar and serve immediately.

v

• BREAKFASTS •

Wholemeal Raspberry Coconut Muffins

SERVES 12 • PREP & COOKING TIME 30 minutes

- 150 g (5 oz) plain flour
- 150 g (5 oz) wholemeal plain flour
- 1 teaspoon baking powder
- 100 g (3½ oz) coconut oil, melted and cooled
- 2 eggs, beaten
- 125 ml (4 fl oz) milk
- 75 g (3 oz) light muscovado sugar
- 225 g (7½ oz) raspberries
- 2 tablespoons desiccated coconut

Loaded with bursting raspberries, these make a lovely morning treat. You can use both fresh raspberries, when they're in season, or frozen. If using frozen, there's no need to defrost them.

- Line a 12-hole muffin tin with paper muffin cases.

- Sift the flours and baking powder into a large bowl. In a separate bowl, whisk together the oil, eggs, milk and sugar, then pour into the dry ingredients and mix together until just combined – do not overmix.

- Gently stir in the raspberries, then spoon the mixture into the paper cases and sprinkle with the desiccated coconut.

- Bake in a preheated oven, 200°C (400°F), Gas Mark 6, for 20 minutes. Transfer to a wire rack to cool.

· LIGHT BITES ·

Picnic Loaf

SERVES 6 • PREP TIME 30 minutes

- 1 medium cottage loaf
- 125 g (4 oz) salami
- 125 g (4 oz) sliced turkey
- handful of basil leaves
- 3 tomatoes, sliced
- 150 g (5 oz) mozzarella cheese, drained and sliced
- 1 small red onion, cut into rings
- 2 handfuls of rocket leaves
- 75 g (3 oz) pitted black olives
- 75 g (3 oz) Cheddar cheese, thinly sliced

A loaf of bread hollowed out and stuffed to the brim with layers of delicious ingredients, this is not your average sandwich. Get creative and add whatever you fancy: roasted peppers, Parma ham or prosciutto, olive tapenade, pesto, cucumber… Make it up to 24 hours ahead to let the flavours mingle, if you like.

- Cut the top off the loaf, about 3.5 cm (1½ inches) down from the top, and hollow out the inside of the loaf, pulling the soft bread out with your hands and leaving about a 2.5 cm (1 inch) edge.

- Start by layering the salami into the base of the hollowed-out loaf, then cover with the turkey slices. Place a layer of basil leaves on top of the turkey, then layer the tomato and mozzarella slices.

- Cover with the red onion rings and scatter over the rocket leaves. Top with the olives and finish with a layer of the Cheddar. Place the cottage loaf top back on and press down firmly.

- Wrap in greaseproof paper and refrigerate until needed. Cut into wedges to serve.

• MAINS •

Sweet & Sour Pork with Fresh Pineapple

SERVES 4 • PREP & COOKING TIME 20 minutes

- 1 tablespoon vegetable oil
- ½ pineapple, skinned, cored and cut into bite-sized chunks
- 1 onion, cut into chunks
- 1 orange pepper, deseeded and cut into chunks
- 375 g (12 oz) pork fillet, cut into strips
- 100 g (3½ oz) mangetout, halved lengthways
- 6 tablespoons tomato ketchup
- 2 tablespoons soft light brown sugar
- 2 tablespoons white wine or malt vinegar

Fresh and juicy pineapple takes this classic dish to a new level. Balancing the sweet and sour flavours is what will make this dish really work, so taste as you go and add more sugar or vinegar as needed. Serve it with egg noodles, if you like.

- Heat the oil in a large, heavy-based frying pan or wok and stir-fry the pineapple chunks over a very high heat for 3–4 minutes until browned in places. Remove with a slotted spoon.

- Add the onion and orange pepper and cook over a high heat, stirring frequently, for 5 minutes until softened. Add the pork strips and stir-fry for 5 minutes until browned and cooked through.

- Return the pineapple to the pan with the mangetout and cook, stirring occasionally, for 2 minutes. Mix the tomato ketchup, sugar and vinegar together in a jug and pour over the pork mixture. Toss and cook for a further 1 minute to heat the sauce through.

- Serve immediately.

Make the most of your leftovers...
Save the juice that comes out when cutting the pineapple. It's a great marinade for chicken or beef as the enzymes tenderize meat. Mix with chilli, garlic and a splash of soy sauce.

V

· BREAKFASTS ·

Pesto Scrambled Eggs

SERVES 4 • PREP & COOKING TIME 10 minutes

- 12 eggs
- 100 ml (3½ fl oz) single cream
- 25 g (1 oz) butter
- 4 slices of granary bread, toasted
- 4 tablespoons ready-made pesto
- salt and black pepper

Pep up scrambled eggs with a little pesto. You can use shop-bought or try the unusual **Watercress Pesto** on page 118. Be careful not to overcook the eggs – scrambled eggs are best when softly set and velvety.

- Beat the eggs, cream and a little salt and pepper together in a bowl. Melt the butter in a large, nonstick frying pan, add the egg mixture and stir over a low heat with a wooden spoon until cooked to your liking.

- Put a slice of toast on each serving plate. Spoon a quarter of the scrambled eggs on to each slice of toast, make a small indent in the centre and add a tablespoonful of pesto. Serve immediately.

V

· DESSERTS ·

Hazelnut & Blueberry Cakes

MAKES 12 • PREP & COOKING TIME 40 minutes

- 3 eggs
- 150 ml (¼ pint) crème fraîche
- 150 g (5 oz) caster sugar
- 50 g (2 oz) finely ground hazelnuts
- 175 g (6 oz) plain flour
- 1½ teaspoons baking powder
- 125 g (4 oz) fresh blueberries
- 15 g (½ oz) hazelnuts, roughly chopped
- sifted icing sugar, for dusting

Studded with juicy, plump blueberries and topped with crunchy chopped hazelnuts, these light-as-you-like little cakes are a proper treat for Dad on Father's Day. They are best eaten on the day they are made.

- Put the eggs, crème fraîche and sugar in a mixing bowl and whisk together until smooth. Add the ground hazelnuts, flour and baking powder and mix together.

- Spoon the mixture into paper cake cases arranged in a 12-hole deep muffin tin and divide the blueberries evenly among them, pressing lightly into the mixture. Sprinkle with chopped hazelnuts.

- Bake in a preheated oven, 180°C (350°F), Gas Mark 4, for about 20 minutes until well risen and golden. Dust the tops with a little sifted icing sugar and leave to cool in the tin.

VG

• LIGHT BITES •

Aubergine Dip with Crispy Tortillas

SERVES 6 • PREP & COOKING TIME 45 minutes, plus cooling

- 1 large aubergine, about 750 g (1½ lb), trimmed and cut into thick chunks
- 8 tablespoons extra virgin olive oil
- 1 garlic clove, crushed
- ½ teaspoon smoked paprika
- 3 tablespoons tahini
- juice of 1 lemon
- 1 tablespoon chopped flat-leaf parsley
- salt and black pepper

FOR THE CRISPY TORTILLAS
- 6 mini flour tortillas, cut into triangles
- 1 tablespoon olive oil
- 1 teaspoon sea salt flakes

Smoky roasted aubergine is paired with tahini, garlic and lemon for maximum flavour in this dip similar to Middle Eastern baba ganoush. Great with warm pitta bread or spread inside a wrap or sandwich.

- Put the aubergine in a bowl with 6 tablespoons of the extra virgin olive oil and toss well. Transfer to a large roasting tin and roast in a preheated oven, 220°C (425°F), Gas Mark 7, for 25 minutes until soft and lightly charred in places. Leave to cool.

- Transfer the aubergine to a food processor and add the garlic, ¼ teaspoon of the smoked paprika, the tahini, lemon juice, half the chopped parsley and plenty of salt and pepper. Process until smooth, then transfer to a serving bowl.

- Mix the remaining extra virgin olive oil with the remaining paprika and use to swirl over the top of the dip. Scatter with the remaining chopped parsley.

- Brush each tortilla triangle lightly with the olive oil and spread out on 1–2 large baking sheets. Sprinkle with the salt and cook under a preheated medium grill for 1–2 minutes until lightly crisp. Arrange around the bowl of dip and serve.

VG

• MAINS •

Garlicky Bean & Mixed Vegetable Roast

SERVES 4 • PREP & COOKING TIME 1 hour

- 1 green pepper, deseeded and cut into chunks
- 1 red pepper, deseeded and cut into chunks
- 1 yellow pepper, deseeded and cut into chunks
- 1 aubergine, trimmed and cut into chunks
- 1 courgette, trimmed and sliced
- 1 red onion, cut into wedges
- a few rosemary sprigs
- a few thyme sprigs
- 4 tablespoons olive oil
- 4 tomatoes, cut into wedges
- 125 g (4 oz) closed cup mushrooms, trimmed
- 4 garlic cloves, unpeeled
- 400 g (13 oz) can flageolet beans, drained
- 2 tablespoons balsamic vinegar
- 50 g (2 oz) black olives
- salt and black pepper

This full-of-sunshine recipe is lovely served with crusty bread as a main course or as a side alongside slow-roasted lamb. If you have some, crumbling over a little tangy goats' cheese or feta wouldn't go amiss.

- Put the peppers, aubergine, courgette, onion, rosemary and thyme in a large roasting tin. Drizzle over the oil, season with salt and pepper and toss until evenly coated in the oil, then spread out in a single layer. Roast in a preheated oven, 200°C (400°F), Gas Mark 6, for 20 minutes until starting to soften.

- Add the tomatoes, mushrooms and garlic cloves and mix with the other vegetables, then roast for a further 10 minutes until all the vegetables are tender.

- Squeeze the soft garlic out of its skin on to the vegetables in the tin. Add the beans and vinegar and mix well. Return to the oven for a final 10 minutes. Scatter over the olives and serve.

V

• DESSERTS •

Lemon & Poppyseed Cupcakes

SERVES 4 • PREP & COOKING TIME 30 minutes, plus cooling

- 225 g (7½ oz) plain flour
- 2 teaspoons baking powder
- ¼ teaspoon bicarbonate of soda
- ½ teaspoon salt
- 125 g (4 oz) caster sugar
- finely grated zest of 2 lemons and 1 tablespoon lemon juice
- 1 tablespoon poppy seeds, plus 1 teaspoon for decorating
- 75 ml (3 fl oz) sunflower oil
- 7 tablespoons milk

FOR THE FROSTING
- 125 g (4 oz) butter
- 250 g (9 oz) icing sugar
- finely grated zest of 1 lemon
- a few drops of yellow food colouring

Who doesn't love a cupcake? With sunshine-yellow frosting and a zingy lemony flavour, these are especially appealing. So whip up a batch and put the kettle on.

- Sift the flour, baking powder, bicarbonate of soda and salt together into a large bowl. Stir in the sugar, lemon zest and poppy seeds.

- Mix the oil, milk and lemon juice together in a jug. Add to the dry ingredients and stir to mix. Spoon evenly into a 12-hole cupcake tin lined with paper cupcake cases and bake in a preheated oven, 160°C (325°F), Gas Mark 3, for 15 minutes until just firm to the touch. Leave to cool on a wire rack.

- Beat the butter, icing sugar, lemon zest and food colouring for the frosting together in an electric mixer or in a bowl until soft and smooth. Spoon or pipe the frosting on to the cooled cakes and sprinkle with the remaining poppy seeds.

V

• BREAKFASTS •

Souffléd Curried Omelette

SERVES 4 • PREP & COOKING TIME 45 minutes

- 1 tablespoon groundnut oil
- 4 garlic cloves, crushed
- 8 spring onions, finely sliced
- 1 red chilli, finely sliced
- 1 tablespoon medium curry powder
- 4 tomatoes, peeled, deseeded and finely chopped
- small handful of finely chopped coriander leaves
- small handful of finely chopped mint leaves
- 8 large eggs, separated
- salt and black pepper

Chilli, curry powder and fresh herbs add heat and a punchy flavour to this beautifully puffy Indian-inspired omelette. It's one to enjoy any time of day with liberally buttered toast or a crisp green salad alongside.

- Heat half the oil in an ovenproof frying pan over a medium heat. Add the garlic, spring onions and red chilli and stir-fry for 1–2 minutes. Stir in the curry powder, tomatoes and herbs and stir-fry for 20–30 seconds. Remove from the heat, season to taste and allow to cool slightly.

- Place the egg whites in a large bowl and whisk until soft peaks form. Gently beat the egg yolks in a separate bowl, then fold into the egg whites with the tomato mixture until well combined.

- Wipe out the pan with kitchen paper and place over a medium heat. Add the remaining oil and, when hot, pour in the egg mixture. Reduce the heat and cook gently for 8–10 minutes, or until the base starts to set.

- Transfer the pan to a preheated medium-hot grill and cook for 4–5 minutes, or until the top is puffed, lightly golden and almost set. Serve immediately.

v

• LIGHT BITES •

Mediterranean Rice Salad

SERVES 4 • PREP & COOKING TIME 15 minutes

- 75 g (3 oz) broccoli, finely chopped
- 75 g (3 oz) courgettes, finely chopped
- 75 g (3 oz) mixed red and yellow peppers, finely chopped
- 25 g (1 oz) spring onions, finely chopped
- 40 g (1½ oz) mushrooms, finely sliced
- 2 tablespoons water
- 2 tablespoons pesto
- 50 g (2 oz) cooked brown rice
- 50 g (2 oz) cooked wild rice
- salt and black pepper

Full of good-for-you vegetables, this colourful salad is a great way to use up rice from last night's meal. You could also use cooked pasta instead. A lovely summer lunch by itself or as a side for grilled fish or chicken.

- Heat a large frying pan or wok, add the vegetables and the measured water and cook over a high heat for 3–5 minutes, until the vegetables have softened. Remove from the heat and allow to cool.

- Mix the cooled vegetables with the pesto and cooked rice, season well and stir to combine.

V

• LIGHT BITES •

Roasted Red Pepper & Goats' Cheese Salad

SERVES 4 • PREP & COOKING TIME 20 minutes

- 4 red peppers, halved and deseeded
- 3 tablespoons extra-virgin olive oil
- juice of ½ lemon
- 1 teaspoon honey
- 1 teaspoon mustard
- 1 garlic clove, crushed
- 75 g (3 oz) pine nuts
- 150 g (5 oz) soft goats' cheese*
- 10–12 basil leaves
- black pepper

Celebrate the summer solstice and the longest day of the year with this bright, zippy salad. It's a wonderful mix of colours and flavours and ready in just 20 minutes.

- Cook the red peppers, cut-side down, under a preheated hot grill for 8–10 minutes, until the skin turns black.

- Meanwhile, whisk together the olive oil, lemon juice, honey, mustard and garlic in a small bowl or jar and season with pepper.

- Place the red pepper in a large bowl, cover with clingfilm and leave until cool enough to handle, then peel away the blackened skin.

- Toast the pine nuts, in a dry frying pan, until they are golden.

- Cut the red peppers into strips and place on a platter. Crumble and scatter over the goats' cheese and the basil leaves and toss together gently.

- Drizzle over the dressing and serve sprinkled with the pine nuts.

*For guidance on vegetarian cheeses, see page 5.

• MAINS •

Moules Marinière

SERVES 4 • PREP & COOKING TIME 15 minutes

- 2 tablespoons olive oil
- 2 garlic cloves, sliced
- 1.5 kg (3 lb) live mussels, scrubbed and debearded
- 200 ml (7 fl oz) dry white wine
- handful of flat-leaf parsley, chopped

Food doesn't have to be complicated; sometimes a simple one-pot meal is just right. This French classic is a great example. Serve with fresh crusty bread to mop up every last drop of the wine- and garlic-scented cooking juices.

- Heat the oil in a large saucepan. Add the garlic and cook for 30 seconds until lightly golden. Add the mussels, discarding any that are cracked or don't shut when tapped, and the wine.

- Cover the pan and cook for 5 minutes, shaking the pan occasionally, or until the mussels have opened. Discard any that remain closed.

- Stir in the parsley and serve immediately.

V

· BREAKFASTS ·

Honeyed Ricotta with Summer Fruits

SERVES 4 • PREP TIME 10 minutes

- 125 g (4 oz) fresh raspberries
- 2 teaspoons rosewater
- 250 g (8 oz) ricotta cheese
- 250 g (8 oz) fresh mixed summer berries
- 2 tablespoons honey with honeycomb
- 2 tablespoons pumpkin seeds, toasted
- pinch of ground cinnamon

This summery breakfast is worth getting up for: creamy ricotta, fragrant rosewater and fresh berries all topped with honey and crunchy toasted pumpkin seeds.

- Rub the raspberries through a fine nylon sieve to purée and remove the pips, then mix with the rosewater. Alternatively, put the raspberries and rosewater in a food processor or blender and process to a purée, then sieve to remove the pips.

- Slice the ricotta into wedges and arrange on serving plates with the berries. Drizzle over the honey and the raspberry purée, adding a little honeycomb, and serve scattered with the pumpkin seeds and cinnamon.

V

• DESSERTS •

Sticky Cinnamon & Pecan Buns

MAKES 10 • PREP & COOKING TIME 1 hour 15 minutes, plus standing, proving and setting

- 1 tablespoon ground flaxseed
- 200 ml (7 fl oz) milk
- 15 g (½ oz) fast-action dried yeast
- 450 g (14½ oz) strong white bread flour, plus extra for dusting
- ½ teaspoon salt
- 75 g (3 oz) butter, cubed
- 50 g (2 oz) soft light brown sugar
- 125 g (4 oz) icing sugar
- sunflower oil, for oiling

FOR THE FILLING
- 100 g (4 oz) butter
- 8 tablespoons soft light brown sugar
- 2 teaspoons ground cinnamon
- 75 g (3 oz) pecan nuts, roughly chopped
- 6 fresh Medjool dates, stoned and mashed
- 2 tablespoons maple syrup

It's Midsummer's Day, the longest day of the year. Celebrating Midsummer is a cherished tradition in Scandinavian countries, so join the party with these Swedish-style buns.

- Mix the flaxseed with 3 tablespoons water in a small jug and set aside. Heat the milk gently in a saucepan until lukewarm. Stir in the yeast and leave to stand for 10 minutes.

- Combine the flour and salt in a large bowl, add the butter and rub in with the fingertips until the mixture resembles fine breadcrumbs, then stir in the brown sugar. Mix the flaxseed mixture into the yeast mixture, then stir into the flour mixture and mix to a dough. Knead the dough out on to a lightly floured surface until smooth and elastic. Put in a bowl, cover with clingfilm and leave to rise in a warm place for 10 minutes.

- Combine the butter, sugar and cinnamon in a bowl. Add the pecan nuts, mashed dates and maple syrup and mix well.

- Turn the dough on a lightly floured surface and knead for 2 minutes until smooth. Roll out to a rectangle about 30 × 45 cm (12 × 18 inches). Spread the filling over the surface, then roll up tightly from one of the longer sides of the dough to form a spiral.

- Slice into 10, place on a baking sheet, cover with oiled clingfilm and leave to prove in a warm place for 30 minutes. Remove the clingfilm and bake in a preheated oven, 200°C (400°F), Gas Mark 6, for 25 minutes until golden and cooked through. Cool on a wire rack.

- Put the icing sugar in a bowl, add 2 tablespoons water, mix until soft and smooth. Drizzle over the cooled buns and leave to set for 20 minutes.

· LIGHT BITES ·

Smoked Trout
& Grape Salad

SERVES 2 • PREP TIME 15 minutes

- 200 g (7 oz) smoked trout
- 160 g (5½ oz) red seedless grapes
- 75 g (3 oz) watercress
- 1 fennel bulb

FOR THE DRESSING
- 3 tablespoons mayonnaise
- 4 cornichons, finely diced
- 1½ tablespoons capers, chopped
- 2 tablespoons lemon juice
- salt and black pepper

Smoked trout has a more delicate flavour than the commonly used smoked salmon and pairs beautifully with the sweetness of the grapes in this salad. Serve it as an elegant starter or light lunch.

- Flake the smoked trout into bite-sized pieces, removing any bones, and place in a large salad bowl. Wash and drain the grapes and watercress and add them to the bowl. Finely slice the fennel and add to the mix.

- Make the dressing by mixing the mayonnaise, cornichons, capers and lemon juice. Season to taste with salt and pepper, then carefully mix through the salad and serve.

• MAINS •

Steak Burritos

SERVES 4 • PREP & COOKING TIME 40 minutes, plus marinating

- 2 garlic cloves, crushed
- 1 tablespoon mild chilli powder
- 1 tablespoon olive oil
- 2 teaspoons smoked sweet paprika
- 1 teaspoon ground cumin
- 400 g (14 oz) skirt steak
- 8 wheat tortillas
- salt and black pepper

FOR THE SALSA
- 3 tomatoes, chopped
- 2 tablespoons finely chopped red onion
- juice of ½ lime

FOR THE FILLING
- 200 g (7 oz) cooked white rice
- 150 g (5 oz) black beans, rinsed, drained and warmed through
- sliced iceberg lettuce
- grated Cheddar cheese
- soured cream
- chopped coriander leaves

You could make all the burritos to serve them, or, much more fun, place all the fillings and salsa on the table and let everyone make their own. So fill, roll and tuck in!

- Place the garlic, chilli powder, oil, paprika and cumin in a bowl and mix together. Rub all over the steak, then place in a shallow dish. Cover with clingfilm and leave to marinate in the refrigerator for at least 2 hours and preferably overnight.

- Season the meat well. Heat a griddle pan until smoking hot, add the steak and cook for 3–5 minutes on each side until browned and cooked to your liking. Remove from the pan and cut into thin slices.

- Make the salsa by tossing together all the ingredients in a bowl.

- When ready to serve, heat a dry nonstick frying pan until hot, add 1 tortilla and cook for 30 seconds until pliable. Remove from the heat and spoon a little cooked rice and warmed beans into the centre. Add some strips of steak and top with some tomato salsa, lettuce, cheese, soured cream and coriander. Fold up the outside edges, squashing down the filling a little if necessary, and roll over so the filling is completely enclosed. Repeat with the remaining tortillas.

V

• BREAKFASTS •

Potato & Sweetcorn Hash with Frazzled Eggs

SERVES 4 • PREP & COOKING TIME 30 minutes

- 750 g (1½ lb) large potatoes, peeled and diced
- 3 tablespoons olive oil
- 1 large onion, finely chopped
- 1 large green pepper, deseeded and chopped
- 1 teaspoon smoked paprika
- 200 g (7 oz) can sweetcorn, drained
- 4 large eggs, chilled
- 2 tablespoons snipped chives
- salt and black pepper

Ready in just half an hour, this hearty brunch dish will keep you going through the day. It's also a great way to use up any leftover cooked potatoes.

- Put the potatoes in a large saucepan and cover with lightly salted water. Bring to the boil and cook for 12–15 minutes until tender, then drain in a colander.

- Meanwhile, heat 2 tablespoons of the oil in a large, nonstick frying pan with an ovenproof handle over a medium heat. Add the onion and green pepper and cook, stirring occasionally, for 7–8 minutes until softened and lightly golden.

- Add the cooked potatoes, smoked paprika and sweetcorn, season generously with salt and pepper and cook for 3–4 minutes, stirring frequently.

- Slide the pan under a preheated grill, keeping the handle away from the heat, and grill for 2–3 minutes until crispy.

- While the hash is grilling, heat the remaining olive oil in a large frying pan over a medium heat. Crack the eggs into the pan and fry for 3 minutes until the egg whites are set and crispy.

- Using a fish slice, lift the eggs on to the hash in the pan and return under the grill to cook the yolk, if you like. Serve immediately sprinkled with the chives.

v

• MAINS •

Summer Vegetable Fettuccine

SERVES 4 • PREP & COOKING TIME 25 minutes

- 250 g (8 oz) asparagus, trimmed and cut into 5 cm (2 inch) lengths
- 125 g (4 oz) sugar snap peas
- 400 g (13 oz) dried fettuccine or pappardelle
- 200 g (7 oz) baby courgettes
- 150 g (5 oz) button mushrooms
- 1 tablespoon olive oil
- 1 small onion, finely chopped
- 1 garlic clove, finely chopped
- 4 tablespoons lemon juice
- 2 teaspoons chopped tarragon
- 2 teaspoons chopped parsley
- 100 g (3½ oz) smoked mozzarella cheese, diced
- salt and black pepper

Also called scamorza, mozzarella is smoked over beechwood and has a distinctive nutty flavour and a tawny colour. If you can't find it, use ordinary mozzarella instead.

- Cook the asparagus and sugar snap peas in a saucepan of boiling water for 3–4 minutes, then drain and refresh under cold running water. Drain well and set aside.

- Cook the pasta in a large saucepan of salted boiling water according to the packet instructions until al dente.

- Meanwhile, halve the courgettes lengthways and cut the mushrooms in half. Heat the oil in a large frying pan, add the onion and garlic and cook for 2–3 minutes. Add the courgettes and mushrooms and cook, stirring, for 3–4 minutes. Stir in the asparagus and sugar snap peas and cook for 1–2 minutes before adding the lemon juice and herbs.

- Drain the pasta and return to the pan. Add the vegetable mixture and mozzarella and season to taste with salt and pepper. Toss gently to mix and serve.

• BREAKFASTS •

Eggs Benedict

SERVES 4 • PREP & COOKING TIME 20 minutes

- 8 thick slices of cooked ham
- 4 muffins or brioche
- 25 g (1 oz) butter
- 8 hot poached eggs
- snipped chives, to garnish

FOR THE HOLLANDAISE
- 3 egg yolks
- 1 tablespoon cold water
- 125 g (4 oz) butter, softened
- large pinch of salt
- 2 pinches of cayenne pepper
- 1 teaspoon lemon juice
- 1 tablespoon single cream

One of the world's great classic dishes, this includes Hollandaise sauce, which has the reputation of being tricky to make. For chef-level success, the secret is to keep the heat very low so the water is just at a gentle simmer, and don't stop beating.

- Warm the ham slices under a preheated high grill for 2–3 minutes on each side. Transfer to an ovenproof dish and keep warm in a low oven.

- Make the sauce. Beat the egg yolks and measured water together in the top of a double boiler over simmering water until the mixture is pale. Gradually add the butter, a small amount at a time, and continue beating until the mixture thickens. Add the salt, 1 pinch of cayenne pepper and lemon juice. Stir in the cream. Remove from the heat and keep warm.

- Split the muffins or brioche in half, then toast and spread with the butter. Arrange on plates. Lay a slice of ham on each muffin half and top with a poached egg. Spoon a little of the sauce over each egg.

- Garnish with the remaining cayenne pepper and chives and serve immediately.

V

· DESSERTS ·

Eton Mess with Ginger

SERVES 4 • PREP TIME 10 minutes

- 500 g (1 lb) strawberries, hulled and chopped
- 1 teaspoon ginger cordial
- 400 ml (14 fl oz) double cream
- 3 ready-made meringue nests, lightly crushed
- 2 pieces of preserved stem ginger, diced
- 1 tablespoon shredded mint

It's the start of Wimbledon fortnight when, alongside the action on court, fans will be enjoying that great combination, strawberries and cream. Go one better with a quintessential summer dessert, this version with a hint of ginger.

- Toss the strawberries in a bowl with the ginger cordial.

- Whip the cream to soft peaks, then stir in the strawberries, crushed meringue, ginger and half the shredded mint.

- Divide between 4 glasses and sprinkle over the remaining shredded mint to serve.

July

GOOD TO EAT THIS MONTH

artichokes * aubergines * beetroot * broad beans *
broccoli * new carrots * courgettes * cucumber *
French beans * lettuces * mangetout * new potatoes
* pak choi * peas *radishes * spinach * spring onions
* summer squash * sweetcorn * tomatoes * apricots
* blackcurrants * blueberries* cherries * nectarines *
peaches * raspberries * redcurrants * strawberries *
basil * chillies * coriander * mint * oregano * parsley

DATES TO LOOK FORWARD TO THIS MONTH

American Independence Day

Summer steps up a gear this month and we can look forward to
long evenings and outdoor eating.

July means barbecues, also warm days, light-filled evenings,
friends and great food cooked on the fire. The recipes for **Spiced
Chicken Wings** (page 217), **Thai Chicken Burgers with Coconut
Satay Sauce** (page 225) and **Pork Burgers with Roasted Pears**
(page 237) will get your barbecues off to a sizzling start.

This month cherry season hits its stride, the orchards full of
dark, juicy fruit that will appear in shops and at markets. Make
the most of them with the **Cherry & Almond Traybake** on page
218 and the **Cherry Clafoutis** on page 230.

Cooking is simpler as warm weather beckons us outside as
much as possible and salads take centre stage. A good salad is
so much more than a bowl of leaves, as shown by the recipes
for **Middle Eastern Bread Salad** (page 215), **Crab & Grapefruit
Salad** (page 224) and **Smoked Chicken Salad** (page 228).

V

· BREAKFASTS ·

French Toast with Blueberries

SERVES 4 • PREP & COOKING TIME 15 minutes

- 2 eggs
- 25 g (1 oz) caster sugar
- ½ teaspoon ground cinnamon
- 4 tablespoons milk
- 25 g (1 oz) butter
- 4 thick slices of brioche
- 100 g (3½ oz) blueberries
- 8 tablespoons thick Greek yogurt
- 4 teaspoons honey, to serve

French toast, eggy bread or pain perdu – this breakfast favourite has many names but whatever you call it, it always feels like a treat. You can vary the fruit you top it with, depending on what's in season.

- Beat the eggs in a bowl with the sugar, cinnamon and milk. Heat the butter in a large, heavy-based frying pan.

- Dip the brioche slices, 2 at a time, into the egg mixture on both sides, then lift into the hot pan and fry for 1–2 minutes on each side until golden.

- Repeat with the remaining brioche slices. Mix half the blueberries into the yogurt.

- Serve the warm French toasts with spoonfuls of the yogurt on top, the remaining blueberries scattered over and a thin drizzle of honey on top.

• LIGHT BITES •

Middle Eastern Bread Salad

SERVES 4–6 • PREP TIME 10 minutes, plus cooling

- 2 flatbreads or flour tortillas
- 1 large green pepper deseeded and diced
- 1 Lebanese cucumber, diced
- 250 g (8 oz) cherry tomatoes, halved
- ½ red onion, finely chopped
- 2 tablespoons chopped mint
- 2 tablespoons chopped parsley
- 2 tablespoons chopped coriander
- 3 tablespoons extra virgin olive oil
- juice of 1 lemon
- salt and black pepper

This is a great summer salad when tomatoes are at peak flavour. It's also ideal as a make-ahead dish as the taste improves the longer the vegetable and herb mixture sits, but don't add the flatbreads or tortillas until just before serving, so they stay crunchy.

- Cook the flatbreads or tortillas on a preheated ridged griddle pan or under a preheated hot grill for 2–3 minutes until toasted and charred. Leave to cool, then tear into bite-sized pieces.

- Put the green pepper, cucumber, tomatoes, onion and herbs in a bowl, add the oil, lemon juice and salt and pepper and stir well. Add the bread and stir again. Serve immediately.

· MAINS ·

Lamb Chops with Olive Couscous

SERVES 4 • PREP & COOKING TIME 40 minutes, plus marinating

- 6 anchovy fillets in olive oil, drained and chopped
- 2 tablespoons black olive tapenade
- 2–3 sprigs of thyme, leaves stripped and chopped
- 1 sprig of rosemary, leaves stripped and chopped
- 2 bay leaves, torn
- 2–3 garlic cloves, crushed
- finely grated zest of 1 lemon
- 4 tablespoons white wine
- 125 ml (4 fl oz) olive oil
- 4 lamb loin chops, about 150 g (5 oz) each
- 300 g (10 oz) couscous
- 2 tablespoons salted capers or capers in brine, drained and rinsed
- 100 g (3½ oz) spicy-marinated green olives, chopped
- 75 g (3 oz) rocket leaves, plus extra for serving
- 4 tablespoons lemon juice, plus extra for serving
- salt and black pepper

Lamb chops need to be cooked quickly and over a high heat to get the best from them, so make sure your griddle pan is good and hot and don't be tempted to overcook them.

- Mash the anchovies with a fork and stir them into a bowl with the tapenade. Add the herbs, garlic and lemon zest, then pour in the wine and 4 tablespoons of the oil. Stir thoroughly, then rub the mixture into the lamb chops. Cover and leave at room temperature for about 1 hour.

- Put the couscous into a heatproof bowl and stir in 2 tablespoons of the oil so that the grains are covered. Season with salt and pour over 400 ml (14 fl oz) boiling water. Leave to stand for 5–8 minutes until the grains are soft.

- Season the lamb chops with pepper and cook them for about 2 minutes in a preheated hot griddle pan. Sprinkle with a little salt, then cook the other side for a further 2 minutes. Transfer to a warm dish, cover with foil and leave to rest for 5 minutes.

- Fluff up the couscous with a fork and gently fold in the capers, olives and rocket.

- Sprinkle over the lemon juice, then heap the couscous on to serving plates. Arrange a lamb chop on each heap and spoon over the juices. Sprinkle with rocket leaves, drizzle with the remaining oil and an extra squeeze of lemon juice and serve immediately with lemon wedges.

• MAINS •

Spiced Chicken Wings

SERVES 4 • PREP & COOKING TIME 20 minutes, plus marinating

- 8 large chicken wings
- flat-leaf parsley sprig, to garnish
- lime wedges, to serve

FOR THE MARINADE
- 1 garlic clove
- 5 cm (2 inch) piece of fresh root ginger, peeled and chopped
- juice and finely grated zest of 2 limes
- 2 tablespoons light soy sauce
- 2 tablespoons groundnut oil
- 2 teaspoons ground cinnamon
- 1 teaspoon ground turmeric
- 2 tablespoons honey
- salt

FOR THE YELLOW PEPPER DIP
- 2 yellow peppers
- 2 tablespoons natural yogurt
- 1 tablespoon dark soy sauce
- 1 tablespoon chopped coriander
- black pepper

A must-make for your 4th July barbecue to mark American Independence Day. Ideally, marinate for 2 hours but, if you're short on time, even 30 minutes will help make them moist and tender. The heat will caramelize the sugars in the honey, adding a lovely crust.

- Soak 8 bamboo skewers in cold water for 30 minutes.

- Place the marinade ingredients in a blender or food processor and blend until smooth.

- Arrange the chicken wings in a shallow dish, pour the marinade over and toss to cover. Cover and leave to marinate for 1–2 hours.

- Put the peppers for the dip on a hot barbecue for 10 minutes, turning occasionally, until they are charred and blistered. Remove and place in a plastic bag, then seal and leave until cool. Peel off the skins and remove the seeds and white membrane. Put the flesh into a food processor or blender with the yogurt and blend until smooth. Pour into a bowl, season with soy sauce and pepper to taste and stir in the coriander. Cover and chill until needed.

- Remove the chicken from the marinade, thread on to the skewers and cook on a hot barbecue for 4–5 minutes on each side, basting with the remaining marinade.

- Garnish with a parsley sprig, then serve with the dip and some lime wedges.

V

· DESSERTS ·

Cherry & Almond Traybake

MAKES 10 squares • PREP & COOKING TIME 1 hour

- 225g self-raising flour
- 1 teaspoon baking powder
- 100g unsalted butter, chilled and diced
- 100g golden caster sugar
- 1 egg, beaten
- 125ml milk
- 1 teaspoon almond extract
- 400g fresh, stoned cherries
- 50g flaked almonds
- sifted icing sugar, for dusting

Make the most of fresh, in-season cherries with this crowd-pleasing traybake. It's a moist cake so will need eating up in a day or two – which shouldn't be difficult!

- Combine the flour, baking powder and butter in a bowl or food processor until the mixture resembles breadcrumbs. Add the caster sugar and combine, then tip into a bowl.

- Mix the egg, milk and almond extract together. Add to the dry mixture with half the cherries and stir until combined.

- Spoon the mixture into a greased and lined 23 cm square shallow baking tin and spread in an even layer. Scatter over the remaining cherries, then the flaked almonds.

- Bake in a preheated oven, 180°C, Gas Mark 4, for 25–30 minutes or until golden and just firm to the touch. Leave to cool in the tin, then transfer to a board and peel off the lining paper. Dust with sifted icing sugar and cut into squares.

• BREAKFASTS •

One-Pan Sausage & Egg Brunch

SERVES 2 • PREP & COOKING TIME 40 minutes

- 1 tablespoon sunflower oil
- 4 pork sausages
- 2 potatoes, scrubbed and cut into 1 cm (½ inch) cubes
- 4 portobello mushrooms, trimmed and halved
- 2 tomatoes, halved
- 2 large eggs
- black pepper

Luxuriate in a leisurely brunch with this one-pan pleaser. Add a stack of hot buttered toast, some fresh orange juice and a pot of coffee and tuck in.

- Heat the oil in a nonstick ovenproof dish or roasting dish in a preheated oven, 200°C (400°F), Gas Mark 6, until hot.

- Add the sausages and potatoes to the hot oil and turn to coat. Cook in the oven for 10 minutes.

- Remove the dish from the oven, add the mushrooms and tomatoes and turn with the sausages and potatoes to coat in the oil. Return to the oven and cook for a further 10–12 minutes until the potatoes are golden and the sausages are cooked through.

- Make 2 separate spaces in the baked mixture and break an egg into each. Return to the oven and cook for a further 3–4 minutes until the eggs are softly set. Grind over some pepper and serve immediately.

V

• LIGHT BITES •

French Onion Tarts

MAKES 12 • PREP & COOKING TIME 1 hour, plus chilling

- 1 quantity chilled ready-made shortcrust pastry
- 50 g (2 oz) butter
- 2 onions, thinly sliced
- 4 eggs
- 200 ml (7 fl oz) milk
- 2 teaspoons Dijon mustard
- 125 g (4 oz) Gruyère or vegetarian hard cheese, finely grated*
- salt and black pepper

Sweet onions encased in crispy pastry make these little tarts a crowd-pleaser. Serve warm or cold as finger food for a party or picnic or a light meal with a green salad to add colour and contrast.

- Roll the pastry out thinly on a lightly floured surface, then stamp out 12 × 10 cm (4 inch) circles with a plain biscuit cutter and press into a greased 12-hole muffin tin. Re-knead and reroll the pastry trimmings as needed. Chill for 15 minutes.

- Heat the butter in a frying pan, add the onions and fry over a gentle heat for 10 minutes, stirring from time to time until softened and just beginning to colour.

- Add the eggs, milk and mustard to a large wide-necked jug, and fork together until just mixed. Add the cheese and seasoning and mix together. Divide the mixture between the pastry cases, then spoon in the fried onions.

- Bake in a preheated oven, 190°C (375°F), Gas Mark 5, for 20–25 minutes until golden brown and the filling is just set. Leave to cool for 10 minutes, then loosen the edges of the tarts with a knife and remove from the tins.

*For guidance on vegetarian cheeses, see page 5.

V

• MAINS •

Courgette & Herb Risotto

SERVES 4 • PREP & COOKING TIME 30 minutes

- 4 tablespoons butter
- 2 tablespoons olive oil
- 1 large onion, finely chopped
- 2 garlic cloves, finely chopped
- 350 g (11½ oz) risotto rice
- 200 ml (7 fl oz) white wine
- 1.5 litres (2½ pints) vegetable stock, heated to simmering
- 200 g (7 oz) baby leaf spinach, chopped
- 100 g (3½ oz) courgettes, finely diced
- 50 g (2 oz) Parmesan or vegetarian hard cheese, finely grated*
- 1 small handful of dill, mint and chives, roughly chopped
- salt and black pepper

Courgettes, baby spinach and a medley of fresh herbs make this a plate of gorgeous green goodness. White wine gives any risotto a lovely depth of flavour but if you haven't got any just replace it with stock.

- Melt the butter with the oil in a saucepan, add the onion and garlic and cook for about 3 minutes until soft. Add the rice and stir until coated with the butter mixture. Add the wine and cook rapidly, stirring, until it has evaporated.

- Add the hot stock, a ladleful at a time, and cook, stirring constantly, until each addition has been absorbed before adding the next. Continue until all the stock has been absorbed and the rice is creamy and cooked but still retains a little bite – this will take around 15 minutes.

- Stir in the spinach and courgettes and heat through for 3–5 minutes. Remove from the heat and stir in the Parmesan and herbs. Season to taste with salt and pepper and serve immediately.

Make the most of your leftovers...
Leftover risotto can be used to make arancini, those irresistible deep-fried balls of risotto wrapped around a centre of melting mozzarella.

*For guidance on vegetarian cheeses, see page 5.

V

· DESSERTS ·

Nectarine & Blueberry Cobbler

SERVES 4 • PREP & COOKING TIME 30 minutes

- 12 ripe nectarines, halved and stoned
- 150 g (5 oz) blueberries
- 2 tablespoons light muscovado sugar
- 175 g (6 oz) self-raising flour, plus extra for dusting
- 50 g (2 oz) unsalted butter, diced
- 50 g (2 oz) caster sugar
- 125 ml (4 fl oz) buttermilk
- milk, for brushing

This dessert is full of wonderful ripe nectarines and blueberries that cook under the scone topping to a bubbling, crowd-pleasing treat. Best enjoyed with a scoop of cold vanilla ice cream.

- Place the nectarines and blueberries in a 750 ml (1¼ pint) ovenproof dish and sprinkle over the muscovado sugar.

- Place the flour in a bowl, add the butter and rub in with the fingertips until the mixture resembles fine breadcrumbs. Stir in the caster sugar, then add the buttermilk a little at a time, to form a slightly sticky, soft dough.

- Turn the dough out on to a lightly floured surface and pat out until it is 1 cm (½ inch) thick. Cut out 8 rounds using a 6 cm (2½ inch) cutter.

- Arrange over the top of the fruit and brush with a little milk. Place in a preheated oven, 180°C (350°F), Gas Mark 4, for 20 minutes or until the scones are golden and the fruit is bubbling. Serve immediately.

V

• BREAKFASTS •

Banana & Buttermilk Pancakes

SERVES 4 • PREP & COOKING TIME 20 minutes

- 125 g (4 oz) plain flour
- 1 teaspoon baking powder
- pinch of salt
- 200 ml (7 fl oz) buttermilk
- 1 egg
- 2 small bananas, thinly sliced
- 1 tablespoon vegetable oil, for frying

TO SERVE
- 1 banana, sliced
- 25 g (1 oz) pecan nuts, chopped
- honey, for drizzling

Naturally sweet bananas elevate these fluffy pancakes. Add a pinch of cinnamon for extra depth of flavour. See page 68 for an easy hack if you don't have any buttermilk.

- Sift the flour, baking powder and salt into a large bowl and make a well in the centre.

- Whisk together the buttermilk and egg in a jug, then gradually whisk into the flour mixture to form a smooth batter. Stir in the sliced bananas.

- Heat a large nonstick frying pan over a medium heat. Using a scrunched-up piece of kitchen paper, dip into the oil and use to wipe over the pan.

- Drop 3 large tablespoons of the batter into the pan to make 3 pancakes, spreading the batter out slightly with a spoon. Cook for 2–3 minutes until bubbles start to appear on the surface and the underside is golden brown, then flip over and cook for a further 2 minutes.

- Remove from the pan and keep warm. Repeat with the remaining batter to make 8 pancakes.

- Serve the pancakes topped with extra sliced banana, sprinkled with pecans and drizzled with a little honey.

• LIGHT BITES •

Crab & Grapefruit Salad

SERVES 4 • PREP TIME 10 minutes

- 400 g (13 oz) white crab meat
- 1 pink grapefruit, peeled and sliced
- 50 g (2 oz) rocket
- 3 spring onions, sliced
- 200 g (7 oz) mangetout, halved
- salt and black pepper

FOR THE
WATERCRESS
DRESSING
- 85 g (3¼ oz) watercress, tough stalks removed
- 1 tablespoon Dijon mustard
- 2 tablespoons olive oil

TO SERVE
- 4 chapattis
- lime wedges

Zesty grapefruit tumbled together with sweet crab and dressed with an unusual watercress dressing, this is a refreshing light lunch and would work as a starter shared with friends.

- Combine the crab meat, grapefruit, rocket, spring onions and mangetout in a serving dish. Season to taste.

- Make the dressing by blending together the watercress, mustard and oil. Season with salt.

- Toast the chapattis. Stir the dressing into the salad and serve with the toasted chapattis and lime wedges on the side.

• MAINS •

Thai Chicken Burgers with Coconut Satay Sauce

SERVES 4 • PREP & COOKING TIME 35 minutes, plus chilling

- 500 g (1 lb) skinless chicken breast fillets, minced
- 1–2 tablespoons Thai red curry paste
- 1 small onion, finely chopped
- 2 tablespoons chopped coriander
- olive oil, for brushing
- 4 oval buns, halved
- 50 g (2 oz) mixed Asian salad leaves
- handful of Thai basil, coriander and mint leaves

FOR THE COCONUT
SATAY SAUCE
- 6 tablespoons coconut cream
- 3 tablespoons smooth peanut butter
- juice of ½ lime
- 2 teaspoons Thai fish sauce
- 2 teaspoons sweet chilli sauce

These burgers are something special for a summer barbecue. If you don't have Thai basil, you can use ordinary basil mixed with coriander and mint leaves for a similar flavour.

- Place the chicken, curry paste, onion, coriander and some salt and pepper in a food processor or blender and blend until smooth. Transfer to a bowl and chill for 30 minutes. Divide the mixture and shape into 8 even-sized patties.

- Meanwhile, put all the satay sauce ingredients in a small saucepan and heat gently, stirring until combined. Simmer gently for 12 minutes until thickened, then set aside to cool.

- Brush the patties lightly with oil and cook on a hot barbecue for 5–6 minutes on each side until cooked through. Test one by inserting a skewer into the centre: it should feel hot to the touch when the burger is cooked.

- Fill the buns with the chicken burgers, Asian salad leaves and mixed herbs and spoon the coconut satay sauce over the top.

VG

• DESSERTS •

Strawberry Sorbet

SERVES 6 • PREP TIME 15 minutes, plus freezing

- 750 g (1½ lb) strawberries, hulled and roughly chopped
- 150 g (5 oz) caster sugar
- juice of 1 lemon
- 300 ml (½ pint) boiling water

Using just a few ingredients, this intensely flavoured and bright-hued sorbet is super-easy – no ice-cream maker needed. Once you've nailed the method, experiment with other flavours such as raspberry, peach, pineapple and melon.

- Add the strawberries, caster sugar and lemon juice to a bowl and pour over the measured boiling water. Set aside to cool.

- Once the mixture has cooled, blitz in a food processor until smooth, then push the purée through a sieve.

- Pour the liquid into a freezerproof container and cover with clingfilm. Freeze until frozen around the edges and slushy in the middle. Use a fork to break up the ice into smaller crystals. Return the container to the freezer.

- Repeat the breaking-up process every 30 minutes, at least three times, until the sorbet is completely frozen and the texture of snow. Scoop into glasses or small bowls and serve.

V

· BREAKFASTS ·

Sweetcorn & Pepper Frittata

SERVES 4 • PREP & COOKING TIME 20 minutes

- 2 tablespoons olive oil
- 4 spring onions, thinly sliced
- 200 g (7 oz) can sweetcorn, drained
- 150 g (5 oz) bottled roasted red peppers in oil, drained and cut into strips
- 4 eggs, lightly beaten
- 125 g (4 oz) strong Cheddar cheese, grated
- 1 small handful of chives, finely chopped
- salt and black pepper

When the fridge is looking a bit bare on a Saturday morning, whip up this colourful and easy-to-make frittata for brunch using a few storecupboard standbys. For a spicy, Mexican-inspired version, add a sliced jalapeño pepper.

- Heat the oil in a nonstick frying pan with an ovenproof handle, add the spring onions, sweetcorn and red peppers and cook for 30 seconds.

- Add the eggs, Cheddar, chives, and salt and pepper to taste and cook over a medium heat for 4–5 minutes until the base is set.

- Remove from the hob, place under a preheated grill and cook for 3–4 minutes or until golden and set.

- Cut into wedges and serve.

Smoked Chicken & Red Onion Salad

SERVES 4 • PREP TIME 10 minutes

- 300 g (10 oz) skinless smoked chicken breast
- 2 red onions, finely sliced
- 150 g (5 oz) cherry tomatoes, halved
- 50 g (2 oz) pumpkin seeds, roasted
- 75 g (3 oz) mixed salad leaves
- salt and black pepper

FOR THE DRESSING
- 1 ripe avocado, peeled, stoned and diced
- 2 tablespoons lime juice
- 1 tablespoon of Dijon mustard

When you want lunch without faff, this is a great choice. Rinsing the raw red onion in cold water will make it less pungent, taming some of the harshness.

- Dice or shred the smoked chicken. Rinse the red onions in water.

- Make the dressing by blending together the avocado, lime juice, mustard and seasoning.

- Toss together the chicken, onion, tomatoes, pumpkin seeds and salad leaves, drizzle over the dressing and serve.

· MAINS ·

Blackened Cod with Orange Salsa

SERVES 4 • PREP & COOKING TIME 25 minutes

- 4 cod fillets, about 175 g (6 oz) each
- 1 tablespoon jerk seasoning

FOR THE ORANGE SALSA
- 1 large orange
- 1 garlic clove, crushed
- 2 large tomatoes, deseeded and diced
- 2 tablespoons chopped basil, plus extra to garnish
- 75 g (3 oz) pitted black olives, chopped
- 5 tablespoons olive oil
- salt and black pepper

Jerk seasoning adds a punch of flavour to mild and delicious cod, while the citrussy salsa gives it a refreshing twist. Serve with a green salad or brown rice.

- Cut the skin and the white membrane off the orange. Working over a bowl to catch the juice, cut between the membranes to remove the segments. Halve the segments and mix them with the reserved juice and the garlic, tomatoes, basil, olives and 4 tablespoons of the oil. Season to taste with salt and pepper and set aside to infuse.

- Brush the cod with the remaining oil and coat with the jerk seasoning. Heat a large, heavy-based frying pan and cook the cod, skin-side down, for 5 minutes. Turn the fish over and cook for a further 3 minutes.

- Transfer to a preheated oven, 150°C (300°F), Gas Mark 2, to rest for about 5 minutes. Garnish the fish with basil and serve with the salsa.

v

· DESSERTS ·

Cherry Clafoutis

SERVES 2 • PREP & COOKING TIME 40 minutes

- 250 g (8 oz) cherries, stoned
- 200 ml (7 fl oz) full-fat milk
- 3 tablespoons single cream
- few drops of vanilla extract
- 2 eggs
- 50 g (2 oz) caster sugar
- 25 g (1 oz) plain flour
- 1 tablespoon roughly chopped blanched almonds
- icing sugar, to dust

This classic French dessert features a thick, custard-like batter over fruit. It is traditionally made with cherries but other stone fruit, such as peaches, plums and apricots, work well also. No cherry pitter? Try using a chopstick or sturdy straw for stoning the cherries.

- Butter a medium-sized ovenproof dish and put the cherries in it. Heat the milk, cream and vanilla extract in a small pan.

- Whisk together the eggs and sugar until light and fluffy, then stir in the flour.

- Gradually stir in the heated milk, then pour this batter mix over the cherries and scatter the almonds over the top.

- Bake in a preheated oven, 190°C (375°F), Gas Mark 5, for 25–30 minutes until golden and puffy. Dust the top with icing sugar and serve.

• BREAKFASTS •

Bacon & Egg Crispy Bread Tarts

SERVES 4 • PREP & COOKING TIME 45 minutes

- 16 slices of white bread
- 75 g (3 oz) butter, melted
- 150 g (5 oz) smoked bacon rashers, rind removed, diced
- 2 eggs
- 125 ml (4 fl oz) double cream
- 2 tablespoons freshly grated Parmesan cheese
- 8 vine cherry tomatoes
- salt and black pepper

Such an ingenious idea: here ordinary white bread takes the place of pastry to create very pretty, guest-worthy breakfast tarts, rich with egg, bacon, cream and cheese.

- Cut the crusts off the bread and discard. Flatten each bread slice by rolling over it firmly with a rolling pin. Brush each slice with the melted butter and place 8 of the slices diagonally on top of the others to form the bases. Carefully press each base into a hole of an oiled muffin tray, making sure that they fit evenly (they need to reach up the sides).

- Bake in a preheated oven, 200°C (400°F), Gas Mark 6, for 12–15 minutes until crisp and golden.

- Meanwhile, heat a dry frying pan until hot, add the bacon and cook for 2–3 minutes until crisp and golden.

- Divide the bacon between the baked bread cases. Beat together the eggs, cream, cheese and salt and pepper to taste in a bowl. Spoon into the cases and top each with a cherry tomato. Bake in the oven for 15 minutes until set.

v

• LIGHT BITES •

Gado Gado Salad

SERVES 4 • PREP & COOKING TIME 25 minutes

- 4 eggs
- 1 iceberg lettuce, finely shredded
- 2 carrots, peeled and cut into matchsticks
- ½ cucumber, peeled and cut into matchsticks
- ½ red pepper deseeded and cut into matchsticks

FOR THE PEANUT DRESSING
- 4 tablespoons crunchy peanut butter
- juice of 1 lime
- 1 tablespoon clear honey
- 1 tablespoon soy sauce
- ½ teaspoon finely chopped red chilli

Gorgeous gado gado is an Indonesian salad that is endlessly versatile – you can make it with a medley of any crunchy veg. The star of this salad by far is the spicy peanut dressing; it's addictive stuff.

- Put the eggs in a saucepan of cold water and bring to the boil. Cook for 10 minutes, then plunge into cold water to cool. Shell the eggs, then cut them in half lengthways.

- Combine all the remaining salad ingredients in a bowl, then add the egg halves.

- Put all the dressing ingredients in a saucepan and heat gently, stirring, until combined. Drizzle the dressing over the salad and serve immediately or serve the dressing as a dipping sauce for the salad.

• MAINS •

Beef & Mixed Peppercorn Stroganoff

SERVES 4 • PREP & COOKING TIME 20 minutes

- 2 tablespoons butter
- 1 red onion, thinly sliced
- 250 g (8 oz) button mushrooms, halved
- 3 tablespoons tomato purée
- 2 teaspoons Dijon mustard
- 1 tablespoon pink peppercorns in brine, drained
- 1 tablespoon green peppercorns in brine, drained
- 1 teaspoon smoked paprika
- 300 ml (½ pint) hot beef stock
- 500 g (1 lb) beef fillet, cut into thin strips
- 200 ml (7 fl oz) soured cream
- salt and pepper
- 2 tablespoons chopped flat-leaf parsley, to garnish

So quick but so delicious, this is one for a speedy meal for friends, served with steamed rice. For a change, pile the beef and mushroom mixture into an ovenproof dish, top with warm mashed potato and cook under a hot grill for a few minutes until the topping is golden.

- Heat a frying pan until hot, then add half the butter. When foaming, add the red onion and fry for 2–3 minutes or until just softened. Add the mushrooms, tomato purée, mustard, pink and green peppercorns and paprika and fry, stirring, for a further 1–2 minutes.

- Pour in the beef stock and bring to the boil, then reduce the heat to low and simmer for 1–2 minutes.

- Meanwhile, heat a separate frying pan and add the remaining butter. Season the beef. When the butter is foaming, add the beef and cook, stirring, for 2–3 minutes or until browned all over.

- Add the soured cream and beef to the onion and mushroom mixture and mix well, then season to taste.

- Spoon into bowls, scatter over the parsley and serve.

V

· DESSERTS ·

Blueberry & Lemon Frozen Yogurt

SERVES 4 • PREP TIME 10 minutes, plus freezing

- 500 g (1 lb) frozen blueberries
- 500 g (1 lb) Greek yogurt
- 125 g (4 oz) icing sugar, plus extra to decorate
- grated zest of 2 lemons
- 1 tablespoon lemon juice

This tangy fro-yo is a speedy choice for a hot summer day. It's lighter and healthier than ice cream and has just four ingredients. Use full-fat yogurt for the best results.

- Reserve a few blueberries for decoration. Put the remainder of the blueberries in a food processor or blender with the yogurt, icing sugar and lemon zest and juice and process until smooth.

- Spoon the mixture into a 600 ml (1 pint) freezerproof container and freeze.

- Eat when the frozen yogurt is softly frozen and easily spoonable. Before serving, decorate with the reserved blueberries and a sprinkling of icing sugar.

V

· BREAKFASTS ·

Apricot & Sunflower Seed Muffins

MAKES 12 • PREP & COOKING TIME 40 minutes

- 300 g (10 oz) self-raising wholemeal flour
- 1 teaspoon baking powder
- 150 g (5 oz) light muscovado sugar
- grated zest of 1 orange
- 3 eggs
- 200 ml (7 fl oz) full-fat crème fraîche
- 225 g (7½ oz) can apricot halves in natural juice, drained and roughly chopped, the juice reserved
- 3 tablespoons sunflower seeds

Just the thing to go with a morning cup of tea. Best eaten on the day they're made and equally delicious hot or cold, these are beautifully moist, thanks to the canned apricots and the crème fraîche.

- Arrange paper muffin cases in a 12-hole muffin tin.

- Stir the flour, baking powder, sugar and orange zest together in a mixing bowl.

- Beat the eggs in a smaller bowl then mix in the crème fraîche. Add to the flour mixture with the chopped apricots and fork together until just mixed, adding 2–3 tablespoons of the reserved canned apricot juice to make a soft spoonable consistency.

- Spoon the mixture into the paper muffin cases and sprinkle with the sunflower seeds.

- Bake in a preheated oven, 200°C (400°F), Gas Mark 6, for 15–18 minutes until well risen and the tops are cracked. Leave to cool in the tin for 5 minutes then transfer to a wire rack.

VG

· LIGHT BITES ·

Summer Vegetable Tempura

SERVES 4 • PREP & COOKING TIME 30 minutes

- vegetable oil, for deep-frying
- 75 g (3 oz) plain flour
- 2 tablespoons cornflour
- pinch of salt
- 200 ml (7 fl oz) ice-cold sparkling water
- 1 red pepper, deseeded and cut into strips
- 150 g (5 oz) thin asparagus spears, trimmed
- 1 courgette, trimmed and sliced

FOR THE DIPPING SAUCE
- 2 tablespoons sweet chilli sauce
- 2 tablespoons soy sauce
- 1 teaspoon finely grated lemon zest
- 1 tablespoon lemon juice

Cold sparkling water is important for making tempura – the bubbles add lift and make the batter airy for a delicate, crunchy coating.

- Mix the dipping sauce ingredients together in a serving bowl and set aside.

- Half-fill a deep saucepan with vegetable oil and heat to 180–190°C (350–375°F), or until a cube of bread dropped into the oil browns in 30 seconds. Just before the oil is hot enough, using a hand whisk, quickly beat the flour, cornflour, salt and sparkling water together in a bowl to make a slightly lumpy batter.

- Dip one-third of the vegetables into the batter until coated and then drop straight into the hot oil. Fry for 2 minutes until crisp. Remove from the pan with a slotted spoon, drain on kitchen paper and keep warm in a low oven.

- Fry the remaining vegetables in 2 more batches. Serve hot with the dipping sauce.

• MAINS •

Pork Burgers with Roasted Pears

SERVES 4 • PREP & COOKING TIME 25 minutes

- 25 g (1 oz) butter
- 2 pears, cut into quarters
- 6 tablespoons maple syrup
- 1 tablespoon red wine vinegar
- 1 tablespoon wholegrain mustard
- 2 teaspoons peeled and grated fresh root ginger
- 1 tablespoon chopped sage leaves
- 4 pork loin medallions, about 125 g (4 oz) each
- 4 soft rolls, halved
- salad leaves
- salt and black pepper

If you're firing up the barbecue to cook for friends this weekend, this is a great recipe to try. The sweetness of the maple-glazed roasted pears works so well with the pork.

- Heat the butter in a frying pan, add the pears and fry until lightly browned. Add 2 tablespoons of the maple syrup and cook until lightly caramelized.

- Transfer the pears to a roasting dish and bake in a preheated oven, 200°C (400°F), Gas Mark 6, for 10 minutes or until cooked through. Keep warm until needed.

- Meanwhile, whisk together the remaining maple syrup with the vinegar, mustard, ginger, sage and a little salt and pepper in a small bowl until they form a sauce.

- Place the pork fillets on a hot barbecue and brush with the sauce. Cook for 4–5 minutes on each side, basting with the sauce at regular intervals, until the pork is glossy and cooked through.

- Toast the rolls on the barbecue for 1 minute on each side until browned. Fill each one with salad leaves, a pork steak and some of the baked pears.

V

· DESSERTS ·

Hazelnut & Apricot Roulade

SERVES 6–8 • PREP & COOKING TIME 50 minutes, plus cooling

- 125 g (4 oz) hazelnuts
- 5 eggs, separated
- 175 g (6 oz) caster sugar, plus extra for sprinkling
- 1 just-ripe pear, peeled and coarsely grated
- 200 g (7 oz) mascarpone cheese
- 2 tablespoons icing sugar
- 250 g (8 oz) fresh apricots, roughly chopped

Roulades look tricky but are surprisingly easy and very satisfying to make – the trick is to use the baking paper to help you roll it. This dinner-party dazzler combines a nutty, light-as-air sponge with juicy apricots and rich mascarpone.

- Place the nuts on a piece of foil and toast under the grill for 3–4 minutes until golden. Roughly chop 2 tablespoons and reserve for decoration, then finely chop the remainder.

- Whisk the yolks and sugar until they are thick and pale and the whisk leaves a trail. Fold in the finely chopped hazelnuts and pear.

- Whisk the whites into stiff, moist-looking peaks. Fold a large spoonful into the nut mix to loosen it, then gently fold in the remaining egg whites.

- Spoon the mixture into a greased 30 × 23 cm (12 × 9 inch) roasting tin, the sides and base lined with nonstick baking paper. Bake the roulade in a preheated oven, 180°C (350°F), Gas Mark 4, for 15 minutes until golden brown and the top feels spongy. Cover and leave to cool for at least 1 hour.

- Beat the mascarpone and icing sugar together until soft. On a work surface, cover a damp tea towel with baking paper and sprinkle with sugar. Turn the roulade on to the paper and remove the tin and lining paper.

- Spread the roulade with the mascarpone mixture, then with the apricots. Roll up the roulade, starting from the short end nearest you, using the paper and tea towel to help.

- Carefully transfer the roulade to a serving plate, sprinkle over the reserved hazelnuts and cut into thick slices.

V

• BREAKFASTS •

Feta Omelettes with Spicy Tomato Sauce

SERVES 4 • PREP & COOKING TIME 25 minutes

- 2 tablespoons olive oil
- 6 eggs, beaten
- salt and black pepper
- 25 g (1 oz) feta cheese, crumbled, to serve

FOR THE SAUCE
- 1 shallot
- 3 ripe tomatoes
- 1 fresh jalapeño chilli, deseeded, if liked
- 1 garlic clove, peeled and left whole
- 1 tablespoon olive oil
- pinch of dried oregano
- splash of red wine vinegar

Sometimes you need to kickstart the day with a little heat and this spicy tomato sauce is just the thing. The cold, creamy, salty feta provides a lovely contrast.

- Make the sauce. Heat a large, dry nonstick frying pan until hot, add the shallot and cook for 2 minutes. Add the tomatoes and cook for a further 2 minutes, then add the chilli and continue to cook for 2–3 minutes until starting to char. Stir in the garlic and cook until all the vegetables are lightly charred.

- Leave to cool slightly, then remove the blackened skin from the tomatoes and chilli. Transfer the flesh to a food processor or blender with the shallot and garlic and whizz to a coarse purée.

- Heat the oil in saucepan, add the vegetable purée, oregano, vinegar and a little water if necessary and simmer for 10 minutes until thickened. Season well.

- Meanwhile, heat a little oil in a small nonstick frying pan, add one-quarter of the eggs, season and swirl around the pan, then cook for 1–2 minutes until just set. Fold the omelette in half, slide on to a plate and keep warm. Repeat with the remaining eggs.

- Spoon a little of the sauce over each omelette and serve sprinkled with the feta.

VG

• LIGHT BITES •

Cucumber & Pepper Relish

MAKES 6 small jars • PREP & COOKING TIME 55 minutes, plus soaking

- 2 cucumbers, diced
- 50 g (2 oz) salt
- 1 tablespoon sunflower oil
- 2 onions, chopped
- 2 red peppers, deseeded and diced
- 300 ml (½ pint) distilled malt vinegar
- 300 g (10 oz) granulated sugar
- 1 teaspoon dried crushed red chillies
- ½ teaspoon turmeric
- 2 teaspoons mustard powder
- 2 tablespoons cornflour
- 2 tablespoons water
- ½ teaspoon peppercorns, roughly crushed

Add a welcome zing to salads, sandwiches and cold meat with this tangy relish that has a whisper of mustard and chilli heat. It's a great way to use up a glut of homegrown cucumbers and peppers.

- Layer the cucumbers in a bowl with the salt, cover with a plate, weigh down and leave to soak for 4 hours. Tip into a colander, drain off the liquid, then rinse with cold water and drain well.

- Heat the oil in a large, heavy-based saucepan, add the onions and fry for 5 minutes, stirring until softened. Add the red peppers and fry for a further 5 minutes.

- Add the vinegar and sugar to the pan. Mix the chillies, turmeric, mustard powder and cornflour in a bowl, then stir in the measured water and mix until smooth. Stir into the vinegar mixture and mix again until smooth. Cook gently for 10 minutes, stirring from time to time, until thickened. Stir in the cucumber and peppercorns and cook for 5 minutes.

- Ladle into sterilized, warm, dry jars, pressing down well and making sure that the vinegar mixture covers the vegetables. Disperse any air pockets with a skewer or small knife and cover with screw-top lids. Label and leave to mature in a cool, dark place for at least 3 weeks.

v

• MAINS •

Melanzane alla Parmigiana

SERVES 6 • PREP & COOKING TIME 1 hour 30 minutes, plus draining

- 6 aubergines, cut lengthways into thick slices
- 2 tablespoons extra virgin olive oil
- 250 g (8 oz) Cheddar cheese, grated
- 50 g (2 oz) Parmesan or vegetarian hard cheese, grated*
- salt

FOR THE TOMATO SAUCE
- 1 kg (2 lb) ripe tomatoes, roughly chopped
- 2 tablespoons extra virgin olive oil
- 2 garlic cloves, chopped
- 2 tablespoons chopped basil
- 1 teaspoon grated lemon zest
- pinch of sugar
- salt and black pepper

This flavour-packed Italian classic is a good recipe to have up your sleeve for feeding a crowd as it can be made well ahead of time. All it needs alongside is crusty bread to mop up the tomato sauce.

- Sprinkle the aubergines with salt and leave to drain in a colander for 30 minutes. Wash well, drain and pat dry on kitchen paper.

- Bring all the ingredients for the tomato sauce to the boil. Cover and simmer for 30 minutes. Remove the lid and cook for a further 20 minutes until the sauce is thick. Adjust the seasoning.

- Meanwhile brush the slices of aubergine with the oil and place on 2 large baking sheets. Roast at the top of a preheated oven, 200°C (400°F), Gas Mark 6, for 10 minutes on each side until golden and tender.

- Spoon a little tomato sauce into 6 lightly greased individual ovenproof dishes (or 1 lasagne dish) and top with a layer of aubergines and some Cheddar. Continue the layers, finishing with the Cheddar. Sprinkle the Parmesan over the top and bake at 200°C (400°F), Gas Mark 6, for 30 minutes until bubbling and golden.

*For guidance on vegetarian cheeses, see page 5.

V

• DESSERTS •

Nectarine & Orange Fool

SERVES 6 • Prep & cooking 15 minutes, plus chilling

- 5 ripe nectarines, halved, stoned and chopped
- 75 g (3 oz) caster sugar
- 4 tablespoons fresh orange juice
- 150 ml (¼ pint) double cream
- 135 g (4½ oz) can or carton custard

A delicious, fruity dessert that takes hardly any time to make. It is fabulous served with the **Mini Orange Shortbreads** on page 77. If you don't have a food processor, you can push the cooked nectarine mix through a sieve.

- Cook the nectarines, sugar and orange juice in a covered saucepan for 10 minutes until soft.

- Add to a food processor and purée until smooth. Leave to cool.

- Whip the cream until it forms soft swirls, then fold in the nectarine purée and the custard. Spoon into 6 glasses and chill for 20 minutes.

V

• BREAKFASTS •

Grilled Peaches with Passion Fruit & Yogurt

SERVES 4 • PREP & COOKING TIME 10 minutes

- 6 large ripe peaches
- 2 tablespoons honey, plus extra to serve
- 2 teaspoons ground cinnamon

TO SERVE
- 125 g (4 oz) Greek yogurt
- pulp from 2 passion fruit

When glorious peaches are abundant, you want to make the most of them. For a fruity breakfast or dessert try grilling them and serving with cold yogurt and sharp passion fruit as in this recipe.

- Cut the peaches in half and discard the stones. Arrange the peach halves cut-side up in a foil-lined grill pan, drizzle over the honey and dust with the cinnamon.

- Cook under a preheated high grill for 4–5 minutes until lightly charred.

- Spoon into bowls and serve each one topped with Greek yogurt, an extra drizzle of honey and the passion fruit pulp.

· LIGHT BITES ·

Chicken Liver Pâté

SERVES 6 • PREP & COOKING TIME 30 minutes, plus cooling

- 1 tablespoon olive oil
- 1 shallot, finely chopped
- 250 g (8 oz) chicken livers
- 100 ml (3½ fl oz) vin santo or other dessert wine
- 250 ml (8 fl oz) double cream
- ½ baguette, thinly sliced
- salt and black pepper

TO SERVE
- red onion, finely chopped
- capers

This classic French recipe makes a lovely starter served with thin slices of toasted baguette, or a simple lunch, piled thickly on hot buttered toast. If making ahead and chilling, remove it from the fridge about 20 minutes before you eat as chilling will deaden the flavours.

- Heat the oil in a frying pan, add the shallot and cook for 3 minutes until softened. Wash the chicken livers and trim away any sinews. Pat dry and add to the pan. Season to taste and cook until browned all over but still soft to the touch. Pour in the wine and cook for 5 minutes. Add the cream and cook for a further 5–10 minutes until reduced by half.

- Whizz in a food processor until smooth, then check and adjust the seasoning if necessary. If you want it extra smooth, press the mixture through a sieve. Transfer to a serving bowl and leave to cool to room temperature.

- Meanwhile, toast the baguette slices until golden and crisp and leave to cool. Serve alongside the pâté with the chopped red onion and capers scattered over.

· DRINKS ·

Sangria

SERVES 10–12 • PREP TIME 5 minutes

- ice cubes
- 2 bottles light Spanish red wine, chilled
- 5 measures brandy
- orange, lemon and apple wedges
- cinnamon sticks
- about 450 ml (¾ pint) chilled lemonade, to top up
- lemon slices

This is fruity, light and delicious, quick to prep and perfect when entertaining a crowd. You can vary the fruit you include, but opt for ones that won't disintegrate while sitting in the jug.

- Put some ice cubes into a very large jug. Add the wine, brandy, fruit wedges and 1 cinnamon stick and stir well.

- Top up with lemonade when you are ready to serve, and stir. Serve in glasses decorated with lemon slices and cinnamon sticks.

August

GOOD TO EAT THIS MONTH

aubergines * beetroot * broccoli * courgettes *
cucumbers * French beans * garlic * lettuce *
mangetout * marrow * mushrooms * peppers *
potatoes * radishes * rocket * runner beans * shallots
* sweet corn * Swiss chard * tomatoes * apricots *
blackcurrants * blueberries * cherries * damsons * figs
* mangoes * melons *plums * raspberries * redcurrants
* strawberries * watermelon * basil * chillies * chives
* coriander * fennel * marjoram * mint * parsley *
rosemary * sage

Luscious plums, cherries, figs and watermelon, juicy tomatoes, crunchy, cool cucumbers – there's so much to enjoy this month.

When you want an easy supper for a balmy night when it's too hot to be in the kitchen, look no further than the **No-cook Tomato Spaghetti** on page 262 or the **Gazpacho** on page 261. No cooking, no fuss, all flavour.

This month ushers us outdoors to enjoy life, so the barbecue, rather than the oven, is a go-to. **Rosemary Lamb Kebabs** (page 250) and **Thai Chickpea Burgers** (page 274) are the recipes to try for relaxed outdoor dining.

Watermelons are at their best and everywhere. A thirst-quenching, chilled slice on a hot day is hard to beat, but enjoy them also in the **Watermelon Cooler** on page 279 and the refreshing salad on page 257.

Basil, the herb that sums up summer, is growing happily in pots by the back door. Use it to add a punch of sunny flavour to salads, pasta dishes and the wonderful ice cream on page 271.

v

· BREAKFASTS ·

On-the-Go Breakfast Granola Bars

MAKES 9 • PREP & COOKING TIME 30 minutes

- 75 g (3 oz) butter, plus extra for greasing
- 75 ml (3 fl oz) clear honey
- ½ teaspoon ground cinnamon
- 100 g (3½ oz) ready-to-eat dried apricots, roughly chopped
- 50 g (2 oz) ready-to-eat dried papaya or mango, roughly chopped
- 50 g (2 oz) raisins
- 4 tablespoons mixed seeds, such as pumpkin, sesame, sunflower
- 50 g (2 oz) pecan nuts, roughly broken
- 150 g (5 oz) rolled oats

When breakfast has to be eaten on the run, you'll want one of these bars. Full of sweet fruit, nuts and seeds, they'll keep you going until lunchtime, and are so much better than any you can buy.

- Place the butter and honey in a saucepan and bring to the boil, stirring continuously, until the mixture bubbles. Add the cinnamon, dried fruit, seeds and nuts, then stir and heat for 1 minute.

- Remove from the heat and add the oats. Stir well, then transfer to a greased shallow 20 cm (8 inch tin) and press down well.

- Bake in a preheated oven, 190°C (375°F), Gas Mark 5, for 15 minutes until the top is just beginning to brown.

- Leave to cool in the tin, then cut into 9 squares or bars.

V

• LIGHT BITES •

Cheesy Summer Veg Pies

MAKES 4 • PREP & COOKING TIME 1 hour

- 1 tablespoon olive oil
- 1 onion, chopped
- 2 garlic cloves, finely chopped
- 1 courgette, diced
- ½ yellow pepper, deseeded and diced
- ½ red pepper, deseeded and diced
- 400 g (13 oz) can chopped tomatoes
- 1 tablespoon chopped rosemary or basil
- ½ teaspoon caster sugar
- beaten egg, to glaze
- salt and black pepper

FOR THE PASTRY
- 175 g (6 oz) bread flour
- 75 g (3 oz) butter, diced
- 75 g (3 oz) mature Cheddar cheese, diced, plus extra, grated, for sprinkling
- 2 egg yolks
- 2 teaspoons water

Summertime means picnic time, so add these Mediterranean-style, veg-filled pies, with their unusual cheesy pastry, to your portable feast. They're equally delicious warm or cold so spread out that picnic blanket and tuck in.

- Heat the oil in a saucepan, add the onion and fry for 5 minutes until softened. Add the garlic, courgette and diced peppers and fry briefly, then add the tomatoes, herbs, sugar and a little salt and pepper. Simmer, uncovered, for 10 minutes, stirring from time to time until thickened. Cool.

- Make the pastry. Add the flour, butter and a little salt and pepper to a bowl, rub in the butter until you have fine crumbs, then stir in the cheese. Add the egg yolks and water and mix to form a smooth dough.

- Knead lightly, then cut the dough into 4 pieces. Roll one of the pieces out between 2 sheets of clingfilm, patting into a neat shape until you have an 18 cm (7 inch) circle. Remove the top sheet of clingfilm, spoon one-quarter of the filling in the centre, brush the pastry edges with beaten egg, then fold the pastry circle in half while still on the lower piece of clingfilm.

- Peel the pastry off the film, lift on to an oiled baking sheet, press the edges together well and press together any breaks in the pastry. Repeat with the remaining pastry pieces and filling until 4 pies have been made.

- Brush with beaten egg, sprinkle with a little extra cheese and bake in a preheated oven, 190°C (375°F), Gas Mark 5, for 20 minutes until golden brown. Loosen and transfer to a wire rack.

· MAINS ·

Rosemary Lamb Kebabs

SERVES 4 • PREP & COOKING TIME 15 minutes, plus chilling

- 500 g (1 lb) boneless leg of lamb, minced
- 1 small onion, finely chopped
- 1 garlic clove, crushed
- 1 tablespoon chopped rosemary
- 6 anchovies in oil, drained and chopped
- olive oil, for brushing
- salt and black pepper

Lamb, anchovies and rosemary were made for each other. The saltiness of the anchovies brings out the meatiness of the lamb, while bittersweet rosemary complements them both.

- Combine the lamb, onion, garlic, rosemary, anchovies and some salt and pepper in a bowl and use your hands to work them together. Divide into 12 and shape into even-sized, sausage-shaped patties. Chill for 30 minutes.

- Thread the patties on to metal skewers, brush lightly with oil and cook on a barbecue or under a preheated hot grill for 3–4 minutes on each side until cooked through. Serve hot.

V

• DESSERTS •

Blueberry Bakewell

SERVES 18 • PREP & COOKING TIME 1 hour 20 minutes

- 350 g (11½ oz) ready-made sweet shortcrust pastry
- 6 tablespoons blueberry jam
- 125 g (4 oz) slightly salted butter, softened
- 125 g (4 oz) caster sugar
- 2 eggs
- 125 g (4 oz) self-raising flour, plus extra for dusting
- ½ teaspoon baking powder
- 1 teaspoon almond extract
- 100 g (3½ oz) ground almonds
- 4 tablespoons flaked almonds
- 75 g (3 oz) icing sugar, sifted

A new take on that teatime favourite, the Bakewell tart. Here it's a crowd-friendly traybake made with blueberry jam, instead of raspberry.

- Roll out the pastry on a lightly floured surface and use to line a greased 28 × 18 cm (11 × 7 inch) shallow baking tin. Line the pastry case with baking parchment and baking beans (or dried beans reserved for the purpose). Bake in a preheated oven, 200°C (400°F), Gas Mark 4, for 15 minutes. Remove the paper and beans and bake for a further 5 minutes. Reduce the oven temperature to 180°C (350°F), Gas Mark 4.

- Spread the base of the pastry with the jam.

- Beat together the butter, caster sugar, eggs, flour, baking powder and almond extract in a bowl until smooth and creamy. Beat in the ground almonds. Spoon the mixture over the jam and spread gently in an even layer.

- Scatter with the flaked almonds and bake in the oven for about 40 minutes until risen and just firm to the touch. Leave to cool in the tin.

- Beat the icing sugar with a dash of water in a bowl to give the consistency of thin cream. Spread in a thin layer over the cake. Allow to set, then cut into squares or fingers.

VG

• BREAKFASTS •

Plum & Grape Juice

SERVES 1 • PREP TIME 5 minutes

- about 300 g (10 oz) plums, plus extra to serve (optional)
- 150 g (5 oz) seedless red grapes
- 2–3 crushed ice cubes

Make the most of juicy plums and sweet red grapes with this antioxidant-packed juice. You could top it up with sparkling water if you like, to make a longer drink.

- Remove the stones from the plums then cut the flesh into even-sized pieces. Add to a juicer along with the grapes and juice.

- Pour the juice into a tall glass, add a couple of crushed ice cubes, decorate with grapes or slices of plum, if liked, and serve immediately.

Make the most of your leftovers...
Any tired-looking plums in your fruit bowl can be speedily turned into compote for dolloping on yogurt or porridge. Simply chop, add to a small saucepan with sugar to taste, a sprinkle of ground cinnamon, a squeeze of lemon juice and a dash of water. Simmer for 5–10 minutes. Remove from the heat, allow to cool (it will thicken as it cools) and store in the fridge for up to 5 days.

V

• LIGHT BITES •

Halloumi with Pomegranate Salsa

SERVES 4 • PREP & COOKING TIME 15 minutes

- 500 g (1 lb) halloumi cheese, sliced
- 1 tablespoon honey

FOR THE POMEGRANATE SALSA

- ½ pomegranate
- 4 tablespoons extra virgin olive oil
- 2 tablespoons chopped parsley
- 1 tablespoon lemon juice
- 1 small red chilli, deseeded and finely chopped
- 1 small garlic clove, crushed
- 1 teaspoon pomegranate molasses
- salt and black pepper

Hot, salty fried halloumi and sweetly sharp pomegranates are an incredible combination. You can leave out the pomegranate molasses, but it does add a tangy complexity to the salsa.

- First make the salsa. Carefully scoop the pomegranate seeds into a bowl, discarding all the white membrane. Stir in the remaining ingredients and season with salt and pepper.

- Heat a large nonstick frying pan for 2–3 minutes until hot. Add the halloumi slices, in batches, and cook over a high heat for 1 minute on each side until browned and softened.

- Meanwhile, warm the honey in a small saucepan until runny.

- Transfer the halloumi to serving plates and spoon over the salsa. Drizzle over the honey and serve immediately.

• MAINS •

Mackerel with Cucumber & Avocado Salsa

SERVES 4 • PREP & COOKING TIME 20 minutes

- 8 mackerel fillets
- 2 lemons, plus extra wedges to serve
- salt and black pepper

FOR THE CUCUMBER & AVOCADO SALSA
- 2 avocados, peeled, stoned and finely diced
- juice and zest of 1 lime
- 1 red onion, finely chopped
- ½ cucumber, finely diced
- 1 handful of coriander leaves, finely chopped

This easy recipe combines good-for-you mackerel – we should all eat oily fish every week – with vitamin-filled avocado for a super-healthy meal.

- Make 3 diagonal slashes across each mackerel fillet on the skin side and season well with salt and pepper. Cut the lemons in half, then squeeze the juice over the fish.

- Lay on a grill rack, skin-side up, and cook under a preheated grill for 6–8 minutes or until the skin is lightly charred and the flesh is just cooked through.

- Meanwhile, to make the salsa, mix together the avocados and lime juice and zest, then add the onion, cucumber and coriander. Toss well to mix and season to taste with salt and pepper.

- Serve the mackerel hot with the salsa and lemon wedges for squeezing over.

V

· DESSERTS ·

Honeyed Figs

SERVES 4 • PREP & COOKING TIME 30 minutes

- 12 figs
- 20 g (¾ oz) unsalted butter
- 4 tablespoons honey
- ¼ teaspoon ground cinnamon
- 50 g (2 oz) toasted flaked almonds, to serve

So simple, so delicious. Serve these baked figs with Greek yogurt, mascarpone or thick cream whipped with a splash of vanilla extract. Chopped walnuts sprinkled over work well instead of the almonds.

- Cut a cross in the top of each fig, not quite cutting all the way through. Place in an ovenproof dish.

- Melt together the butter, honey and cinnamon in a saucepan and pour over the figs.

- Bake in a preheated oven, 200°C (400°F), Gas Mark 6, for 20 minutes.

- Serve the figs sprinkled with flaked almonds.

v

• BREAKFASTS •

Mixed Seed
Soda Bread

MAKES 1 small loaf • PREP & COOKING TIME 1 hour

- 350 g (11½ oz) wholemeal plain flour, plus extra for dusting and sprinkling
- 50 g (2 oz) sunflower seeds
- 2 tablespoons poppy seeds
- 1 teaspoon bicarbonate of soda
- 1 teaspoon salt
- 1 teaspoon caster sugar
- 300 ml (½ pint) buttermilk

Buttermilk is the key to this bread as it reacts with the bicarbonate of soda to make the bread rise. You can replace the buttermilk with a half-and-half mix of milk and plain yogurt.

- Mix the flour, sunflower seeds, poppy seeds, bicarbonate of soda, salt and sugar together in a bowl. Make a well in the centre, add the buttermilk and gradually work into the flour mixture to form a soft dough.

- Turn the dough out on a lightly floured work surface and knead for 5 minutes. Shape into a flattish round. Transfer to a lightly oiled baking sheet. Using a sharp knife, cut a cross in the top of the bread. Sprinkle a little extra flour over the surface.

- Bake in a preheated oven, 230°C (450°F), Gas Mark 8, for 15 minutes, then reduce the temperature to 200°C (400°F), Gas Mark 6, and bake for a further 25–30 minutes until risen and the loaf sounds hollow when tapped underneath.

- Leave to cool completely on a wire rack.

v

• LIGHT BITES •

Watermelon & Feta Salad

SERVES 4 • PREP & COOKING TIME 20 minutes

- 1 tablespoon black sesame seeds
- 500 g (1 lb) watermelon, peeled, deseeded and diced
- 175 g (6 oz) feta cheese, diced
- 875 g (1¾ lb) rocket
- sprigs of mint, parsley and coriander
- 6 tablespoons olive oil
- 1 tablespoon orange flower water
- 1½ tablespoons lemon juice
- 1 teaspoon pomegranate molasses (optional)
- ½ teaspoon caster sugar
- salt and black pepper

If you're looking for a cooling summer lunch, this one is amazing. The bright pink watermelon, white feta, green rocket and black seeds all contrast on the plate. It's tastes amazing too. Serve with toasted pitta bread.

- Heat a frying pan and dry-fry the sesame seeds for 2 minutes until aromatic, then set aside.

- Arrange the watermelon and feta on a large plate with the rocket and herbs.

- Whisk together the oil, orange flower water, lemon juice, pomegranate molasses, if using, and sugar. Season to taste with salt and pepper, then drizzle over the salad.

- Scatter over the sesame seeds and serve.

Make the most of your leftovers...
If you buy pomegranate molasses for this recipe, there are lots of other ways to use it. Try some of these:
- Use it in the **Halloumi with Pomegranate Salsa** on page 253
- Add it instead of all or some of the lemon or vinegar in a salad dressing
- Brush it on meat as a glaze
- Add it to hummus for a burst of acidity
- Drizzle a little over vanilla ice cream

· MAINS ·

Rolled Stuffed Chicken Breasts

SERVES 4 • PREP & COOKING TIME 30 minutes

- 4 boneless, skinless chicken breasts, about 150 g (5 oz) each
- 4 slices of Parma ham
- 4 thin slices of buffalo mozzarella cheese
- 4 asparagus tips, plus extra to serve
- 75 g (3 oz) plain flour
- 1 tablespoon olive oil
- 50 g (2 oz) butter
- 50 ml (2 fl oz) dry white wine
- 75 ml (3 fl oz) chicken stock
- 200 g (7 oz) baby leaf spinach
- 200 g (7 oz) chilled pack sun-blush tomatoes in oil, drained
- salt and black pepper

When you want to impress but are pushed for time, this will be a go-to recipe. The vibrant colours and flavours are beautiful, it only takes 30 minutes and all you need to serve alongside are a bowl of steamed new potatoes and a glass of something chilled.

- Place each chicken breast between 2 sheets of greaseproof paper and flatten to about 2½ times its original size by pounding with a rolling pin.

- Season the chicken with salt and pepper, place a slice of Parma ham, a slice of mozzarella and an asparagus tip on top and tightly roll up the chicken breasts. Tie with a piece of strong thread or spear with wooden toothpicks.

- Season the flour with salt and pepper. Dip the chicken rolls into the flour to coat evenly.

- Heat the oil and half of the butter in a frying pan, add the chicken rolls and sauté over a low heat for 15 minutes or until golden all over and cooked through, turning frequently to brown the chicken evenly.

- Remove the chicken, place in a serving dish and keep warm. Pour the wine and stock into the pan, bring to the boil and simmer for 3 minutes.

- Remove the thread or toothpicks just before serving the chicken. Add the remaining butter to the pan, mix quickly with a small whisk to emulsify the sauce, add the spinach and tomatoes and cook for 2 minutes until the spinach has just wilted. Spoon on to plates, slice the chicken and arrange in a line down the centre.

V

• DESSERTS •

Cantaloupe Melon Sorbet

SERVES 4–6 • PREP TIME 15 minutes, plus freezing

- 1 cantaloupe melon, weighing 1 kg (2 lb)
- 50 g (2 oz) icing sugar
- juice of 1 lime or small lemon
- 1 egg white

This summery, palate-cleansing sorbet can also be made using honeydew or watermelon. For a pretty as picture bowl of icy treats, make three batches, each using a different melon, and serve a different-coloured scoop of each.

- Cut the melon in half and scoop out and discard the seeds. Scoop out the melon flesh with a spoon and discard the shells.

- Place the flesh in a food processor or blender with the icing sugar and lime or lemon juice and process to a purée. (Alternatively, rub through a sieve.)

- Pour into a freezer container, cover and freeze for 2–3 hours. If using an ice-cream maker, purée then pour into the machine, churn and freeze until half-frozen.

- Whisk the melon mixture to break up the ice crystals, then whisk the egg white until stiff and whisk it into the half-frozen melon mixture. Return to the freezer until firm.

- Alternatively, add whisked egg white to the ice-cream machine and churn until very thick.

- Transfer the sorbet to the fridge 20 minutes before serving to soften slightly, or scoop straight from the ice-cream machine. Scoop the sorbet into glass dishes to serve.

• BREAKFASTS •

Baked Eggs
with Chorizo

SERVES 4 • PREP & COOKING TIME 45 minutes

- 5 tomatoes
- 2 red chillies, deseeded, if liked
- 1 garlic clove, peeled and left whole
- 75 ml (3 fl oz) water
- ½ teaspoon dried oregano
- 1 tablespoon olive oil
- 125 g (4 oz) chorizo sausage, chopped
- 4 eggs
- salt and black pepper

Fiery chillies and spicy chorizo pack a punch of flavour in these little pots of breakfast heaven. Serve with crunchy corn tortillas or pitta bread for dipping.

- Place the tomatoes in a grill pan and cook under a preheated hot grill for 5 minutes until starting to char. Turn the tomatoes over, then add the chillies and cook for a further 5–10 minutes, turning frequently, until they are softened and charred.

- Leave to cool slightly, then transfer to a food processor or blender, add the garlic and measured water and whizz to a chunky sauce. Season well and add the dried oregano.

- Heat the oil in a small frying pan, add the chorizo and cook for 2 minutes, stirring frequently. Add the tomato sauce and cook for 5 minutes until slightly thickened. Divide the sauce into 4 individual ramekins, then crack an egg into each one.

- Place the ramekins on a baking sheet and bake in a preheated oven, 200°C (400°F), Gas Mark 6, for 12 minutes, or until the eggs are just set.

VG

• LIGHT BITES •

Gazpacho

SERVES 4 • PREP & COOKING TIME 45 minutes, plus chilling

- 750 g (1½ lb) ripe tomatoes
- 1 large fennel bulb
- ¾ teaspoon coriander seeds
- ½ teaspoon mixed peppercorns
- 1 tablespoon extra virgin olive oil
- 1 large garlic clove, crushed
- 1 small onion, chopped
- 1 tablespoon balsamic vinegar
- 1 tablespoon lemon juice
- 1 tablespoon chopped oregano
- 1 teaspoon tomato purée
- 1 rounded teaspoon rock salt
- green olives, finely sliced, to garnish

Take a lesson from the Spanish and make this your go-to on a hot summer day. The tomatoes are key so use the ripest, juiciest ones you can find and serve the soup ice cold straight from the fridge.

- Put the tomatoes in a large pan or bowl and pour over enough boiling water to cover. Leave for about 1 minute, then drain, skin carefully and roughly chop the flesh.

- Trim the green fronds from the fennel and discard. Finely slice the bulb and put it in a saucepan with 300 ml (½ pint) lightly salted boiling water. Cover and simmer for 10 minutes.

- Meanwhile, crush the coriander seeds and peppercorns using a pestle and mortar. Gently heat the oil in a large pan and add the crushed spices, garlic and onion. Cook gently for 5 minutes.

- Add the vinegar, lemon juice, tomatoes and oregano, reserving a few oregano leaves to garnish. Give the mixture a good stir and add the fennel along with the cooking liquid, tomato purée and salt. Bring to a simmer and leave to cook, uncovered, for 10 minutes.

- Transfer the soup to a food processor or blender and process lightly. Cool and chill overnight and serve garnished with the reserved oregano leaves and green olives.

V

· MAINS ·

No-Cook
Tomato Spaghetti

SERVES 4 • PREP & COOKING TIME 25 minutes, plus standing

- 750 g (1½ lb) very ripe tomatoes, quartered
- 2 garlic cloves
- 10 basil leaves
- 2 teaspoons fennel seeds
- 5 tablespoons extra virgin olive oil
- 400 g (13 oz) dried spaghetti
- 2 × 150 g (5 oz) mozzarella cheese balls, cut into cubes
- salt and black pepper

When it's too hot to cook, this is the recipe you want. Use really ripe, red tomatoes and leave the sauce to sit on the counter for as long as you can to let the flavours meld.

- Put the tomatoes, garlic cloves and basil in a food processor and process until the tomatoes are finely chopped but not smooth. Transfer to a large bowl and add the fennel seeds and oil. Season with salt and pepper. Leave the flavours to infuse for at least 15 minutes before cooking the pasta.

- Cook the pasta in a large saucepan of salted boiling water according to the packet instructions until al dente. Drain, stir into the prepared tomato sauce, then toss in the mozzarella. Serve immediately.

v

• DESSERTS •

White Chocolate & Apricot Blondies

MAKES 20 • PREP & COOKING TIME 55 minutes

- 300 g (10 oz) white chocolate
- 125 g (4 oz) butter
- 3 eggs
- 175 g (6 oz) caster sugar
- 1 teaspoon vanilla extract
- 175 g (6 oz) self-raising flour
- 1 teaspoon baking powder
- 125 g (4 oz) ready-to-eat dried apricots, chopped

Dense, delicious and a doddle to make. Switch things up by replacing the dried apricots with the same quantity of dried cranberries or dried cherries, if you like. They will keep in an airtight tin for up to 3 days.

- Break half the chocolate into pieces, place in a saucepan with the butter and heat gently until melted. Dice the remaining chocolate.

- Whisk the eggs, sugar and vanilla together in a bowl, using an electric whisk, for about 5 minutes until very thick and foamy and the whisk leaves a trail when lifted above the mixture. Fold in the melted chocolate mixture and then the flour and baking powder. Gently fold in half the chopped chocolate and apricots.

- Pour the mixture into an 18 × 28 cm (7 × 11 inch) roasting tin lined with nonstick baking paper, and ease into the corners. Sprinkle with the remaining chocolate and apricots.

- Bake in a preheated oven, 180°C (350°F), Gas Mark 4, for 25–30 minutes until well risen, the top is crusty and the centre still slightly soft.

- Leave to cool in the tin then lift out using the lining paper and cut into 20 small pieces. Peel off the paper.

VG

• BREAKFASTS •

Very Berry Fruit Salad

SERVES 4 • PREP & COOKING TIME 20 minutes, plus cooling

- 3 oranges
- 50 g (2 oz) granulated sugar
- 1 vanilla pod, split
- 1 cinnamon stick, lightly bruised
- 250 g (8 oz) fresh strawberries
- 200 g (7 oz) fresh cherries
- 125 g (4 oz) fresh raspberries
- 125 g (4 oz) fresh blueberries

When the temperatures soar, start a sunny day with this rather special fruit salad. Packed with sweet fresh berries and cherries and with a hint of vanilla, it would work equally well as a refreshing dessert.

- Squeeze the juice from the oranges into a measuring jug and make up to 300 ml (½ pint) with cold water. Put in a saucepan with the sugar, vanilla pod and cinnamon stick. Heat over a low heat, stirring, until the sugar has dissolved, then simmer gently for 5 minutes until a light syrup is reached.

- Remove from the heat and leave to cool completely. Remove the vanilla pod and cinnamon stick.

- Hull and halve the strawberries, then put in a large bowl with the remaining berries and pour over the syrup. Stir well and leave to marinate at room temperature for 30 minutes before serving.

v

• LIGHT BITES •

White Bean, Feta & Pepper Salad

SERVES 4 • PREP & COOKING TIME 30 minutes, plus cooling

- 2 red peppers, deseeded
- 4 tablespoons olive oil
- 2 tablespoons balsamic vinegar or red wine vinegar
- 3 teaspoons sun-dried tomato paste
- 4 teaspoons capers
- 2 × 410 g (13¼ oz) cans cannellini beans
- ½ red onion, finely chopped
- 4 celery sticks, sliced
- 125 g (4 oz) feta cheese
- 1 cos lettuce
- salt and black pepper

You can use any white beans for this salad: butterbeans, haricot beans and even chickpeas all work well. Putting the roasted peppers into a plastic bag until they are cool will make them so much easier to peel, so be patient!

- Put the peppers, skin-side up, on a foil-lined grill rack. Brush them with a little of the oil and cook under a preheated grill for 10–12 minutes or until they are softened and the skins charred. Put the peppers in a plastic bag, fold over the top to seal and leave to cool.

- Meanwhile, make the dressing by mixing the remaining oil with the vinegar, tomato paste and chopped capers. Season to taste with salt and pepper.

- Rinse and drain the beans or chickpeas. Stir them into the dressing with the onion and celery.

- Peel the skins off the peppers and cut the flesh into strips. Add to the beans and gently toss together. Crumble the feta cheese over the top and serve the salad on a bed of lettuce leaves.

· MAINS ·

Baked Trout with Olives

SERVES 4 • PREP & COOKING TIME 30 minutes

- 4 trout, about 225 g (7½ oz) each, scaled
- 4 tablespoons flour
- 2 tablespoons olive oil
- 1 onion, sliced
- 30 g (1¼ oz) pimento-stuffed green olives
- 400 g (13 oz) tomatoes, chopped
- juice of 1 lemon
- 1 tablespoon capers
- 2 tablespoons chopped parsley, to garnish

Salty olives, juicy fresh lemon juice and sharp capers make this easy weekday dinner burst with flavour. Trout is a great source of heart- and brain-healthy omega-3 fatty acids plus vitamins and protein, so a good choice for a nutritious family meal.

- Dust the trout with flour. Heat the olive oil in a frying pan and brown the trout for 2–3 minutes on each side. Place the fish in an ovenproof dish big enough for them to sit in a single layer.

- Add the onion and olives to the frying pan, sauté for 3–4 minutes and then spoon over the fish. Scatter over the chopped tomatoes, lemon juice and capers and bake in a preheated oven, 190°C (375°F), Gas Mark 5, for 15–18 minutes, until the fish is cooked through.

- Serve scattered with chopped parsley.

V

• DESSERTS •

Cherry Almond Ice Cream

SERVES 6 • PREP & COOKING TIME 40 minutes,
plus cooling and freezing

- 150 ml (¼ pint) milk
- 50 g (2 oz) ground almonds
- 1 egg
- 1 egg yolk
- 75 g (3 oz) caster sugar
- 2–3 drops almond extract
- 500 g (1 lb) cherries, stoned
- 25 g (1 oz) slivered almonds
- 150 ml (¼ pint) double cream

This is a lovely combination of sweet fresh cherries – choose the darkest, ripest ones you can find – with cream and crunchy almonds. For a boozy version, you could add a dash of Amaretto to the mixture. Serve with the biscotti on page 383 and perhaps decorated with a few cherries.

- Pour the milk into a small saucepan and stir in the ground almonds. Bring to the boil, then set aside.

- Put the egg and the yolk into a heatproof bowl with the sugar and beat until pale and thick. Pour on the milk and almond mixture. Place the bowl over a pan of gently simmering water and stir until thick. Stir in the almond extract and leave to cool.

- Purée the cherries in a food processor or blender, then stir into the custard.

- Toss the slivered almonds in a heavy pan over a low heat to toast them. Leave to cool.

- Whip the cream until it forms soft peaks. Fold the whipped cream into the cherry mixture.

- Transfer the mixture to a freezer container, cover and freeze until firm, beating twice at hourly intervals. Stir the slivered almonds into the mixture at the last beating. (If using an ice-cream machine, pour the cherry mixture into the machine, add the cream, churn and freeze. Once frozen, fold through the slivered almonds.)

• BREAKFASTS •

Smoked Salmon Scrambled Eggs

SERVES 1 • PREP & COOKING TIME 15 minutes

- 15 g (½ oz) butter
- 3 large eggs
- 1 tablespoon milk
- 1 tablespoon single cream (optional)
- 25–40 g (1–1½ oz) smoked salmon, cut into narrow strips
- 1 teaspoon finely snipped chives
- 1–2 slices of hot buttered toast
- salt and black pepper

A classic and luxurious breakfast that is hard to beat: smoked salmon and silky scrambled eggs with a sprinkle of chives. This recipe is a treat for one but it's easy to double or triple up to share.

- Melt the butter in a saucepan over a gentle heat until foaming.

- Put the eggs in a bowl and mix well with a fork. Add the milk and season with salt and pepper.

- Pour the eggs into the foaming butter and cook, stirring constantly with a wooden spoon, scraping the bottom of the pan and bringing the eggs from the outside to the centre. The eggs are done when they form soft, creamy curds and are barely set.

- Remove the pan from the heat and stir in the cream, if using, salmon and chives. Pile on to the hot toast on a serving plate. Serve immediately.

• LIGHT BITES •

Chicken, Apricot & Almond Salad

SERVES 4 • PREP TIME 10 minutes

- 200 g (7 oz) celery
- 75 g (3 oz) almonds
- 3 tablespoons chopped parsley
- 4 tablespoons mayonnaise
- 3 poached or roasted chicken breasts, each about 150 g (5 oz)
- 12 fresh apricots
- salt and black pepper

Make the most of this month's juicy apricots with this salad, full of the crunch of celery and almonds. Great for a summery lunch or supper, perhaps with some bread on the side.

- Thinly slice the celery sticks diagonally, reserving the yellow inner leaves. Transfer to a large salad bowl together with half the leaves. Roughly chop the almonds and add half to the bowl with the parsley and mayonnaise. Season to taste with salt and pepper.

- Arrange the salad on a serving plate. Shred the chicken and halve and stone the apricots. Add the chicken and apricots to the salad and stir lightly to combine. Garnish with the remaining almonds and celery leaves and serve.

· MAINS ·

Beef Skewers with Satay Sauce

SERVES 4 · PREP & COOKING TIME 30 minutes

- 350 g (12 oz) rump or sirloin steak
- 6 tablespoons dark soy sauce
- 2 tablespoons sesame oil
- 2 tablespoons rice vinegar or mirin
- 1 tablespoon dark brown soft sugar
- 2.5 cm (1 inch) piece of fresh root ginger, peeled and finely grated
- 1 garlic clove, crushed
- crudités, such as carrots, sugar snap peas and cucumber

FOR THE SAUCE
- 6 tablespoons crunchy peanut butter
- 3 tablespoons dark soy sauce
- 1 small red chilli, finely chopped
- 150 ml (¼ pint) boiling water

These skewers with a very moreish peanut sauce are a great choice to whip up when you have friends coming round and not a lot of time. They can be cooked under the grill or on the barbecue.

- Cut the steak into long, thin strips. Mix together the soy sauce, oil, vinegar or mirin, sugar, ginger and garlic in a non-metallic bowl. Add the steak and toss well to coat. Cover and leave to marinate for 15 minutes.

- Meanwhile, heat all the ingredients for the sauce in a pan over a very gentle heat, stirring constantly with a wooden spoon, until smooth and thick. Transfer to a small serving bowl and place on a serving platter with the crudités.

- Thread the beef on to 8 metal skewers, or bamboo skewers pre-soaked in cold water for 30 minutes, and cook under a preheated high grill for 2 minutes on each side until browned and just cooked.

- Transfer to the serving platter with the sauce and crudités and serve immediately.

V

• DESSERTS •

Tropical Fruit & Basil Ice Cream

SERVES 4–6 • PREP TIME 10 minutes

- 450 g (14½ oz) frozen tropical fruits, such as mango, papaya and pineapple
- 1 tablespoon lime juice
- 200 g (7 oz) mascarpone cheese
- 2 tablespoons icing sugar
- 2 tablespoons chopped basil, plus 4–6 basil sprigs, to decorate

This amazing 'cheat' ice cream is so simple to make. Just whizz up frozen fruit with rich mascarpone and sweetly scented basil and it's done. The basil adds a herby note to the sweet fruit.

- Place half the fruit and the lime juice in a food processor and whizz until roughly chopped. Add the mascarpone and icing sugar and blend until fairly smooth.

- Add the remaining fruit and the basil and pulse until no large lumps of fruit remain.

- Scoop into bowls and serve immediately, decorated with basil sprigs.

VG

• BREAKFASTS •

No-Cook
Strawberry Conserve

MAKES 6 POTS • PREP TIME 20 minutes, plus standing and freezing

- 600 g (1¼ lb) strawberries, hulled and sliced
- 1 kg (2 lb) caster sugar
- 4 tablespoons freshly squeezed lemon juice (about 2 lemons)
- 150 ml (¼ pint) liquid pectin

This unusual fresh strawberry conserve is super-easy to make – no boiling or endless stirring needed here! – and perfect atop hot buttered toast or the **Sunflower Seed & Rye Bread** on page 75.

- Crush the strawberries with a potato masher, or by blending briefly in a food processor using the pulse setting so that there are pieces of strawberry rather than a fine purée.

- Add to a large bowl and stir in the sugar, then cover and leave to stand for 1½–2 hours, stirring from time to time, until the sugar has dissolved.

- Stir in the lemon juice, then add the pectin and continue stirring for 2 minutes. Ladle into small clear plastic pots leaving a gap of 1 cm (½ inch) at the top. Clip or press on lids. Label and leave at room temperature overnight for the conserve to 'gel'.

- Transfer to the freezer to store until required. Defrost overnight in the refrigerator, then transfer to attractive jars and serve in the same way as a conventional jam.

• LIGHT BITES •

Chilli-Seared Squid & Herb Salad

SERVES 4 • PREP & COOKING TIME 15 minutes, plus marinating

- large pinch of sea salt
- 1 teaspoon ground coriander
- 1 teaspoon ground cumin
- 1 teaspoon hot chilli powder
- 8 tablespoons lemon juice
- 1 teaspoon tomato purée
- 1 fresh red chilli, deseeded and finely sliced
- 1 teaspoon peeled and finely grated fresh root ginger
- 1 garlic clove, crushed
- 750 g (1½ lb) squid, cut into bite-sized pieces
- 1 small red onion, very thinly sliced
- large handful of chopped coriander leaves
- small handful of chopped mint leaves

Tender squid is achieved by gentle, slow cooking or quick cooking over a very high heat, as here. The salad element of this spicy dish is the fresh herbs which will wilt quickly so serve as soon as you have mixed them with the hot squid.

- Mix the salt, ground spices, chilli powder, lemon juice, tomato purée, chilli, ginger and garlic in a large bowl and add the squid. Toss to coat evenly, cover and leave to stand at room temperature for 15 minutes.

- Heat a nonstick ridged griddle pan over a very high heat. Working in batches, lift the squid from the marinade and sear in the hot pan for 1–2 minutes, then remove from the pan and keep warm while you cook the remaining squid.

- Add the red onion and herbs to the cooked squid, toss to mix well and serve immediately.

VG

• MAINS •

Thai Chickpea Burgers

SERVES 4 • PREP & COOKING TIME 30 minutes

- 4 spring onions
- 1 stalk lemon grass, outer leaves removed
- 1.5 cm (¾ inch) piece of fresh ginger, peeled and chopped
- 1 red chilli, halved and deseeded
- 1 garlic clove
- handful of coriander leaves
- 400 g (13 oz) can chickpeas, drained
- 2 tablespoons wholemeal plain flour
- 3 tablespoons rapeseed oil
- salt and black pepper

Low in fat, high in fibre and big on flavour, these vegan burgers are delicious in burger buns piled high with your favourite toppings – try avocado for a creamy contrast – or served with a salad. They're sturdy so a good choice for cooking on the barbecue too.

- Pulse together the spring onions, lemon grass, ginger, chilli, garlic and coriander leaves in a food processor until finely chopped. Add the chickpeas and then pulse again until roughly blended.

- Add the flour and season with salt and pepper, then process until the mixture forms a coarse thick paste. Shape the mixture into 4 burgers.

- Heat the oil in a frying pan, add the burgers and fry for 2–3 minutes on each side until browned.

V

• BREAKFASTS •

Fried Eggs with Sage

SERVES 4 • PREP & COOKING TIME 15 minutes

- 1 tablespoon olive oil
- small handful of sage leaves
- 100 g (3½ oz) mushrooms, sliced
- 4 large eggs
- salt and black pepper

The earthiness of the sage, fried until crispy and fragrant, pairs beautifully with the other ingredients in this recipe, elevating the humble fried egg to something special for breakfast. Sage has a strong flavour so a little goes a long way.

- Heat the olive oil in a large frying pan over a medium heat and add the sage leaves. When they begin to lose colour and become crisp at the edges, remove from the pan and drain on kitchen paper.

- Add the mushrooms to the pan and cook for 3–5 minutes until just tender. Remove from the pan and set aside. Increase the heat and fry the eggs until the whites are set.

- Divide the mushrooms between 4 plates, top each portion with a fried egg then sprinkle with the toasted sage leaves. Season to taste and serve.

• MAINS •

Chilli Pork Ribs

SERVES 2–4 • PREP & COOKING TIME 2 hours, plus marinating

- 1 small onion
- 2 garlic cloves, crushed
- 1 tablespoon chipotle paste
- 1 tablespoon tamarind paste
- 2 teaspoons tomato purée
- 1 teaspoon dried oregano
- ¼ teaspoon ground cinnamon
- 2 tablespoons olive oil
- 1 rack of pork ribs
- salt and black pepper

Chipotle paste and tamarind paste give these succulent and sticky ribs a fantastic hit of smoky, tangy flavour. They're great for a barbecue but can be cooked in a griddle pan. Leave them to marinate overnight if you can.

- Place all the ingredients except the pork in a food processor or blender and whizz until smooth.

- Pierce the meat of the ribs a few times with a sharp knife, then place in a shallow dish. Rub over the marinade, cover with clingfilm and leave to marinate in the refrigerator for at least 4 hours and preferably overnight.

- Remove about 3 tablespoons of the marinade and reserve. Wrap the ribs in a double layer of foil and place on a baking sheet. Bake in a preheated oven, 150°C (300°F), Gas Mark 2, for 1½ hours.

- Remove the foil and baste all over the ribs with the reserved marinade. Heat a griddle pan until smoking hot or cook over a barbecue for 3–5 minutes on each side until charred all over.

v

• BREAKFASTS •

Vanilla, Bran & Blueberry Muffins

MAKES 12 • PREP & COOKING TIME 30 minutes

- 250 g (8 oz) plain flour
- 50 g (2 oz) bran
- 1 teaspoon baking powder
- 1 teaspoon bicarbonate soda
- 3 eggs
- 1 teaspoon vanilla extract
- 250 ml (8 fl oz) buttermilk
- 50 ml (2 fl oz) rice bran oil or groundnut oil
- 125 g (4 oz) frozen or fresh blueberries

The secret to baking the best muffins is simple – don't overmix the batter as this will make them tough. Fold the wet ingredients into the dry and mix gently and briefly. Try these sweet treats with raspberries in place of the blueberries.

- Line a 12-hole muffin tin with paper muffin cases.

- In a large bowl mix together the dry ingredients until well combined. Break the eggs into a large jug and beat lightly, then add the vanilla extract, buttermilk and oil.

- Pour the egg mixture into the dry ingredients, add the blueberries and fold gently using a large, metal spoon just until barely combined.

- Spoon the mixture into the muffin cases. Bake in a preheated oven, 180°C (350°F), Gas Mark 4, for 18–20 minutes, until risen, golden and firm.

- Remove from the oven and transfer to a wire rack to cool slightly before serving warm.

v

· DESSERTS ·

Easy Pecan Pie

SERVES 6 • PREP & COOKING TIME 30 minutes

- 25 g (1 oz) unsalted butter, plus extra for greasing
- 150 g (5 oz) golden syrup
- 1 tablespoon lemon juice
- 1 teaspoon finely grated lemon zest
- 50 g (2 oz) soft light brown sugar
- 200 g (7 oz) pecan halves
- 225 g (7 oz) ready-rolled shortcrust pastry
- 2 large eggs

Using ready-made shortcrust pastry means this sweetly crunchy classic pie is a breeze to make. Serve it warm with a cup of coffee or with scoops of vanilla ice cream or whipped cream for dessert.

- Place the butter and golden syrup in a small saucepan over a low heat and warm until just melted. Pour into a bowl and stir in the lemon juice and zest, sugar and pecan halves. Leave to cool for 1–2 minutes.

- Meanwhile, unroll the pastry and use to line a greased 23 cm (9 inch) pie dish, trimming away the excess pastry. Beat the eggs into the cooled butter mixture, then pour into the pastry case.

- Bake in a preheated oven, 200°C (400°F), Gas Mark 6, for 20 minutes, or until golden and just set. Leave to cool in the dish for 5 minutes, then cut into slices and serve warm.

• DRINKS •

Watermelon Cooler

SERVES 2 • PREP TIME 5 minutes, plus freezing

- 100 g (3½ oz) watermelon
- 100 g (3½ oz) strawberries
- 100 ml (3½ fl oz) still water
- small handful of mint or tarragon leaves, plus extra to serve (optional)

Heaven on a hot day, this refreshing fruity cooler is a breeze to make – a bit of chopping, freezing and blending is all it takes. You can ring the changes by using cantaloupe melon instead of watermelon.

- Skin and deseed the melon and chop the flesh into cubes. Hull the strawberries. Freeze the melon and strawberries until solid.

- Put the frozen melon and strawberries in a food processor or blender, add the water and the mint or tarragon and process until smooth.

- Pour the mixture into 2 short glasses, decorate with mint or tarragon leaves, if liked, and serve immediately.

September

GOOD TO EAT THIS MONTH

aubergines * beetroot * broccoli * butternut squash *
celeriac * celery * courgettes * cucumber * lettuces *
peppers * potatoes * rocket * runner beans *spinach
* sweetcorn * tomatoes * apples * blackberries *
chestnuts * cobnuts * damsons * figs * pears * plums
* raspberries * chillies * mint * oregano * parsley *
rosemary * sage * thyme

DATES TO LOOK FORWARD TO THIS MONTH

Rosh Hashanah

Summer is over and we're heading into the colder months.
September is the month that bridges summer and the start of
real autumn – often a fickle month. The beginning of the month
feels like summer's last hurrah and can still be warm, but towards
the end of the month, when we really notice the nights drawing
in, we know autumn is coming.

There's still plenty of summer veg available and figs are at
their best. Ripe, enjoyed by themselves or with a chunk of blue
cheese, they are wonderful, but try them also in the **Fig & Honey
Pots** on page 286 and the **Fig, Raspberry & Prosciutto Salad** on
page 283.

The recipes on pages 285 and 309 celebrate the arrival of
classic hedgerow treat, blackberries. Whether you forage your
own or buy them at the supermarket or farmers' market, their
dark juiciness is brilliant in salads, bakes and desserts.

For Rosh Hashanah this month there's **Honey Cake**, full of
spices that will make your kitchen smell like autumn as it bakes
(page 301).

V

• BREAKFASTS •

Cornbread Muffins

MAKES 12 • PREP & COOKING TIME 40 minutes

- 75 g (3 oz) butter
- 1 large sweetcorn cob, kernels sliced off
- 1 small onion, diced
- ½ red chilli, deseeded and diced
- 140 g (43/4 oz) plain flour
- 140 g (43/4) polenta
- 2 teaspoons baking powder
- 50g (2 oz) grated Cheddar cheese
- pinch of salt
- 2 eggs
- 300 ml (½ pint) buttermilk
- 100 ml (3½ fl oz) milk

Whip up a batch of these cornbread muffins for a breakfast treat to serve with crispy bacon or scrambled or poached eggs. They're best eaten warm but also freeze well and are great for lunchboxes and picnics.

- Melt 25g (1 oz) butter in a saucepan over a medium heat, add the sweetcorn, onion and chilli and cook for 2–3 minutes.

- Sift together the flour, polenta and baking powder. Stir in the grated Cheddar and a pinch of salt.

- Melt the remaining butter in a small saucepan. In a bowl, whisk together the eggs, melted butter, buttermilk and milk. Stir the wet ingredients into the dry, add the sweetcorn mixture and mix lightly. Divide between the holes of a greased 12-hole muffin tin.

- Bake in a preheated oven, 190°C (375°F), Gas Mark 5, for 18–20 minutes until golden and cooked through.

• LIGHT BITES •

Fig, Raspberry & Prosciutto Salad

SERVES 4–6 • PREP TIME 5 minutes

- 150 g (5 oz) rocket and beetroot salad mix
- 6 ripe figs, halved
- 150 g (5 oz) raspberries
- 8 slices of prosciutto
- 2 large buffalo mozzarella balls, each about 150 g (5 oz)

FOR THE DRESSING
- 2 tablespoons aged balsamic vinegar
- 2 tablespoons olive oil

Recipes don't have to be complicated or time-consuming to deliver spectacular results. This simple 5-minute salad is all about great ingredients – perfect for lunch in the garden.

- Put the rocket and beetroot leaves in a large bowl, add the halved figs, the raspberries and the prosciutto, toss carefully and transfer to a large serving plate.

- Make the dressing by whisking together the vinegar and oil.

- Tear each mozzarella ball into 3 pieces and arrange them on the salad. Drizzle the dressing over the salad and serve.

v

· MAINS ·

Provençale Tart

SERVES 6 • PREP & COOKING TIME 1 hour 20 minutes, plus proving

- 225 g (7½ oz) strong white bread flour, plus extra for dusting
- 1 teaspoon salt
- 1 teaspoon caster sugar
- 1 teaspoon fast-action dried yeast
- 1 tablespoon olive oil
- 150 ml (¼ pint) lukewarm water

FOR THE TOPPING
- 4 tablespoons olive oil
- 1 kg (2 lb) onions, sliced
- 1 garlic clove, crushed
- 1 teaspoon thyme leaves, plus extra to garnish
- 1 teaspoon dried mixed herbs
- 12 pitted black olives
- 12 cherry tomatoes, halved
- 2 tablespoons capers
- salt and black pepper

This vegan tart is an absolute stunner for al fresco dining with friends. Pour yourself a glass of cold wine and imagine you're in the south of France. If you're not catering for vegans, you could scatter over a big handful of grated mozzarella before cooking.

- Mix the flour, salt, sugar and yeast together in a bowl. Add the oil and measured lukewarm water and mix with your hand until the mixture comes together into a dough and leaves the sides of the bowl clean. If too dry, add a little more lukewarm water.

- Turn the dough out on to a lightly floured surface and knead for about 10 minutes until smooth and stretchy. Put in a clean bowl, cover with clingfilm and leave to rise in a warm place for about 1 hour until doubled in size.

- Meanwhile, make the topping. Heat the oil in a large frying pan, add the onions, garlic, thyme and dried herbs and cook, covered, over a gentle heat, stirring occasionally, for about 30 minutes until the onions are meltingly soft.

- Turn the dough out on to a lightly floured surface and knead for 1 minute. Roll out the dough and use to line a 33 × 23 cm (13 × 9 inch) Swiss roll tin. Spread the cooked onions over the top, scatter over the olives, tomatoes and capers and season with salt and pepper.

- Bake in a preheated oven, 180°C (350°F), Gas Mark 4, for 25 minutes until golden. Garnish with thyme leaves and serve warm or cold.

V

• DESSERTS •

Easy Blackberry Fool

SERVES 4 • PREP TIME 20 minutes

- 300 g (10 oz) blackberries, plus extra to decorate
- 50 g (2 oz) icing sugar
- 1 tablespoon lemon juice
- 250 g (8 oz) fromage frais
- 200 g (7 oz) fat-free Greek yogurt

A good-for-you take on traditional blackberry fool, this uses fromage frais and fat-free Greek yogurt in place of double cream but is no less delicious. Serve it in pretty little glasses or glass dishes, decorated with extra blackberries.

- Place the blackberries, icing sugar and lemon juice in a food processor or blender and blend to a purée, then press through a sieve into a large bowl to remove the pips. Beat in the fromage frais and yogurt.

- Spoon into 4 little glasses or glass dishes and chill for 10 minutes. Decorate with extra blackberries before serving.

V

• BREAKFASTS •

Fig & Honey Pots

SERVES 4 • PREP TIME 10 minutes, plus chilling

- 6 ripe fresh figs, thinly sliced, plus 2 extra, cut into wedges, to decorate (optional)
- 450 ml (¾ pint) Greek yogurt
- 4 tablespoons honey
- 2 tablespoons chopped pistachio nuts

When figs are in season, these pots make a sweet and tangy breakfast or a light dessert. The green of the pistachios looks very pretty against the white of the yogurt but you could use any nuts.

- Arrange the fig slices snugly in the bottom of 4 glasses or glass bowls. Spoon the yogurt over the figs and chill in the refrigerator for 10–15 minutes.

- Just before serving, drizzle 1 tablespoon honey over each and sprinkle the pistachio nuts on top. Decorate with the wedges of fig, if liked.

• LIGHT BITES •

Potted Crab & Prawns

SERVES 4 • PREP & COOKING TIME 30 minutes, plus chilling

- 200 g (7 oz) butter, diced
- finely grated zest and juice of 1 lime
- 3 tablespoons chopped coriander
- generous pinch of cayenne pepper
- 200 g (7 oz) peeled, cooked prawns, roughly chopped
- 1 dressed crab, about 175 g (6 oz)
- salt

TO SERVE
- ½ small wholemeal baguette, sliced
- 2 heads of chicory
- a few tiny radishes

Much easier to make than they look, these little pots are a great way to kick off a dinner party, especially as they can be made several hours ahead and just sit in the fridge until you are ready to serve. You could use chives in place of the coriander, and all prawns rather than a mix of shellfish.

- First clarify the butter. Heat a small saucepan of water, add the butter and heat gently until melted. Cool, then freeze until the butter has formed a set layer on top of the water. Lift the disc of hardened butter off the water and discard the water.

- Remove any droplets of water from the underside of the butter with kitchen paper.

- Melt half the clarified butter in a saucepan. Add the lime zest, chopped coriander, cayenne and a little salt. Stir the prawns into the butter with the crab meat and lime juice. Heat until piping hot. Spoon into 4 small china ramekins and press down well so there are no air pockets. Chill for 15 minutes.

- Melt the remaining butter in a clean pan then spoon over the top of the fish mixture in a thin even layer. Chill for 3–4 hours until set. Sprinkle with a little extra cayenne.

- When ready to serve, toast the bread then arrange on plates with the dishes of potted fish, the chicory leaves and tiny radishes.

• MAINS •

Grilled Hoisin Pork

SERVES 4 • PREP & COOKING TIME 30 minutes, plus marinating

- 8 boneless lean pork loin steaks, about 100 g (3½ oz) each
- 4 tablespoons hoisin sauce
- 3 tablespoons dark soy sauce
- 4 garlic cloves, crushed
- 2 teaspoons peeled and finely grated fresh root ginger
- 1 teaspoon Szechuan peppercorns, crushed
- 2 tablespoons tomato purée
- 2 tablespoons cider vinegar

TO GARNISH
- 4 spring onions, finely shredded
- 1 red chilli, deseeded and finely shredded

Made with lean pork loin steaks with a hit of warmth from the ginger and peppercorns, this is a lovely healthy dish. Serve the pork with rice and a pile of steamed Asian greens.

- Place the pork steaks in a shallow glass or ceramic dish in a single layer. Mix together the hoisin sauce, soy sauce, garlic, ginger, crushed Szechuan peppercorns, tomato purée and vinegar, then brush or spoon the mixture on to the pork. Cover and leave to marinate in the refrigerator for 2–3 hours.

- Arrange the pork on a grill rack in a single layer and cook under a preheated medium-high grill for 5–6 minutes on each side, or until cooked through.

- Remove from the grill, garnish with the spring onions and red chilli and serve.

V

• DESSERTS •

Plum Tarts with Saffron Custard

SERVES 6 • PREP & COOKING TIME 45 minutes

- 200 g (7 oz) chilled ready-rolled puff pastry
- 50 g (2 oz) butter, softened
- 50 g (2 oz) caster sugar
- 50 g (2 oz) ground almonds
- 1 egg yolk
- 6 ripe red plums, about 300 g (10 oz), pitted and thickly sliced
- sifted icing sugar, to decorate

FOR THE SAFFRON CUSTARD
- 4 egg yolks
- 50 g (2 oz) caster sugar
- 1 teaspoon cornflour
- large pinch of saffron threads
- 300 ml (½ pint) semi-skimmed milk

Make the most of summer's bounty with these lovely little tarts. The edges of the tarts are fluted: to do this, press your first and second fingers on to the tart edge, then make small cuts with a knife between them to create a scalloped edge all the way around.

- Cut the pastry into 6 even rectangles. Flute the edges with a sharp knife then transfer to a lightly greased baking sheet. Prick the centres of the pastries.

- Cream the butter and sugar together, then mix in the ground almonds and egg yolk.

- Divide the mixture between the pastry rectangles, then spread into a thin layer, leaving a border of pastry around the edges.

- Arrange the plums on top of the almond mixture, then bake in a preheated oven, 200°C (400°F), Gas Mark 6, for 12–15 minutes until the pastry is well risen and golden.

- Meanwhile, make the custard. Whisk the egg yolks, sugar, cornflour and saffron together in a bowl.

- Heat the milk in a saucepan until just boiling then gradually whisk into the egg yolks. Pour the milk mixture back into the pan then heat gently, stirring continuously, until almost boiling, and thickened and smooth. Pour into a jug.

- Remove the tarts from the oven and loosen the bases with a palette knife, then dust with a little sifted icing sugar and serve with the custard.

V

• BREAKFASTS •

Raspberry & Oatmeal Scotch Pancakes

MAKES 8 • PREP & COOKING TIME 20 minutes

- 125 g (4 oz) self-raising flour
- 2 tablespoons golden caster sugar
- 2 tablespoons oatmeal
- 1 egg, beaten
- ½ teaspoon vanilla extract
- 150 ml (¼ pint) milk
- 75 g (3 oz) raspberries, halved
- oil, for frying
- maple syrup or honey, to serve

Raspberries give a pop of colour and sweet tartness to these pancakes, which can be on the breakfast table in only 20 minutes. Drizzle over some maple syrup or honey and tuck in!

- Place the flour in a bowl with the sugar and oatmeal and stir well. Make a well in the centre and set aside.

- Beat together the egg, vanilla extract and milk in a jug, then pour into the dry ingredients and beat lightly to make a batter the consistency of thick cream. Carefully fold in the raspberries.

- Lightly oil a heavy-based frying pan or flat griddle pan. Drop tablespoons of the batter on to the pan surface until covered, and cook over a medium heat for 1–2 minutes until bubbles rise to the surface and burst. Turn the pancakes over and cook for a further 1–2 minutes until golden and set. Remove from the pan and keep warm.

- Repeat with the remaining batter to make 8 pancakes.

- Serve warm with maple syrup or honey spooned over each.

• LIGHT BITES •

Pork Larb

SERVES 4 • PREP & COOKING TIME 30 minutes

- 1 tablespoon groundnut oil
- 2 cm (¾ inch) fresh root ginger, peeled and finely chopped
- 2 lemon grass stalks, white stems chopped
- 3 kaffir lime leaves, finely sliced
- 600 g (1¼ lb) minced pork
- 2 tablespoons Thai fish sauce
- juice of 1½ limes
- ½ cucumber
- 1 iceberg lettuce

TO GARNISH
- 30 g (1¼ oz) roasted peanuts, chopped
- small bunch of mint, finely chopped
- small bunch of coriander, finely chopped
- 1 red chilli, deseeded and finely chopped

Larb is a Southeast Asian speciality, spiked with chillies and fresh herbs. It includes Thai fish sauce, nam pla, which gets its concentrated, pungent fishy flavour from anchovies fermented in sugar and water.

- Heat the oil in a large, nonstick frying pan or wok over a high heat, add the ginger, lemon grass and lime leaves and fry for 1 minute.

- Add the pork and stir-fry for 4–5 minutes until slightly browned and cooked through. Add the fish sauce and lime juice to taste then remove the pan from the heat.

- Cut the cucumber into very fine strands and arrange on serving plates next to a lettuce leaf. Serve the pork on the lettuce, garnished with the chopped peanuts, herbs and red chilli.

V

• MAINS •

Vegetable Moussaka

SERVES 4 • PREP & COOKING TIME 1 hour

- 5 tablespoons olive oil
- 1 onion, chopped
- 2 garlic cloves, finely chopped
- 500 g (1 lb) courgettes, cut into chunks
- 250 g (8 oz) closed cup mushrooms, quartered
- 1 red pepper, deseeded and cut into chunks
- 1 orange pepper, deseeded and cut into chunks
- 2 × 400 g (13 oz) cans chopped tomatoes
- 2–3 rosemary stems, leaves stripped from stems
- 1 teaspoon caster sugar
- 2 aubergines, sliced, sprinkled with salt for 15 minutes
- 3 eggs
- 300 g (10 oz) natural yogurt
- large pinch of grated nutmeg
- 75 g (3 oz) feta cheese, grated
- salt and black pepper

Put this vegetarian version of the Greek favourite in the middle of the table and let everyone dig in. All it needs to go with it is a crisp green salad with a lemony dressing and perhaps a loaf of garlic bread.

- Heat 1 tablespoon of the oil in a frying pan, add the onion and fry for 5 minutes, stirring until just beginning to brown. Add the garlic, courgettes, mushrooms and peppers and fry for 2–3 minutes.

- Stir in the tomatoes, rosemary and sugar, season, then bring to the boil, cover and simmer for 15 minutes. Tip into a shallow ovenproof dish, leaving enough space to add the aubergines and topping.

- Rinse and dry the aubergines. Heat 2 tablespoons of the oil in a clean frying pan and fry half the aubergine slices until softened and golden on both sides. Arrange, overlapping, on top of the tomato mixture. Repeat with remaining oil and aubergines.

- Stir the eggs, yogurt, nutmeg and a little pepper together in a bowl, then pour over the aubergines. Sprinkle with the feta and bake in a preheated oven, 180°C (350°F), Gas Mark 4, for 30–35 minutes until piping hot.

V

• DESSERTS •

Lemon & Honey Ice

SERVES 4–6 • PREP & COOKING TIME 25 minutes,
plus cooling and freezing

- 4 large or 6 medium lemons
- about 4 tablespoons water
- 2 tablespoons honey
- 50 g (2 oz) caster sugar
- 1 bay leaf or lemon balm sprig
- 475 ml (16 fl oz) natural yogurt or fromage frais
- strips of lemon rind to decorate

A tangy, icy and refreshing dessert, with a light texture and vibrant flavour. The bay leaf may seem an unusual addition but it complements the lemon really well.

- Slice off the top of each lemon. Carefully scoop out all the pulp and juice with a teaspoon. Discard any white pith, skin and pits, then purée the pulp and juice in a food processor or blender. You will need 150 ml (5 fl oz). If there is less than this, top it up with water.

- Put the measured water, honey, sugar and bay leaf into a saucepan. Stir over a low heat until the sugar has dissolved, then leave to cool. Blend the mixture with the lemon purée and the yogurt. Do not remove the herb at this stage.

- Pour into a freezer tray or shallow dish and freeze until lightly frozen, then gently fork the mixture and remove the bay leaf. Return the ice to the freezer.

- Transfer the ice to the refrigerator about 20 minutes before serving. Serve in bowls, decorated with strips of lemon rind.

VG

• BREAKFASTS •

Coconut Toasted Muesli

SERVES 8 • PREP & COOKING TIME 45 minutes, plus cooling

- 350 g (11½ oz) rolled oats
- 75 g (3 oz) coconut chips
- 75 g (3 oz) sunflower seeds
- 200 g (7 oz) pumpkin seeds
- 150 g (5 oz) flaked almonds
- 100 g (3½ oz) hazelnuts
- 4 tablespoons maple syrup
- 2 tablespoons sunflower oil
- 250 g (8 oz) sultanas
- 75 g (3 oz) dried figs, roughly chopped

Crunchy coconut chips, sticky maple syrup and sweet sultanas give this muesli a varied texture. Great for breakfast with milk or yogurt or by the handful as a satisfying snack. Store in an airtight container.

- Mix together the oats, coconut chips, sunflower and pumpkin seeds, flaked almonds and hazelnuts in a large bowl.

- Transfer half the muesli mixture to a separate bowl. Mix the maple syrup and oil together in a jug, then pour over the remaining half of the muesli and toss really well to lightly coat all the ingredients.

- Line a large roasting tin with baking parchment, scatter over the syrup-coated muesli and spread out in a single layer. Bake in a preheated oven, 150°C (300°F), Gas Mark 2, for 15–20 minutes, stirring occasionally, until golden and crisp.

- Leave to cool completely, then toss with the uncooked muesli and the dried fruit.

VG

• LIGHT BITES •

Avocado & Cucumber Sushi

SERVES 4 • PREP TIME 30 minutes, plus standing/steaming

- 200 g (7 oz) sushi rice
- 4 tablespoons rice vinegar
- 2 tablespoons granulated sugar
- 2 tablespoons sesame seeds, toasted
- 4 sheets of nori seaweed
- 1 small avocado, peeled, stoned and cut into slim wedges
- ¼ cucumber, cut into long thin sticks

TO SERVE
- soy sauce
- wasabi
- pickled ginger

Rolling sushi neatly takes practice – a bamboo mat really helps but you could try using a clean tea towel lined with a sheet of clingfilm. But no matter if it doesn't look perfect, this vegan sushi will still taste delicious.

- Cook and leave the rice to stand/steam according to the packet instructions, then transfer to a bowl.

- Put the vinegar and sugar in a cup and microwave for 30 seconds until hot. Pour into the cooked rice and mix well – the rice should be sticky. Stir in the sesame seeds.

- Lay out the sheets of nori seaweed and divide the rice between them. Spread evenly to the edges, then arrange the avocado wedges and cucumber strips across the length of the rice in the bottom third of each sheet.

- Starting at the filled end, gently roll each nori sheet up tightly until a neat roll is formed, brushing with a little water to hold the seaweed tightly in place.

- Use a very sharp knife to slice the rolls into 2.5 cm (1 inch) thick pieces. Serve with soy sauce and wasabi for dipping, along with some pickled ginger.

· MAINS ·

Haddock, Tomato & Tamarind Fish Curry

SERVES 4 • PREP & COOKING TIME 30 minutes

- 750 g (1 lb 10 oz) skinless haddock fillets, boned and cut into chunks
- 1 tablespoon tamarind paste
- 4 tablespoons rice wine vinegar
- 2 tablespoons cumin seeds
- 1 teaspoon ground turmeric
- 2 teaspoons hot curry powder
- 1 teaspoon salt
- 4 tablespoons sunflower oil
- 1 onion, finely chopped
- 3 garlic cloves, finely grated
- 2 teaspoons peeled and grated fresh root ginger
- 2 teaspoons black mustard seeds or nigella seeds
- 600 g (1 lb 5 oz) canned chopped tomatoes
- 1 teaspoon caster sugar
- 200 g (7 oz) cherry tomatoes
- chopped coriander, to garnish

When you feel like curry in a hurry, this is a winner every time. Infused with spices and with a rich tomatoey sauce as a backdrop to the meaty fish, it's great served with plain steamed basmati rice or naan bread.

- Put the fish in a shallow non-reactive bowl. Mix together the tamarind, vinegar, cumin seeds, turmeric, curry powder and salt in a small bowl. Spoon over the fish and toss to coat evenly, then cover and leave to marinate.

- Meanwhile, heat the oil in a large wok or frying pan over a high heat until hot, add the onion, garlic, ginger and mustard or nigella seeds, then reduce the heat to medium and stir-fry for 1–2 minutes.

- Add the chopped tomatoes and sugar, stir through and bring to the boil. Reduce the heat again, cover and cook gently, stirring occasionally, for 15–20 minutes.

- Add the cherry tomatoes and the fish with its marinade and stir gently to mix. Cover and simmer gently for 5–6 minutes or until the fish is cooked through and flakes easily.

- Ladle into bowls, scatter with chopped coriander and serve.

V

• DESSERTS •

Fruited Friands

MAKES 12 • PREP & COOKING TIME 45 minutes, plus cooling

- 175 g (6 oz) unsalted butter
- 75 g (3 oz) dried strawberries, sour cherries or cranberries roughly chopped
- 2 tablespoons orange juice
- 6 egg whites
- 225 g (7½ oz) caster sugar, plus extra for sprinkling
- 75 g (3 oz) plain flour
- 125 g (4 oz) ground almonds

Made with egg whites and very little flour, these fruit-spiked friands are beautifully light, while the ground almonds ensure they are moist and just the right kind of chewy. Superb with a cup of coffee.

- Melt the butter and leave to cool.

- Put the strawberries, cherries or cranberries and orange juice in a saucepan and heat until the mixture is hot, then turn into a bowl and leave to cool.

- Whisk the egg whites in a large clean bowl with a hand-held electric whisk until frothy and increased in volume but not peaking. Add the sugar, flour and ground almonds and stir in until almost combined. Drizzle the melted butter over the mixture, then stir together gently until just combined.

- Divide the mixture evenly between the holes of a greased 12-hole muffin tray, then scatter the strawberries, cherries or cranberries on top.

- Bake in a preheated oven, 200°C (400°F), Gas Mark 6, for about 20 minutes until pale golden and just firm to the touch. Leave in the tin for 5 minutes, then transfer to a wire rack to cool. Serve sprinkled with caster sugar.

Make the most of your leftovers...
Rather than throw away the egg yolks left over from this recipe, use them to make homemade mayonnaise or add extra richness to a cake. Or you could try the **Saffron Custard** on page 289 or **Portuguese Custard Tarts** on page 123.

v

• BREAKFASTS •

Cranberry & Yogurt Smoothie

SERVES 1 • PREP TIME 5 minutes

- 100 g (3½ oz) cranberries
- 50 g (2 oz) Greek yogurt
- 100 ml (3½ fl oz) soya milk
- 2–3 ice cubes
- sugar or sweetener, to taste

Start your day the right way with a health-boosting smoothie. Cranberries are packed with antioxidants and vitamin C. They are tart, though, so add sugar or sweetener to taste.

- Put the cranberries in a food processor or blender, add the yogurt, soya milk and ice cubes and process.

- Taste and add sugar or sweetener if required. Process once again. Pour the smoothie into a large glass and serve immediately.

• LIGHT BITES •

Tuna & Borlotti Bean Salad

SERVES 4 • PREP & COOKING TIME 20 minutes, plus marinating

- 400 g (13 oz) can borlotti beans, drained and rinsed
- 1 tablespoon water (optional)
- 2 tablespoons extra virgin olive oil
- 2 garlic cloves, crushed
- 1 red chilli, deseeded and finely chopped
- 2 celery sticks, thinly sliced
- ½ red onion, cut into thin wedges
- 200 g (7 oz) can tuna in olive oil, drained and flaked
- finely grated zest and juice of 1 lemon
- 50 g (2 oz) rocket leaves
- salt and black pepper

The longer you can leave the beans and onion sitting in the marinade, the better this salad will taste. For a vegetarian version of this, omit the tuna and add a can of cannellini beans.

- Heat the borlotti beans in a saucepan over a medium heat for 3 minutes, adding the measured water if starting to stick to the base.

- Put the oil, garlic and chilli in a large bowl. Stir in the celery, onion and hot beans and season with salt and pepper. Cover and leave to marinate at room temperature for at least 30 minutes and up to 4 hours.

- Stir in the tuna and lemon zest and juice. Gently toss in the rocket leaves then serve.

• MAINS •

Roast Chicken with Herbs & Garlic

SERVES 4 • PREP & COOKING TIME about 1 hour

- 8 garlic cloves, unpeeled
- 4 large thyme sprigs
- 3 large rosemary sprigs
- 1 organic or free-range chicken, about 1.75 kg (3½ lb)
- 1 tablespoon olive oil
- salt and black pepper

The smells that will waft through the kitchen when you make this herby roast chicken will be mouth-watering. It's wonderful served with roast or mashed potatoes and some steamed green veg.

- Put the garlic cloves and half the herb sprigs in the body cavity of the chicken. Pat the chicken dry with kitchen paper and rub the oil all over the outside of the bird. Strip the leaves off the remaining herb sprigs and rub over the bird, with a little salt and pepper.

- Place the chicken, breast-side up, in a roasting tin. Roast in a preheated oven, 220°C (425°F), Gas Mark 7, for 10 minutes. Turn the chicken over, breast-side down, reduce the oven temperature to 180°C (350°F), Gas Mark 4, and cook for a further 20 minutes. Finally, turn the chicken back to its original position and roast for another 25 minutes until the skin is crisp and golden. Check that the chicken is cooked by piercing the thigh with a knife. The juices should run clear, with no sign of pink. If not, cook for a further 10 minutes.

- Transfer to a serving plate and leave to rest for 5 minutes before serving with the pan juices.

Make the most of your leftovers...
Use the leftover chicken carcass to make homemade chicken stock. It's really easy to do and tastes so much better than a stock cube. Divide into portions and freeze to use in risottos, soups and stews.

V

• DESSERTS •

Honey Cake

MAKES a 1 kg (2 lb) loaf cake • PREP & COOKING TIME 1¼ hours

- 125 g (4 oz) plain flour
- 50 g (2 oz) wholemeal flour
- 1 teaspoon baking powder
- 1 teaspoon ground cinnamon
- 1 teaspoon mixed spice
- 1 teaspoon ground ginger
- 3 tablespoons golden caster sugar
- 125 g (4 oz) heather honey, plus extra to serve
- 125 g (4 oz) butter, softened
- 3 eggs, lightly beaten
- 1 teaspoon vanilla extract
- 50 ml (2 fl oz) apple juice
- 1 large dessert apple, peeled, cored and chopped

Honey cake, or lekach, is made to celebrate Rosh Hashanah, Jewish New Year. The honey symbolizes hopes for sweetness in the new year. Fragrant with spices and moist from the apples, this version is a delicious treat any time.

- Sift the flours and baking powder into a large bowl. Mix in the cinnamon, mixed spice, ginger, sugar, honey, butter, eggs, vanilla extract and apple juice. Stir through the apple.

- Spoon the mixture into a 1 kg (2 lb) loaf tin lined with nonstick baking paper and bake in a preheated oven, 180°C (350°F), Gas Mark 4, for 1 hour. To see if it is cooked, insert a skewer in the centre of the loaf – if it comes out clean it is done, but if cake mix is attached to the skewer it will need another 10 minutes.

- Remove the cake from the oven and turn out on to a wire rack. Peel off the baking paper and leave to cool. Serve cut into slices with honey drizzled over.

V

· BREAKFASTS ·

Melting Mushrooms

SERVES 4 • PREP & COOKING TIME 20 minutes

- 2 tablespoon olive oil
- 4 large flat mushrooms
- 4 small fresh tomatoes, roughly chopped
- 1 tablespoon tomato purée
- 4 tablespoons canned cannellini beans, drained and rinsed
- 1 tablespoon honey
- 1 tablespoon chopped parsley
- 50 g (2 oz) Gruyère or Edam, thinly sliced*
- 1 tablespoon grated Parmesan or vegetarian hard cheese*

Add some oomph to mushrooms for breakfast with this recipe, full of good-for-you ingredients. Serve with slices of hot buttered wholemeal toast and, if you fancy something a bit more substantial, top with poached eggs.

- Heat the oil in a large, heavy-based frying pan and cook the mushrooms over a moderate heat for 2–3 minutes, turning once, until they are softened. Place the mushrooms, stalk side up, on a foil-lined grill rack.

- Add the tomatoes to the pan juices, and cook, stirring occasionally, for 4–5 minutes until the tomatoes are thick and pulpy. Add the tomato purée, beans and honey and continue to cook for a further 1 minute. Remove from the heat and stir in the parsley.

- Divide the mixture between the mushrooms and arrange the slices of Gruyère or Edam over the top. Sprinkle the mushrooms with the Parmesan and place under a preheated hot grill for 2–3 minutes until golden and bubbling.

*For guidance on vegetarian cheeses, see page 5.

VG

· LIGHT BITES ·

Guacamole

SERVES 4 • PREP TIME 10 minutes

- 2 avocados, peeled, stoned and chopped
- juice of 1 lime
- 6 cherry tomatoes, diced
- 1 tablespoon chopped coriander leaves
- 1–2 garlic cloves, crushed

Heart-healthy, nutrient-dense avocado is the star of the show in this simple, fresh-tasting guacamole recipe. Serve with strips of toasted pitta bread or tortilla chips, or – keeping with the healthy theme – with the **Oatcakes** on page 29 and vegetable crudités, such as cucumber, peppers and carrots.

- Put the avocados and lime juice in a bowl and mash together to prevent discoloration, then stir in the remaining ingredients. Serve immediately.

• MAINS •

Tray-baked Sausages with Apples

SERVES 4 • PREP & COOKING TIME 35 minutes

- 3 red onions, cut into wedges
- 3 red apples, cored and cut into 6 wedges
- 200 g (7 oz) baby carrots, scrubbed
- 3 potatoes, peeled and cut into small cubes
- 4 tablespoons olive oil
- 12 pork sausages
- 2 tablespoons chopped sage leaves
- 1 tablespoon rosemary leaves
- 3 tablespoons honey
- salt and black pepper

A one tray dish that's on the table in just over half an hour, this is a great autumnal midweek meal. It's sure to become a make-on-repeat favourite.

- Place the wedges of onion and apple in a large, shallow roasting tin with the carrots and potatoes. Drizzle over the oil, then toss well to lightly coat all the vegetables. Season generously with salt and pepper. Arrange the sausages in and around the vegetables, scatter over the herbs and toss again.

- Place in a preheated oven, 200°C (400°F), Gas Mark 6, for 20–25 minutes until golden and cooked through.

- Remove from the oven and drizzle over the honey. Toss all the vegetables and sausages in the honey and serve.

V

• BREAKFASTS •

Courgette Fritters with Poached Eggs

SERVES 4 • PREP & COOKING TIME 20 minutes

- 4 courgettes, grated
- 4 tablespoons self-raising flour
- 40 g (1¾ oz) Parmesan or vegetarian hard cheese, grated*
- 2 tablespoons olive oil
- 4 eggs
- black pepper

Crispy on the outside and creamy inside, these little courgette fritters are wonderful accompanied by the soft poached eggs. They also work really well as a snack served with the **Soured Cream Dip** on page 134 or with sweet chilli sauce for dipping.

- Place the grated courgette, flour and grated Parmesan in a bowl and mix together well. Squeeze into walnut-sized balls and then gently flatten.

- Heat the oil in a deep frying pan and, working in batches if necessary, fry the fritters for 2–3 minutes on each side, until golden.

- Meanwhile, bring a large saucepan of water to a gentle simmer and stir with a large spoon to create a swirl. Carefully break 2 eggs into the water and cook for 3 minutes. Remove with a slotted spoon and keep warm. Repeat with the remaining eggs.

- Serve the fritters topped with the poached eggs and sprinkled with pepper.

*For guidance on vegetarian cheeses, see page 5.

• DESSERTS •

Passion Fruit Panna Cotta

SERVES 4 • PREP TIME 20 minutes, plus setting

- 2 gelatine leaves
- 8 passion fruit
- 200 g (7 oz) crème fraîche
- 125 g (4 oz) Greek yogurt
- 1 teaspoon caster sugar
- vanilla pod, split

An elegant, make-ahead option for a stress-free finale to a special dinner. For a coffee version of this delicate dessert, substitute 2 teaspoons of strong coffee for the passion fruit and decorate each one with chocolate coffee beans.

- Soften the gelatine leaves in cold water. Halve the passion fruit and remove the seeds, working over a bowl to catch as much juice as you can. Reserve the seeds for decoration.

- Combine the crème fraîche, yogurt and passion fruit juice.

- Put 100 ml (3½ fl oz) water in a small saucepan, add the sugar and the seeds from the vanilla pod and heat gently, stirring until the sugar has dissolved. Drain the gelatine and add to the pan. Stir until dissolved, then leave to cool to room temperature.

- Mix the gelatine mixture into the crème fraîche, then pour into 4 ramekins or moulds. Refrigerate for 6 hours or until set.

- Turn the panna cotta out of their moulds on to serving plates by briefly immersing each ramekin in very hot water. Spoon over the reserved seeds to decorate.

VG

• LIGHT BITES •

Pickled Peaches

MAKES 1 large jar • PREP & COOKING TIME 30 minutes

- 300 ml (½ pint) white malt vinegar
- 500 g (1 lb) granulated sugar
- 1 teaspoon whole cloves
- 1 teaspoon whole allspice berries
- 7 cm (3 inch) piece cinnamon stick, halved
- 1 kg (2 lb) small peaches, halved and stoned

When ripe peaches are plentiful and cheap in summer, pickle some to have with slices of ham, roast pork or duck, and blue cheese. The recipe works well with nectarines also.

- Pour the vinegar into a large saucepan, add the sugar and spices and heat gently until the sugar has dissolved.

- Add the peach halves and cook very gently for 4–5 minutes until just tender but still firm. Lift out of the syrup with a slotted spoon and pack tightly into a sterilized, warm, large jar.

- Boil the syrup for 2–3 minutes to concentrate the flavours, then pour over the fruit, making sure that the fruit is completely covered and the jar filled to the very top. Top up with a little extra warm vinegar if needed. Add a small piece of crumpled greaseproof paper to stop the fruit from rising out of the vinegar in the jar. Screw or clip on the lid, label and leave to cool.

- After a few hours, the peaches will begin to rise in the jar, but as they become saturated with the syrup they will sink once more; at this point they will be ready to eat.

· MAINS ·

Feta-stuffed Plaice

SERVES 4 • PREP & COOKING TIME 1 hour

- 2 tablespoons chopped mint
- 2 tablespoons chopped oregano
- 25 g (1 oz) Parma ham, finely chopped
- 2 garlic cloves, crushed
- 4 spring onions, finely chopped
- 200 g (7 oz) feta cheese
- 8 plaice fillets, skinned
- 300 g (10 oz) courgettes, sliced
- 4 tablespoons garlic-infused olive oil
- 8 flat mushrooms
- 150 g (5 oz) baby plum tomatoes, halved
- 1 tablespoon capers, rinsed and drained
- salt and black pepper

When you've got friends coming for dinner, a one-dish meal is optimal. Who likes lots of washing-up? The rolls of feta- and ham-stuffed plaice look sophisticated but are so easy to do.

- Put the mint, oregano, ham, garlic and spring onions in a bowl. Crumble in the feta cheese, season with plenty of pepper and mix together well.

- Put the fish fillets skinned-side up on the work surface and press the feta mixture down the centres. Roll up loosely and secure with wooden cocktail sticks.

- Scatter the courgettes into a shallow, ovenproof dish and drizzle with 1 tablespoon of the oil. Place in a preheated oven, 190°C (375°F), Gas Mark 5, for 15 minutes.

- Remove from the oven and add the plaice fillets to the dish. Tuck the mushrooms, tomatoes and capers around the fish and season lightly. Drizzle with the remaining oil.

- Return to the oven for a further 25 minutes or until the fish is cooked through.

V

• DESSERTS •

Blackberry & Apple Crumbles

SERVES 4 • PREP & COOKING TIME 30 minutes

- 4 dessert apples, peeled, cored and thinly sliced
- 125 g (4 oz) blackberries
- 2 teaspoons caster sugar
- 100 g (3½ oz) rolled oats
- 50 g (2 oz) unsalted butter, diced
- 40 g (1¾ oz) dark muscovado sugar
- 25 g (1 oz) flaked almonds

Steaming hot crumble plus lashings of custard equals smiling faces all round. So homely and so comforting. Almonds and oats make for a lovely crispy topping in this recipe.

- Divide the apple slices and blackberries between 4 small ovenproof dishes or ramekins and sprinkle with the caster sugar.

- In a food processor, blitz the oats, butter, sugar and almonds. Spoon the oat mixture over the fruit and bake in a preheated oven, 190°C (375°F), Gas Mark 5, for 22–25 minutes until golden.

· MAINS ·

Greek Lamb with Tzatziki Toasts

SERVES 4 • PREP & COOKING TIME 1 hour 15 minutes

- 750 g (1½ lb) lamb chump chops
- 2 teaspoons dried oregano
- 3 garlic cloves, crushed
- 4 tablespoons olive oil
- 1 medium aubergine, about 300 g (10 oz), diced
- 2 red onions, sliced
- 200 ml (7 fl oz) white or red wine
- 400 g (13 oz) can chopped tomatoes
- 2 tablespoons honey
- 8 kalamata olives
- 8 thin slices French bread
- 200 g (7 oz) tzatziki
- salt and black pepper

Leave the lamb to bubble away gently, filling the kitchen with amazing aromas, until it is meltingly soft. The tzatziki toasts add crunch and tangy contrast. Use ready-made or the homemade version in the introduction on page 93.

- Cut the lamb into large pieces, discarding any excess fat. Mix the oregano with the garlic and a little seasoning and rub into the lamb.

- Heat half the oil in a large saucepan or sauté pan and fry the lamb in batches until browned. Drain to a plate.

- Add the aubergine to the pan with the onions and remaining oil and cook very gently, stirring frequently, for about 10 minutes until softened and lightly browned. Return the meat to the pan with the wine, tomatoes, honey, olives and seasoning. Cover with a lid and cook on the lowest setting for about 1¼ hours or until the lamb is very tender.

- Lightly toast the bread and spoon the tzatziki on top.

- Check the stew for seasoning and turn into shallow bowls. Serve with the toasts on the side.

V

· LIGHT BITES ·

Olive, Onion & Halloumi Bread

SERVES 12 • PREP & COOKING TIME 50 minutes, plus proving

- 500 g (1 lb) strong plain flour, plus extra for sifting
- 7 g (¼ oz) sachet fast-action dried yeast
- pinch of salt
- 2 tablespoons olive oil
- 300 ml (½ pint) warm water
- 1 onion, thinly sliced
- 100 g (3½ oz) pitted olives
- 75 g (3 oz) halloumi cheese, chopped
- 2 tablespoons chopped parsley

A far cry from sliced white, this Mediterranean-inspired bread is delicious warm from the oven with butter or alongside soup or stew, or topped with the **Butter Bean & Anchovy Pâté** on page 41.

- Place the flour, yeast and salt in a large bowl. Combine half the oil with the measured water in a jug and stir into the flour to form a dough.

- Turn the dough out on a lightly floured surface and knead for 5 minutes until smooth and elastic. Place in a lightly oiled bowl, cover with a damp cloth and set aside in a warm place for about 1 hour until doubled in size.

- Meanwhile, heat the remaining oil in a frying pan, add the onion and fry for 7–8 minutes until softened and golden. Leave to cool.

- Turn the risen dough out on the floured surface and add the remaining ingredients, including the onion, kneading it into the dough. Shape into an oval, place on a lightly floured baking sheet and leave to rise for 1 hour.

- When the loaf has risen, slash a few cuts in the top, sift over a little flour, then bake in a preheated oven, 220°C (425°F), Gas Mark 7, for about 25 minutes until hollow-sounding when tapped. Transfer to a wire rack to cool.

October

GOOD TO EAT THIS MONTH

beetroot * broccoli * Brussels sprouts * butternut
squash * cabbage * carrots * cauliflower *celeriac *
kale * leeks * marrows * mushrooms * parsnips * plums
*potatoes * sweet potatoes * apples * blackberries *
chestnuts * cobnuts * pears * plums * quinces * sloes *
mint * rosemary * sage

DATES TO LOOK FORWARD TO THIS MONTH

Sukkot
Diwali
Hallowe'en

The natural world is closing down for the winter's rest. Leaves are turning and starting to fall, days are shortening and this is the month we really feel we are moving into winter, especially as the clocks change at the end of the month.

The kitchen reflects the shifting of the seasons with the autumnal colours of orange pumpkins, butternut squash and sweet potatoes alongside purple blackberries, plums and sloes.

Sweet potatoes are lovely now, enjoyed simply baked and topped with melting butter, salt and pepper or in the **Sausage & Sweet Potato Hash** on page 316. And make the most of the last of the summer vegetables, including any tomatoes that didn't get a chance to ripen, with the **Autumn Harvest Chutney** on page 324.

Use up the flesh from carving Hallowe'en pumpkins in the **Pumpkin, Beetroot & Goats' Cheese Bake** on page 344. And for all your foraged sloes, see the recipe on page 345 for **Spiced Sloe Gin**.

This month, we celebrate Diwali, the Festival of Lights, with **Gulab Jamun** (page 334), delicious fried dumplings steeped in a fragrant rosewater syrup. And for Sukkot celebrations this month, there's a **Hot Blackberry & Apple Trifle** (page 319) – a good choice for reflecting this harvest festival.

v

• BREAKFASTS •

Mixed Mushrooms on Toast

SERVES 4 • PREP & COOKING TIME 15 minutes

- 25 g (1 oz) butter
- 3 tablespoons extra virgin olive oil, plus extra to serve
- 750 g (1½ lb) mixed mushrooms, such as oyster, shiitake, flat and button, trimmed and sliced
- 2 garlic cloves, crushed
- 1 tablespoon chopped thyme
- grated zest and juice of 1 lemon
- 2 tablespoons chopped parsley
- 4 slices of sourdough bread
- 100 g (3½ oz) mixed salad leaves
- salt and black pepper
- fresh Parmesan or vegetarian hard cheese shavings, to serve*

Full-flavoured with a garlicky punch and a lift of lemon zest, this is a quick and easy brunch or lunch dish. Use whatever mushrooms you like but aim for a good mix for maximum taste.

- Melt the butter with the oil in a large frying pan. As soon as the butter stops foaming, add the mushrooms, garlic, thyme, lemon zest and salt and pepper and cook over a medium heat, stirring, for 4–5 minutes until tender. Scatter over the parsley and squeeze over a little lemon juice.

- Meanwhile, toast the bread, then arrange it on serving plates.

- Top the sourdough toast with an equal quantity of the salad leaves and mushrooms, and drizzle over a little more oil and lemon juice. Scatter with Parmesan shavings and serve immediately.

*For guidance on vegetarian cheeses, see page 5.

V

· LIGHT BITES ·

Leeks Milanese

SERVES 4 • PREP & COOKING TIME 35 minutes

- 6 tablespoons olive oil
- 100 g (3½ oz) ciabatta or rustic white bread, torn into pieces
- 1 garlic clove, finely chopped
- 12 baby leeks
- 2 eggs, hard-boiled and roughly chopped
- 1 tablespoon red wine vinegar
- 1 teaspoon Dijon mustard
- 1 tablespoon capers
- 3 tablespoons roughly chopped flat-leaf parsley
- salt and black pepper

Simple ingredients but complex flavours abound in this unusual salad, which is a spin on the classic dish, leeks mimosa. Full of freshness, it's a lovely lunch when you want something not too heavy. It also works well as a dinner-party first course.

- Heat 2 tablespoons of the oil in a frying pan, add the bread and garlic and fry until crisp and golden. Transfer to a plate and allow to cool.

- Cut the leeks into 2 or 3 slices, depending on their length, then steam them over a pan of boiling water for 3–4 minutes until just tender. Arrange the leeks in a salad bowl and sprinkle the chopped eggs over the top.

- Beat the remaining oil with the vinegar, mustard and seasoning. Drizzle over the leeks and add the capers and parsley.

- Toss the salad gently and sprinkle with the croutons. Spoon on to serving plates and serve immediately.

· MAINS ·

Sausage & Sweet Potato Hash

SERVES 4 • PREP & COOKING TIME 1 hour

- 3 tablespoons olive oil
- 8 pork sausages
- 3 large red onions, thinly sliced
- 1 teaspoon caster sugar
- 500 g (1 lb) sweet potatoes, scrubbed and cut into small chunks
- 8 sage leaves
- 2 tablespoons balsamic vinegar
- salt and black pepper

Full of fibre and rich in vitamin A and beta-carotene, the sweet potatoes in this one-pot dish offer a great health boost. Serve with steamed spinach or green beans or a tangle of sharp watercress.

- Heat the oil in a large frying pan or flameproof casserole and fry the sausages, turning frequently, for about 10 minutes, until browned. Drain to a plate.

- Add the onions and sugar to the pan and cook gently, stirring frequently, until lightly browned. Return the sausages to the pan with the sweet potatoes, sage leaves and a little seasoning.

- Cover the pan with a lid or foil and cook over a very gentle heat for about 25 minutes until the potatoes are tender.

- Drizzle with the vinegar and check the seasoning before serving.

v

• DESSERTS •

Peanut Butter Swirl Brownies

MAKES 12–16 • PREP & COOKING TIME 30 minutes

- 175 g (6 oz) unsalted butter
- 200 g (7 oz) plain dark chocolate, broken into small pieces
- 75 g (3 oz) crunchy peanut butter
- 125 g (4 oz) smooth peanut butter
- 3 large eggs
- 175 g (6 oz) caster sugar
- ¼ teaspoon salt
- 50 g (2 oz) self-raising flour

Combine two favourite ingredients – peanut butter and chocolate – to create these irresistible brownies. Leave them to cool fully in the tin, or even overnight in the fridge, for that perfect fudgy consistency.

- Place the butter, chocolate and crunchy peanut butter in a small saucepan over a low heat and warm until just melted. In a separate saucepan, gently warm through the smooth peanut butter.

- Meanwhile, place the eggs, sugar and salt in a large bowl and whisk until combined. Using a rubber spatula, stir in the melted chocolate mixture and flour.

- Scrape the mixture into a greased and lined 30 × 20 cm (12 × 8 inch) brownie tin. Drizzle over the smooth peanut butter in 3–4 straight lines, then 'drag' through the peanut butter with the tip of a sharp knife to create a marbled effect.

- Bake in a preheated oven, 200°C (400°F), Gas Mark 6, for 18–20 minutes until just firm to the touch, but with a slightly fudgy texture.

- Leave to cool in the tin for 1–2 minutes, then lift on to a board using the lining paper and cut into 12–16 squares.

V

· BREAKFASTS ·

Honey-Roasted Granola

SERVES 4 • PREP & COOKING TIME 40 minutes, plus cooling

- 5 tablespoons honey
- 2 tablespoons sunflower oil
- 250 g (8 oz) rolled oats
- 50 g (2 oz) hazelnuts, roughly chopped
- 50 g (2 oz) blanched almonds, roughly chopped
- 50 g (2 oz) dried cranberries
- 50 g (2 oz) dried blueberries

Packed with vitamin-rich dried berries and nuts, this homemade granola just needs your milk of choice and perhaps some fresh fruit. It keeps well in an airtight container.

- Heat the honey and oil together gently in a small saucepan.

- Mix the oats and nuts together thoroughly in a large bowl. Pour over the warm honey mixture and stir well to combine.

- Spread the mixture over a large nonstick baking sheet and bake in a preheated oven, 150°C (300°F), Gas Mark 2, for 20–25 minutes, stirring once, until golden.

- Leave the granola to cool, then stir in the dried berries.

V

• DESSERTS •

Hot Blackberry & Apple Trifle

SERVES 4 • PREP & COOKING TIME 45 minutes, plus cooling

- 150 g (5 oz) fresh or frozen blackberries
- 2 dessert apples, cored, unpeeled and sliced
- 1 tablespoon water
- 50 g (2 oz) caster sugar
- 4 trifle sponges
- 3 tablespoons dry or sweet sherry
- 425 g (14 oz) can or carton custard

FOR THE MERINGUE
- 3 egg whites
- 75 g (3 oz) caster sugar

A harvest-inspired spin on a conventional trifle for Sukkot, the Jewish Festival of Tabernacles, is very versatile: you can enjoy it hot in winter and it's also lovely cold in summer. For an alcohol-free version, replace the sherry with 3 tablespoons of orange juice.

- Put the blackberries, apples, measured water and sugar in a saucepan, then cover and simmer for 5 minutes or until the fruit has softened. Leave the mixture to cool slightly.

- Break the trifle sponges into chunks and arrange in an even layer in the base of a 1.2 litre (2 pint) ovenproof pie or soufflé dish and drizzle with the sherry. Spoon the poached fruit and syrup over the top, then cover with custard.

- Whisk the egg whites in a large, dry bowl until stiffly peaking, then gradually whisk in the sugar, a teaspoonful at a time, until the meringue is stiff and glossy. Spoon over the custard and swirl the top with the back of a spoon.

- Bake in a preheated oven, 180°C (350°F), Gas Mark 4, for 15–20 minutes until heated through and the meringue is golden. Serve immediately if eating the trifle hot.

V

• LIGHT BITES •

Gingered Cauliflower Soup

SERVES 6 • PREP & COOKING TIME 45 minutes

- 1 tablespoon sunflower oil
- 25 g (1 oz) butter
- 1 onion, roughly chopped
- 1 cauliflower, cut into florets, woody core discarded, about 500 g (1 lb) when prepared
- 3.5 cm (1½ inch) piece of fresh root ginger, peeled and finely chopped
- 900 ml (1½ pints) vegetable or chicken stock
- 300 ml (½ pint) milk
- 150 ml (¼ pint) double cream
- salt and pepper

FOR THE SOY-GLAZED SEEDS
- 1 tablespoon sunflower oil
- 2 tablespoons sesame seeds
- 2 tablespoons sunflower seeds
- 2 tablespoons pumpkin seeds
- 1 tablespoon soy sauce

The crunchy seeds glazed with salty soy sauce really make this soup into something worthy of a special occasion. It's unlikely – they are so delicious! – but if there are any left over, they're also great sprinkled over salad.

- Heat the oil and butter in a saucepan, add the onion and fry for 5 minutes until softened but not coloured. Stir in the cauliflower florets and ginger, then the stock. Season with salt and pepper and bring to the boil. Cover and simmer for 15 minutes until the cauliflower is just tender.

- Meanwhile, make the glazed seeds by heating the oil in a frying pan, adding the seeds and cooking for 2–3 minutes, stirring until lightly browned. Add the soy sauce, then quickly cover the pan with a lid until the seeds have stopped popping. Set aside until ready to serve.

- Purée the cooked soup in batches in a blender or food processor, then pour back into the saucepan and stir in the milk and half the cream. Bring just to the boil, then taste and adjust the seasoning if needed.

- Ladle the soup into shallow bowls, drizzle over the rest of the cream and sprinkle with some of the glazed seeds, serving the remaining seeds in a small bowl for further sprinkling.

V

• MAINS •

Wild Mushroom Lasagne

SERVES 6 • PREP & COOKING TIME 1 hour, plus cooling

- 100 g (3½ oz) unsalted butter, plus extra for greasing
- 4 tablespoons plain flour
- 1 litre (1¾ pints) milk
- large pinch of freshly grated nutmeg
- 3 tablespoons roughly chopped flat-leaf parsley
- 5 tablespoons Parmesan or vegetarian hard cheese, grated
- 1 tablespoon olive oil
- 625 g (1¼ lb) mixed wild mushrooms, trimmed and thickly sliced
- 1 garlic clove, crushed
- 100 ml (3½ fl oz) dry white wine
- 25 g (1 oz) dried porcini mushrooms, soaked in 100 ml (3½ fl oz) hot water for 10 minutes
- 300 g (10 oz) fresh lasagne sheets
- truffle oil, for drizzling
- salt and black pepper

A feast for meat-eaters and vegetarians alike, this lasagne gets the gourmet treatment thanks to the wonderfully intense aroma of the dried porcini mushrooms and the truffle oil. The pepperiness of a simply dressed rocket salad would be a good counterbalance to the rich mushrooms.

- Melt half the butter in a saucepan over a low heat. Add the flour and cook, stirring with a wooden spoon, for 1–2 minutes until a pale biscuity colour. Remove from the heat and gradually stir in the milk until smooth. Return to a medium heat and cook, stirring constantly, until thick and velvety. Add the nutmeg and season with salt and pepper, then stir in the parsley and 2 tablespoons of the cheese. Remove from the heat and leave to cool to room temperature.

- Melt the remaining butter with the oil in a large, heavy-based frying pan. Add the fresh mushrooms and cook over a high heat for 2 minutes. Stir in the garlic and cook for 1 minute. Season with salt and pepper. Pour in the wine and porcini and their soaking water. Cook, stirring, until the liquid has evaporated. Stir into the white sauce.

- Grease an ovenproof dish, about 19 × 30 cm (8 × 12 inches). Cover the base with a layer of slightly overlapping lasagne sheets. Top with a quarter of the sauce, then continue layering, finishing with a layer of sauce. Scatter with the remaining cheese. Bake in a preheated oven, 200°C (400°F), Gas Mark 6, for 30 minutes. Drizzle lightly with truffle oil.

V

· DESSERTS ·

Old-Fashioned Coffee Cake

SERVES 8 • PREP & COOKING TIME 50 minutes

- 175 g (6 oz) butter, softened
- 175 g (6 oz) light muscovado or caster sugar
- 175 g (6 oz) self-raising flour
- 1 teaspoon baking powder
- 3 eggs
- 3 teaspoons instant coffee, dissolved in 2 teaspoons boiling water

FOR THE FROSTING
- 75 g (3 oz) butter, softened
- 150 g (5 oz) icing sugar, sifted
- 3 teaspoons instant coffee, dissolved in 2 teaspoons boiling water
- 50 g (2 oz) dark chocolate, melted

Baking doesn't get much easier than this: simply add all the ingredients at once, mix and bake for a perfectly moist and moreish coffee cake. It can be stored in an airtight container for 2–3 days in a cool place.

- Beat all of the cake ingredients in a mixing bowl or a food processor until smooth.

- Divide the mixture evenly between 2 × 18 cm (7 inch) sandwich tins, greased and base-lined with oiled greaseproof paper, and spread the surfaces level.

- Bake in a preheated oven, 180°C (350°F), Gas Mark 4, for 20 minutes until well risen, the cakes are browned and spring back when gently pressed with a fingertip.

- Leave the cakes for a few minutes then loosen the edges, turn out on to a wire rack and peel off the lining paper. Leave to cool.

- Make the frosting. Put the butter and half the icing sugar in a mixing bowl, add the dissolved coffee and beat until smooth. Gradually mix in the remaining icing sugar until creamy.

- Put one of the cakes on a serving plate, spread with half the frosting then cover with the second cake. Spread the remaining frosting over the top. Pipe or drizzle swirls of melted chocolate on top.

• BREAKFASTS •

Poached Egg & Bacon Muffins

SERVES 4 • PREP & COOKING TIME 25 minutes

- 4 ripe tomatoes, thickly sliced
- 2 tablespoons chopped basil
- 2 tablespoons olive oil
- 8 back or streaky bacon rashers
- 4 large eggs
- 1 tablespoon vinegar
- 4 split and toasted English muffins, buttered
- salt and black pepper

A hot, buttery English muffin is a great vehicle for crispy bacon and a perfectly poached egg. All you need to add is a splodge of your favourite sauce and a steaming mug of tea.

- Lay the tomato slices in a grill pan. Mix together the basil and oil in a bowl, then drizzle over the tomatoes. Season with lots of salt and pepper. Cook under a preheated medium grill for 3–4 minutes until starting to soften. Arrange the bacon rashers on top of the tomatoes and grill for 6–8 minutes, turning once.

- Poach the eggs, by breaking 1 of the eggs into a ramekin or cup, making sure not to break the yolk. Bring a large saucepan of water to the boil. Add the vinegar to the boiling water, then stir the water rapidly in a circular motion to make a whirlpool.

- Carefully slide the egg into the centre of the pan while the water is still swirling, holding the ramekin or cup as close to the water as you can. Repeat with the other eggs and cook for 3 minutes. Lift the poached eggs out with a slotted spoon.

- Put the hot buttered muffins on serving plates. Top each muffin half with grilled tomatoes and 2 rashers of bacon, then put a poached egg on top. Serve immediately.

VG

• LIGHT BITES •

Autumn Harvest Chutney

MAKES 6 jars • PREP & COOKING TIME 2 hours

- 1 kg (2 lb) mixed green and red tomatoes, roughly chopped
- 500 g (1 lb) red plums, stoned and roughly chopped
- 1 marrow (about 750 g/ 1½ lb), peeled, halved, deseeded and diced
- 500 g (1 lb) onions, roughly chopped
- 100 g (3½ oz) sultanas or raisins
- 300 ml (½ pint) distilled malt vinegar
- 250 g (8 oz) granulated sugar
- 1 tablespoon tomato purée
- 2 teaspoons hot paprika
- 2 teaspoons English mustard powder
- 1 teaspoon salt
- 2 teaspoons peppercorns, roughly crushed

This is the chutney to make with the last of summer's bounty to brighten up winter meals. It adds a whack of welcome flavour to everything from sandwiches and cheese boards to baked potatoes and sausages.

- Add all the ingredients to a large, heavy-based pan, stir to combine, then cook, uncovered, over a gentle heat for 1½ hours, stirring from time to time, but more frequently towards the end of cooking as the chutney thickens.

- Ladle into sterilized, warm, dry jars, filling to the very top and pressing down well. Disperse any air pockets with a skewer or small knife and cover with screw-top lids. Label and leave to mature in a cool, dark place for at least 3 weeks.

• MAINS •

Chicken, Bacon & Sage Meatballs

SERVES 4 • PREP & COOKING TIME 50 minutes, plus chilling

- 125 g (4 oz) cup mushrooms, finely chopped
- 2 rashers smoked streaky bacon, chopped
- 500 g (1 lb) minced chicken
- 2 tablespoons fresh sage, finely chopped
- 1 egg yolk
- 2 tablespoons sunflower oil
- 2 onions, thinly sliced
- 2 teaspoons caster sugar
- 2 tablespoons plain flour
- 450 ml (¾ pint) chicken stock
- salt and black pepper

These chicken meatballs in a rich, thick gravy are wonderful served with mashed potatoes, peas and green beans. Everyone begging for second helpings is guaranteed!

- Mix the mushrooms and bacon with the chicken, then stir in the sage, egg yolk and seasoning. Shape into 20 small meatballs and chill for 30 minutes.

- Fry the meatballs in 1 tablespoon of the oil for 5 minutes until lightly browned all over, then transfer to a roasting tin and cook in a preheated oven, 190°C (375°F), Gas Mark 5, for 15 minutes.

- Meanwhile, fry the onions in the remaining oil in the cleaned frying pan until softened and just beginning to brown. Sprinkle over the sugar and cook for 5 minutes more, stirring frequently until a deep brown.

- Mix in the flour, then gradually mix in the stock, season and bring to the boil. Simmer for 2–3 minutes until thickened. Add the meatballs to the gravy and gently stir. Spoon into serving bowls and serve.

V

• DESSERTS •

Upside-Down Pineapple Cake

SERVES 8 • PREP & COOKING TIME 1 hour 30 minutes

- 1 small ripe pineapple
- 3 pieces of stem ginger in syrup, chopped
- 125 g (4 oz) polenta
- 1 teaspoon baking powder
- 125 g (4 oz) ground almonds
- 175 g (6 oz) slightly salted butter, softened
- 175 g (6 oz) caster sugar
- finely grated zest of 3 limes
- 2 eggs, beaten

FOR THE SYRUP
- 50 g (2 oz) caster sugar
- 3 tablespoons water
- juice of 3 limes
- 3 tablespoons stem ginger syrup

Serve this delectable cake warm with a scoop of vanilla ice cream or a drizzle of thick cream for dessert, or cold with a mug of tea or coffee. Be sure to buy a really ripe pineapple for maximum flavour.

- Cut away the skin from the pineapple and cut the flesh into 1 cm (½ inch) slices. Chop into small pieces, discarding the core.

- Mix together the pineapple and chopped ginger, then scatter in a greased and base-lined 20 cm (8 inch) round cake tin at least 4.5 cm (1¾ inches) deep.

- Mix together the polenta, baking powder and ground almonds in a bowl. Beat together the butter, sugar and lime zest in a bowl until pale and creamy. Gradually beat in the eggs. Add the dry ingredients and mix well.

- Spoon the mixture into the tin and level the surface. Bake in a preheated oven, 180°C (350°F), Gas Mark 4, for about 35 minutes or until risen, just firm to the touch and a skewer inserted into the centre comes out clean.

- Meanwhile, make the syrup. Put the sugar and measured water in a small saucepan and heat gently until the sugar dissolves. Bring to the boil and boil for about 3 minutes or until thickened. Remove from the heat and stir in the lime juice and ginger syrup.

- Loosen the edge of the cake and invert on to a serving plate, peeling off the lining paper. Spoon the syrup over the top.

• BREAKFASTS •

Piperade with Pastrami

SERVES 6 • PREP & COOKING TIME 45 minutes

- 6 large eggs
- thyme sprigs, leaves removed, or large pinch of dried thyme, plus extra sprigs to garnish
- 1 tablespoon olive oil
- 125 g (4 oz) pastrami, thinly sliced
- salt and black pepper

FOR THE SOFRITO
- 375 g (12 oz), or 3 small, different coloured peppers
- 1 tablespoon olive oil
- 1 onion, finely chopped
- 2 garlic cloves, crushed
- 500 g (1 lb) tomatoes, skinned, deseeded and chopped
- pinch of piment d'Esplette

This Basque dish uses piment d'Esplette – a type of chilli grown in the Esplette commune in southwest France – to add distinctive flavour. If you can't find piment d'Esplette, smoked or sweet paprika is a good substitute.

- Make the sofrito. Grill or cook the peppers directly in a gas flame for about 10 minutes, turning them until the skins have blistered and blackened. Rub the skins from the flesh and discard. Halve and deseed and cut the flesh into strips.

- Heat the oil in a large frying pan, add the onion and cook gently for 10 minutes until softened and transparent. Add the garlic, tomatoes, peppers and piment d'Esplette and simmer for 5 minutes until any juice has evaporated from the tomatoes. Set aside until ready to serve.

- Beat the eggs with the thyme and salt and pepper in a bowl. Reheat the sofrito. Heat the oil in a saucepan, add the eggs, stirring until they are lightly scrambled. Stir into the reheated sofrito and spoon on to serving plates.

- Arrange slices of pastrami around the eggs and serve immediately, garnished with a little extra thyme.

VG

• LIGHT BITES •

Butternut Squash & Rosemary Soup

SERVES 4 • PREP & COOKING TIME 1 hour 30 minutes

- 1 large butternut squash
- 2 tablespoons olive oil
- a few rosemary sprigs, plus extra to garnish
- 150 g (5 oz) red lentils, washed
- 1 onion, finely chopped
- 900 ml (1½ pints) vegetable stock
- salt and black pepper

Thick, nourishing, tasty, filling, comforting. This is everything soup should be so make a big batch and freeze some for another time.

- Cut the squash in half and scoop out the seeds and fibrous flesh. Peel and cut the squash into small chunks and place in a roasting tin. Sprinkle over the oil and rosemary, and season well with salt and pepper. Roast in a preheated oven, 200°C (400°F), Gas Mark 6, for 45 minutes.

- Meanwhile, place the lentils in a saucepan, cover with water, bring to the boil and boil rapidly for 10 minutes. Strain, then return the lentils to the saucepan with the onion and stock and simmer for 5 minutes. Season to taste.

- Remove the squash from the oven, mash the flesh with a fork and add to the soup. Simmer for 20 minutes, then ladle into serving bowls and garnish with rosemary sprigs.

· MAINS ·

Creamy Spiced Lobster Tail

SERVES 4 • PREP & COOKING TIME 20 minutes

- 2 egg yolks, beaten
- 100 ml (3½ fl oz) double cream
- 30 g (1 oz) butter
- 2 tablespoons dry sherry
- ½ teaspoon salt
- 1 tablespoon medium curry powder
- 4 tablespoons finely chopped coriander leaves, plus extra leaves to garnish
- 450 g (14½ oz) cooked lobster tail meat, cut into bite-sized pieces
- lemon wedges, to serve

When time is short but you deserve a little luxury, this is the recipe to turn to. It features tender chunks of lobster stirred through a heavenly creamy, spicy, sherry-laced sauce and – best of all – it will be on the table in 20 minutes. Serve with steamed rice.

- Whisk together the egg yolks and double cream in a small bowl until well blended. Melt the butter in a saucepan over a low heat, then stir in the egg mixture and sherry. Cook, stirring, for about 10–12 minutes or until the mixture thickens, but do not allow to boil.

- Remove from the heat, then stir in the salt, curry powder and coriander. Stir in the lobster, then return the pan to a low heat and cook gently until heated through.

- Spoon into serving bowls, scatter with coriander leaves and serve with lemon wedges to squeeze over.

· DESSERTS ·

Cidered Apple Jellies

SERVES 6 • PREP & COOKING TIME 40 minutes, plus chilling

- 1 kg (2 lb) cooking apples, peeled, cored and sliced
- 300 ml (½ pint) cider
- 150 ml (¼ pint) water, plus 4 tablespoons
- 75 g (3 oz) caster sugar
- finely grated zest of 2 lemons
- 4 teaspoons powdered gelatine
- 150 ml (¼ pint) double cream

Your inner child will love these boozy jellies, served daintily in tea cups or small glasses, and they're a great make-ahead dessert option when entertaining. They're also lovely served with buttery shortbread to provide a contrasting crunch.

- Put the apples, cider, 150 ml (¼ pint) of water, sugar and the zest of one of the lemons into a saucepan. Cover and simmer for 15 minutes until the apples are soft.

- Meanwhile put the 4 tablespoons of water into a small bowl and sprinkle over the gelatine, making sure that all the powder is absorbed by the water. Set aside.

- Add the gelatine to the hot apples and stir until completely dissolved. Purée the apple mixture in a blender or food processor until smooth, then pour into 6 tea cups or small glasses. Allow to cool then chill for 4–5 hours until fully set.

- When ready to serve, whip the cream until it forms soft peaks. Spoon over the jellies and sprinkle with the remaining lemon zest.

• BREAKFASTS •

Brunch Bacon & Leek Tortilla

SERVES 4–6 • PREP & COOKING TIME 40 minutes

- 4 tablespoons olive oil
- 2 leeks, trimmed and thickly sliced
- 350 g (11½ oz) new potatoes, sliced
- 4 back bacon rashers, chopped
- 6 large eggs
- 75 g (3 oz) mature Cheddar cheese, grated
- salt and black pepper

Sweet leeks, tender potatoes and crispy bacon combine for a wonderful one-pan brunch. It's also delicious served cold.

- Heat the oil in a large flameproof frying pan, add the leeks and potatoes and sauté, stirring frequently, for 8–10 minutes until golden and tender. Add the bacon and fry for a further 5 minutes.

- Meanwhile, beat the eggs in a large bowl and add the cheese. Season well.

- Stir the potato mixture into the beaten eggs, then return to the pan and cook over a low heat for 8–10 minutes, making sure the bottom does not overcook.

- Place the pan under a preheated hot grill and cook for a further 3–4 minutes until the tortilla is cooked through and golden.

- Serve cut into wedges.

V

· LIGHT BITES ·

Brie & Thyme Melts

SERVES 4 · PREP & COOKING TIME 10 minutes

- 1 ciabatta-style loaf, cut in half horizontally
- 6 tablespoons onion or caramelized onion chutney
- 200 g (7 oz) Brie or Camembert cheese, sliced*
- 1 teaspoon dried thyme
- 4 teaspoons chilli, garlic or basil oil

Take cheese on toast to a whole new level with these deliciously cheesy melts. Serve them with a tomato salad or green salad for a more substantial meal.

- Cut the 2 pieces of bread in half to give 4 portions. Arrange, cut-side up, on a baking sheet and spread each piece with the onion chutney.

- Lay the Brie slices on top and sprinkle with the thyme. Drizzle with the flavoured oil and cook under a preheated grill for 3–4 minutes, until the cheese begins to melt.

- Serve immediately.

*For guidance on vegetarian cheeses, see page 5.

• MAINS •

Lamb Ragu with Toasted Walnuts

SERVES 4 • PREP & COOKING TIME 2 hours

- 1 tablespoon olive oil
- 500 g (1 lb) diced lamb
- 1 onion, chopped
- 2 garlic cloves, finely chopped
- 50 g (2 oz) walnut pieces, plus extra to garnish
- 1 tablespoon plain flour
- 450 ml (¾ pint) lamb stock
- 200 ml (7 fl oz) red wine
- 2 tablespoons tomato purée
- 1 bouquet garni
- 250 g (8 oz) rigatoni or penne
- handful of chopped flat-leaf parsley
- salt and black pepper

Here slow-cooked, rich ragu is piled on top of pasta. Serve with a salad of rocket, watercress and spinach dressed with lemon juice and sprinkled with Parmesan shavings, if you like.

- Heat the oil in a flameproof casserole, add the lamb a few pieces at a time, then add the onion. Fry for about 5 minutes, stirring until browned all over.

- Add the garlic and walnuts and fry for a couple of minutes more until the nuts are lightly toasted. Stir in the flour then add the stock, wine, tomato purée, bouquet garni and a little seasoning. Bring to the boil, stirring occasionally.

- Cover and cook in a preheated oven, 160°C (325°F), Gas Mark 3, for 1½ hours or until the lamb is tender.

- Meanwhile, cook the pasta in a large saucepan of boiling water according to the packet instructions until al dente.

- Drain the pasta then toss with the lamb and sprinkle with chopped parsley and a few extra walnuts. Spoon into shallow bowls and serve.

V

• DESSERTS •

Gulab Jamun

SERVES 6–8 • PREP & COOKING TIME 1 hour, plus soaking

- 100 g (3½ oz) full-cream milk powder
- 40 g (1½ oz) plain flour
- 1 teaspoon caster sugar
- ½ teaspoon baking powder
- 50 g (1¾ oz) ghee or softened unsalted butter
- 1 tablespoon natural yogurt
- squeeze of lemon juice
- 4–5 tablespoons milk
- sunflower oil, for deep-frying
- 1 tablespoon chopped pistachios, to serve

FOR THE SYRUP
- 5 cardamom pods, lightly crushed
- 500 g (1 lb 2 oz) caster sugar
- 500 ml (18 fl oz) water
- 1 teaspoon rosewater
- 2 cloves
- small pinch of saffron threads, soaked in 2 tablespoons of warm water

Celebrate Diwali with these doughnut-like dumplings soaked in a rose- and cardamom-scented syrup. Serve them just as they are or with vanilla ice cream.

- To make the syrup, gently heat the cardamom pods, caster sugar and measured water in a large saucepan. Simmer for 5 minutes, then remove from the heat and allow to cool slightly.

- Add the rosewater, cloves, saffron and its soaking liquid, stir and keep warm.

- Sieve the milk powder, flour, caster sugar and baking powder into a large mixing bowl. Rub in the ghee or butter with your fingertips until the mixture resembles coarse crumbs.

- Add the yogurt, lemon juice and enough milk to form a soft dough, taking care not to overwork the mixture as this will make the balls dense.

- Oil your hands with a little sunflower oil and shape small portions of the dough into walnut-sized balls. Make sure the balls are smooth and have no cracks.

- Pour the oil in to a large, heavy-based saucepan to the depth of 5 cm (2 inches) and heat to 140°C (275°F) or until a small piece of dough dropped in turns golden in 40 seconds. Fry the balls in batches, moving them around with a slotted spoon, for about 5 minutes or until they are golden brown all over. Remove from the saucepan using a slotted spoon, drain well on kitchen paper and allow to cool.

- Add them to the warm syrup, cover and leave them to soak for 3 hours or preferably overnight. They will expand as they soak up the syrup. When ready to eat, gently reheat the balls and their syrup. Serve hot with the syrup generously spooned over and scattered with the pistachios.

v

• BREAKFASTS •

Breakfast Smoothie

SERVES 2 • PREP TIME 10 minutes

- 1 tablespoon pomegranate juice
- 1 banana, chopped
- 300 ml (½ pint) soya milk
- 1 tablespoon almonds
- ½ teaspoon honey
- ½ tablespoon ground linseeds
- 2 tablespoons natural yogurt

You can whizz up this smoothie in no time. It's a super-healthy blend of oats, almonds, linseeds, yogurt and fruit. An excellent way to begin your day.

- Place all the ingredients in a blender and blend until smooth and creamy.

- Pour into 2 glasses and serve immediately.

V

• LIGHT BITES •

Chicory, Walnut & Blue Cheese Salad

SERVES 4 • PREP & COOKING TIME 20 minutes

- 50 g (2 oz) walnut halves
- 2 tablespoons icing sugar
- 2 chicory heads
- 50 g (2 oz) rocket
- 1 radicchio, separated into leaves
- 125 g (4 oz) blue cheese, such as Roquefort*

FOR THE DRESSING
- 1 teaspoon Dijon mustard
- 2 tablespoons cider vinegar
- 4 tablespoons olive oil

Bitter leaves are such a brilliant foil for the rich blue cheese and crunchy walnuts in this recipe. You could skip candying the walnuts but the sweetened flavour adds an extra dimension to a classic salad.

- Put the walnuts in a plastic bag with the icing sugar and 1 tablespoon water and shake them until coated. Arrange the nuts on a baking sheet and roast in a preheated oven, 180°C (350°F), Gas Mark 4, for 5 minutes or until gold and crusted.

- Separate the chicory leaves and put them into a large salad bowl with the rocket and radicchio. Crumble over the cheese and add the walnuts. Toss carefully.

- Make the dressing by whisking together the mustard, vinegar and oil. Drizzle the dressing over the salad, mix lightly and serve.

*For guidance on vegetarian cheeses, see page 5.

• MAINS •

Sea Bass & Spicy Potatoes

SERVES 2 • PREP & COOKING TIME 1 hour 15 minutes

- 500 g (1 lb) baking potatoes
- 3 tablespoons olive oil
- 2 tablespoons sun-dried tomato tapenade
- ½ teaspoon mild chilli powder
- 2 small whole sea bass, scaled and gutted
- 2 tablespoons mixed chopped herbs, e.g. thyme, parsley, chervil, tarragon
- 1 garlic clove, crushed
- 2 bay leaves
- ½ lemon, sliced
- handful of pitted black olives
- salt and black pepper

A restaurant-quality meal for two that looks impressive but isn't hard to do. To test if the fish is cooked, pierce the thick end of the fish with a knife; the flesh should be cooked through to the bone.

- Cut the potatoes into 1 cm (½ inch) thick slices – you can peel them first if you wish to, but this isn't necessary. Cut into chunky chips. Mix 2 tablespoons of the oil with the tapenade, chilli powder and plenty of salt. Toss in a bowl with the potatoes until evenly coated.

- Tip the potatoes into a shallow ovenproof dish or roasting pan and bake in a preheated oven, 200°C (400°F), Gas Mark 6, for 30 minutes until pale golden, turning the potatoes once or twice during cooking.

- Meanwhile, score the fish several times on each side. Mix the remaining oil with 1 tablespoon of the herbs, the garlic and a little salt and pepper. Pack the bay leaves, lemon slices and remaining herbs into the fish cavities and lay the fish over the potatoes in the dish, pushing the potatoes to the edges of the dish.

- Brush the garlic and herb oil over the fish and scatter the olives over the potatoes.

- Return to the oven for a further 30 minutes until the fish is cooked through.

v

· DESSERTS ·

Pine Nut & Honey Tart

SERVES 8–10 • PREP & COOKING TIME 1 hour 20 minutes

- 400 g (13 oz) chilled ready-made sweet shortcrust pastry
- 100 g (3½ oz) unsalted butter
- 100g (3½ oz) caster sugar
- 3 eggs
- 175 g (6 oz) flower honey, warmed
- grated zest and juice of 1 lemon
- 200 g (7 oz) pine nuts

This unusual tart is a delicately balanced combination of sweet and nutty. Serve with ice cream, cream or a blob of crème fraîche and drizzled with a little extra honey for a cheffy flourish.

- Roll out the pastry thinly on a lightly floured surface and line a 23 cm (9 inch) loose-bottomed baking tin. Prick the base, line with nonstick baking paper, add baking beans and bake blind in a preheated oven, 190°C (375°F), Gas Mark 5, for 15 minutes. Remove the paper and beans and bake for 5 minutes more. Reduce the oven temperature to 180°C (350°F), Gas Mark 4.

- Cream together the butter with the caster sugar. Beat in the eggs, one at a time, then mix in the warmed honey, the lemon zest and juice and the pine nuts. Pour into the tart case and bake for about 40 minutes until browned and set.

- Let the tart cool for 10 minutes before serving.

• LIGHT BITES •

Lamb Pasties

MAKES 6 • PREP & COOKING TIME 50 minutes, plus chilling

- 375 g (12 oz) plain flour, plus extra for dusting
- ½ teaspoon salt
- 175 g (6 oz) butter, cubed
- 2–3 tablespoons cold water
- 1 tablespoon vegetable oil
- ½ small onion, chopped
- 175 g (6 oz) lean lamb, finely sliced
- 1 small potato or 2 baby new potatoes, peeled and diced
- 300 ml (½ pint) hot lamb stock
- 1 teaspoon Dijon mustard, optional
- 2 tablespoons finely chopped mint
- beaten egg, for brushing

These golden beauties are a great all-in-one option for lunch on the run but also perfect as a main meal served with steamed green veg and redcurrant jelly.

- Sift the flour and salt into a large mixing bowl and add the butter. Rub the butter into the flour until the mixture resembles fine breadcrumbs. Add the measured water and mix to form a rough dough. Turn on to a lightly floured work surface and knead until smooth. Place in a food bag and refrigerate for 30 minutes.

- Meanwhile, heat the oil in a frying pan and cook the onion and lamb over a moderate heat for 5 minutes, stirring occasionally, until beginning to brown. Add the potato, reduce the heat and cook for a further 2 minutes, stirring occasionally until beginning to brown.

- Mix the lamb stock with the mustard and pour into the pan. Cover with a tight-fitting lid and simmer gently for 15 minutes, stirring occasionally until the potatoes are soft yet still retaining their shape, and the meat is tender. Stir in the mint and set aside to cool.

- Roll out the pastry to 5 mm (¼ inch) thick, and using a 15 cm (6 inch) saucer as a template, cut out 6 rounds.

- Lightly brush the edges of the circles with a little water and place 2 tablespoons of the mixture in the centre of each. Fold up to enclose the filling and pinch and gently twist the edges to seal.

- Place on a baking sheet and lightly glaze each one with the beaten egg. Bake in a preheated oven, 200°C (400°F), Gas Mark 6, for 20–25 minutes until the pastry is golden and crisp. Wrap loosely in foil to keep warm.

· MAINS ·

Caribbean Lamb Stoba

SERVES 4 • PREP & COOKING TIME 2 hours

- 2 tablespoons sunflower oil
- 750 g (1½ lb) boneless leg of lamb, cut into bite-sized cubes
- 2 onions, finely chopped
- 2 teaspoons peeled and finely grated fresh root ginger
- 1 Scotch bonnet chilli, thinly sliced
- 1 red pepper, deseeded and roughly chopped
- 2 teaspoons ground allspice
- 3 teaspoons ground cumin
- 1 cinnamon stick
- pinch of grated nutmeg
- 400 g (13 oz) can chopped tomatoes
- 300 g (10 oz) cherry tomatoes
- finely grated zest and juice of 2 limes
- 65 g (2½ oz) soft brown sugar
- 200 g (7 oz) fresh or frozen peas
- salt and black pepper

Stoba, a popular stew throughout the Caribbean, is usually made with goat. This recipe uses lamb because it's easier to find, but if you can get goat, do try it with that. Serve this with rice or roti.

- Heat half the oil in a large, heavy-based saucepan. Brown the lamb, in batches, for 3–4 minutes. Remove with a slotted spoon and set aside.

- Heat the remaining oil in the saucepan and add the onions, ginger, chilli, red pepper and spices. Stir-fry for 3–4 minutes and then add the lamb with the canned and cherry tomatoes, lime zest and juice, and sugar. Season and bring to the boil.

- Reduce the heat, cover tightly and simmer gently for 1½ hours or until the lamb is tender.

- Stir in the peas 5 minutes before serving.

V

· DESSERTS ·

Mint Choc Chip Cheesecake

SERVES 4–6 • PREP TIME 20 minutes, plus chilling

- 200 g (7 oz) chocolate biscuits
- 100 g (3½ oz) mint-flavoured dark chocolate, chopped
- 50 g (2 oz) butter, melted
- 200 g (7 oz) cream cheese
- 200 g (7 oz) mascarpone cheese
- 50 g (2 oz) caster sugar
- 1 tablespoon crème de menthe or peppermint extract
- 2 drops green food colouring
- 50 g (2 oz) plain dark chocolate chips

Desserts don't get much simpler or speedier to make than this. If you don't have a food processor, break the biscuits for the base into a ziplock bag and bash and roll with a rolling pin until you have fine crumbs. Very therapeutic!

- Put the biscuits and chocolate in a food processor or blender and process to make fine crumbs. Mix with the melted butter and press the mixture gently over the base of a 20 cm (8 inch), round, springform cake tin. Place in the freezer to set while making the cream cheese mixture.

- Beat together the cream cheese, mascarpone, sugar, mint liqueur or extract and food colouring in a large bowl. Stir in 40 g (1½ oz) of the chocolate chips and spoon the mixture over the biscuit base, smoothing with the back of a spoon.

- Place in the refrigerator to chill for about 1 hour.

- Loosen the edge with a knife, then remove the cheesecake from the tin carefully. Scatter over the remaining chocolate chips, roughly chopped.

· LIGHT BITES ·

Pork & Apple Balls

SERVES 4 • PREP & COOKING TIME 20 minutes

- 1 small Cox's apple, cored and grated (with skin on)
- 1 small onion, grated
- 250 g (8 oz) minced pork
- 50 g (2 oz) wholemeal breadcrumbs
- 3 tablespoons vegetable oil

Pork and apple pair very happily together in these juicy mini meatballs. They're great as a snack, dipped in tomato chutney or your favourite relish, and can also be served with mashed potato and some crunchy green veg for a speedy supper.

- Place the apple and onion in a bowl with the pork and, using a fork, mash all the ingredients together well. Shape into 16 rough balls. Place the breadcrumbs on a plate and roll the balls in the breadcrumbs to lightly coat.

- Heat the oil in a large heavy-based frying pan and cook the balls over a medium-high heat for 8–10 minutes, turning frequently, until cooked through. Drain on kitchen paper and serve warm.

• DESSERTS •

Red Wine Poached Pears

SERVES 6 • PREP & COOKING TIME about 50 minutes

- 850 ml (1½ pints) red wine
- 300 g (10 oz) caster sugar
- 2 tablespoons lemon juice
- 1 cinnamon stick
- 2 star anise
- 6 pears

The cooking time for this simple classic dessert will depend on how ripe your pears are − they need to be tender all the way through when pierced with a cocktail stick. Serve with thick cream or crème fraîche.

- Put the wine, sugar, lemon juice, cinnamon stick and star anise in a heavy-based saucepan and bring to a low simmer.

- Peel the pears, leaving the stalks in place, put them in the saucepan and cook for 20–25 minutes, turning occasionally, until they are soft. Remove the pears from the saucepan with a slotted spoon and set aside to cool.

- Meanwhile, return the poaching liquor to the heat and boil to reduce for about 10 minutes until it is thick and syrupy. Serve the pears, drizzled with the syrup.

V

· MAINS ·

Pumpkin, Beetroot & Goats' Cheese Bake

SERVES 4 · PREP & COOKING TIME 50 minutes

- 400 g (13 oz) raw beetroot, peeled and diced
- 625 g (1¼ lb) pumpkin or butternut squash, peeled, deseeded and cut into slightly larger dice than the beetroot
- 1 red onion, cut into wedges
- 2 tablespoons olive oil
- 2 teaspoons fennel seeds
- ½ teaspoon chipotle chilli flakes
- 2 small goats' cheeses, 100 g (3½ oz) each
- salt and pepper
- chopped rosemary, to garnish

Earthy beetroot and sweet pumpkin contrast beautifully with the creamy, tangy goats' cheese in this one-tin vegetarian dish. A great recipe to use up pumpkin left over from carving your Hallowe'en pumpkin.

- Put the vegetables into a roasting tin, drizzle with the oil and sprinkle with the fennel seeds, chilli flakes and salt and pepper. Roast in a preheated oven, 200°C (400°F), Gas Mark 6, for 20–25 minutes, turning once, until well browned and tender.

- Cut the goats' cheeses into thirds and nestle among the roasted vegetables. Sprinkle the cheeses with a little salt and pepper and drizzle with some of the pan juices.

- Return the dish to the oven and cook for about 5 minutes until the cheese is just beginning to melt. Sprinkle with rosemary and serve immediately.

• DRINKS •

Spiced Sloe Gin

MAKES 750 ml (1¼ pints) • PREP TIME 15 minutes, plus standing

- 250 g (8 oz) sloes, stalks removed and soft ones discarded
- 125 g (4 oz) caster sugar
- 3 whole cloves
- pared rind of 1 orange
- 1 cinnamon stick, halved
- about 750 ml (1¼ pints) inexpensive gin

Make the most of the sloes that are around this month with this lovely recipe. The longer you leave it to mature, the mellower and more delicious it will be, and it makes a great gift.

- Prick each sloe with a fork and drop them into a clean, dry 1 litre (1¾ pint) wide-necked, screwtop bottle.

- Using a plastic funnel or a cone of paper, pour the sugar into the bottle. Stick the cloves into the orange rind and add to the bottle along with the halved cinnamon stick.

- Pour in the gin, seal with an airtight top and turn the bottle upside down 2–3 times.

- Stand the bottle in a cool place and turn it once a day for 7 days until the sugar has completely dissolved.

- Label the bottle and leave to mature in a cool, dark place for 6 months or longer if you can. The sloes should be discarded before the gin is served.

November

GOOD TO EAT THIS MONTH

beetroot * Brussels sprouts * butternut squash *
cabbage * carrots * cauliflower * celeriac * celery *
kale * leeks * wild mushrooms * parsnips * potatoes *
pumpkin * salsify * swede * sweet potatoes * apples *
chestnuts * cobnuts * cranberries * pears * quince *
rosemary * sage

DATES TO LOOK FORWARD TO THIS MONTH

Day of the Dead (Día de los Muertos)
Bonfire Night
Stir-up Sunday
Thanksgiving
St Andrew's Day

There's plenty to enjoy this month: crisp days and, if we're lucky,
clear blue skies and the last of the autumn leaves in their glorious
colours. These are days for pulling on a cosy jacket for a brisk walk,
kicking through fallen leaves, and coming home for something
warming to eat.

It's that time of the year when we turn to the comfort that
only a hot pudding – preferably with lots of custard – can bring,
like the **Orchard Fruit Crumble** on page 357 and the **Orange &
Cranberry Puddings** on page 353.

Leeks and sweet parsnips shine in abundance and Brussels
sprouts are plentiful and crisply delicious. Try them in the **Stilton
& Leek Tarts** on page 350, the spicy **Parsnip Soup** on page 352
and the **Colcannon** on page 356.

There are a lot of celebrations to relish this month and we have
the recipes worthy of them: **Mexican Three-Milk Cake** for the
Day of the Dead (page 348), all-American favourite **Pumpkin
Pie**, of course, for Thanksgiving (page 374) and traditional
Scottish soup **Cullen Skink** for St Andrew's Day (page 377).

It's even time to start thinking about Christmas on Stir-up
Sunday when everyone in the family gets to have a stir of the
Christmas pud mix and make a wish (see page 370).

v

• DESSERTS •

Mexican Three-Milk Cake

SERVES 8–10 • PREP & COOKING TIME 50 minutes, plus cooling

- 5 eggs
- 175 g (6 oz) caster sugar
- 1 teaspoon vanilla extract
- 150 g (5 oz) plain flour
- 2 teaspoons baking powder
- 125 g (4 oz) butter, melted
- 200 ml (7 fl oz) sweetened condensed milk
- 200 ml (7 fl oz) evaporated milk
- 200 ml (7 fl oz) milk

TO DECORATE
- 200 ml (7 fl oz) double cream
- 1 tablespoon caster sugar
- selection of fruit, such as strawberries, blueberries and oranges

The Day of the Dead – a joyful time to remember departed loved ones – is a big occasion in South America and what better to celebrate with than a rich, indulgent three-milk cake?

- Beat together the eggs and sugar in a bowl until pale and thickened. Add the vanilla extract, then gradually stir in the flour and baking powder. Carefully stir in the melted butter until well combined.

- Pour the mixture into a lightly greased and base-lined 23 cm (9 inch) cake tin. Bake in a preheated oven, 180°C (350°F), Gas Mark 4, for 30–35 minutes until golden and a skewer inserted into the centre comes out clean.

- Whisk together all 3 milks in a bowl. Prick all over the warm cake with a skewer, then spoon over the milk mixture, letting it sink in. Leave to cool.

- When ready to serve, whisk together the cream and 1 tablespoon sugar in a bowl until soft peaks form. Spoon over the cake, then top with the fruit.

V

• BREAKFASTS •

Porridge with Prune Compote

SERVES 4–8 • PREP & COOKING TIME 25 minutes

- 1 litre (1¾ pints) milk
- 500 ml (17 fl oz) water
- 1 teaspoon vanilla extract
- pinch of ground cinnamon
- pinch of salt
- 200 g (7 oz) rolled oats
- 3 tablespoons flaked almonds, toasted

FOR THE COMPOTE
- 250 g (8 oz) ready-to-eat dried Agen prunes
- 125 ml (4 fl oz) apple juice
- 1 small cinnamon stick
- 1 clove
- 1 tablespoon honey
- 1 unpeeled orange quarter

When it's cold outside, a steaming bowl of porridge is a great way to start the day. The compote can be prepared in advance and chilled and works well as a topping for yogurt too.

- Place all the compote ingredients in a small saucepan over a medium heat. Simmer gently for 10–12 minutes or until softened and slightly sticky. Leave to cool.

- Put the milk, measured water, vanilla extract, cinnamon and salt in a large saucepan over a medium heat and bring slowly to the boil. Stir in the oats, then reduce the heat and simmer gently, stirring occasionally, for 8–10 minutes until creamy and tender.

- Spoon the porridge into bowls, scatter with the almonds and serve with the prune compote.

V

• LIGHT BITES •

Stilton & Leek Tarts

SERVES 4 • PREP & COOKING TIME 40 minutes

- 1 teaspoon olive oil
- 8 small leeks, finely sliced
- 50 g (2 oz) Stilton cheese, crumbled*
- 1 teaspoon chopped thyme
- 2 eggs, beaten
- 4 tablespoons crème fraîche
- 12 × 15 cm (6 inch) squares filo pastry
- milk, for brushing

All these easy-to-make little tarts need is a simple side salad of lightly dressed green leaves and you've got lunch or a starter for when friends gather. You can use any strong blue cheese instead of Stilton or try grated Cheddar instead.

- Heat the oil in a saucepan, add the leeks and fry for 3–4 minutes until softened.

- Stir half the Stilton and the thyme into the leek mixture, then blend together the remaining Stilton, the eggs and crème fraîche in a bowl.

- Brush the filo squares with a little milk and use them to line 4 fluted flan tins, each 10 cm (4 inches) across. Spoon the leek mixture into the tins, then pour over the cheese and egg mixture.

- Place the tins on a baking sheet and bake in a preheated oven, 200°C (400°F), Gas Mark 6, for 15–20 minutes until the filling is set.

*For guidance on vegetarian cheeses, see page 5.

VG

• MAINS •

Thai Massaman Pumpkin Curry

SERVES 4 • PREP & COOKING TIME 20 minutes

- 2 tablespoons vegetable oil
- 2 tablespoons Thai massaman curry paste
- 6 shallots, thinly sliced
- 8 cm (3 inch) length of trimmed lemon grass stalk, finely chopped
- 6 green cardamom pods
- 2 teaspoons black mustard seeds
- 800 g (1¾ lb) pumpkin flesh, cut into 1 cm (½ inch) cubes
- 200 ml (7 fl oz) hot vegetable stock
- 400 ml (14 fl oz) can coconut milk
- juice of 1 lime

TO GARNISH
- small handful of Thai basil leaves
- red chilli slivers

This fragrant, mild curry uses massaman curry paste, a spicy blend of gorgeous flavours that include cardamom and tangy lemon grass. If you can't get hold of Thai basil for the garnish, use mint instead. Steamed jasmine rice is the perfect accompaniment and perhaps a few lime wedges for squeezing over.

- Heat the oil in a heavy-based saucepan, add the curry paste, shallots, lemon grass, cardamom and mustard seeds and fry over a medium heat for 1–2 minutes until fragrant.

- Add the pumpkin and pour over the stock and coconut milk. Bring to a simmer, then cook for 10–12 minutes or until the pumpkin is tender.

- Remove from the heat and stir in the lime juice. Ladle into bowls, scatter with Thai basil leaves and red chilli slivers.

V

· LIGHT BITES ·

Curried Parsnip Soup

SERVES 4 • PREP & COOKING TIME 45 minutes

- 25 g (1 oz) butter
- 1 tablespoon sunflower oil
- 1 onion, chopped
- 2 garlic cloves, crushed
- 2.5 cm (1 inch) piece of fresh root ginger, peeled and chopped
- 1 tablespoon medium curry powder
- 1 teaspoon cumin seeds
- 750 g (1½ lb) parsnips, peeled and chopped
- 1 litre (1¾ pints) vegetable stock
- salt and black pepper

TO SERVE
- natural yogurt
- 2 tablespoons chopped coriander

Velvety smooth and comforting, this is a gently spiced mug of warming goodness to wrap your cold hands around on Bonfire Night. Serve hot naan breads on the side for dunking.

- Melt the butter and oil in a large saucepan, add the onion, garlic and ginger and cook over a medium heat for 4–5 minutes until softened.

- Stir in the curry powder and cumin seeds and cook, stirring, for 2 minutes, then stir in the parsnips, making sure they are well coated in the spice mixture.

- Pour over the stock and bring to the boil, then cover and simmer for 20–25 minutes until the parsnips are tender. Season with salt and pepper.

- Blend the soup with a stick blender until smooth. Reheat gently if necessary.

- Serve with dollops of yogurt, garnished with the coriander.

V

• DESSERTS •

Orange & Cranberry Puddings

SERVES 4 • PREP & COOKING TIME 30 minutes

- 100 g (3½ oz) unsalted butter, softened, plus extra for greasing
- grated zest of ½ small orange
- 100 g (3½ oz) caster sugar
- 1 tablespoon golden syrup
- 2 eggs
- 125 g (4 oz) self-raising flour, sifted
- 75 g (3 oz) dried cranberries

FOR THE SAUCE
- 3 tablespoons chunky orange marmalade
- 1 tablespoon cranberry jelly
- 2 tablespoons orange juice

It's cold, it's dark and you crave something sweet and comforting. These little fruit-studded puds are ready in just half an hour and lovely with a dollop or two of whipped cream or some custard. You could use shop-bought marmalade or, even better, try the **Dark Oxford Marmalade** on page 37.

- To make the sauce, place all the ingredients in a saucepan and heat gently until the marmalade and cranberry jelly are dissolved. Bring to the boil, then reduce the heat and simmer gently for 5 minutes to form a thick syrup.

- Spoon the sauce into the bottom of 4 greased and base-lined 200 ml (7 fl oz) ramekins or metal pudding moulds and place the moulds on a baking sheet.

- Place the butter, orange zest, sugar and golden syrup in a large bowl and beat together with a hand-held electric whisk until light and fluffy. Beat in the eggs, one at a time, then gently fold in the flour and cranberries.

- Spoon the pudding mixture into the ramekins and place in a preheated oven, 190°C (375°F), Gas Mark 5, for 20 minutes or until risen and set.

- Turn out the puddings on to serving plates and serve.

V

• BREAKFASTS •

Huevos Rancheros

SERVES 4 • PREP & COOKING TIME 20 minutes

- 2 tablespoons olive oil
- 1 large onion, diced
- 2 red peppers, deseeded and diced
- 2 garlic cloves, crushed
- ¾ teaspoon dried oregano
- 400 g (13 oz) can chopped tomatoes
- 4 eggs
- 20 g (¾ oz) feta cheese, crumbled

Mexican favourite huevos rancheros – also known as ranch eggs – is a vibrant, flavour-packed brunch dish that will bring a smile to all at the table. Serve with warm flatbreads or toasted pitta breads.

- Heat the oil in a frying pan over a medium heat, then add the onion, peppers, garlic and oregano and cook for 5 minutes.

- Add the tomatoes and cook for a further 5 minutes. Pour the tomato mixture into a shallow ovenproof dish and make 4 dips in the mixture.

- Crack the eggs into the dips, sprinkle with the feta and cook under a preheated hot grill for 3–4 minutes.

V

· LIGHT BITES ·

Baked Mushrooms with Taleggio & Pesto

SERVES 4 • PREP & COOKING TIME 20 minutes

- 8 large flat mushrooms, stalks trimmed
- 8 slices of Taleggio cheese
- 75 g (3 oz) dried breadcrumbs
- 1 garlic clove, crushed
- 6 tablespoons olive oil
- bunch of basil leaves, finely chopped
- 25 g (1 oz) Parmesan cheese or vegetarian hard cheese, finely grated
- 25 g (1 oz) toasted pine nuts, chopped, plus extra to serve
- salt and black pepper

To toast the pine nuts in this recipe to enhance their flavour, add to a dry frying pan in a single layer and cook over a low-medium heat, stirring constantly, until fragrant and golden brown. Tip on to a plate to stop them cooking.

- Put the mushrooms on a baking sheet and top each one with a slice of Taleggio. Mix together the breadcrumbs and garlic and scatter a little over each mushroom. Drizzle with olive oil and bake in a preheated oven, 200°C (400°F), Gas Mark 6, for 15–20 minutes until golden and crispy.

- Meanwhile, mix together the basil, Parmesan, pine nuts and remaining oil and season to taste. Drizzle the pesto over the mushrooms and scatter over a few extra pine nuts to serve.

*For guidance on vegetarian cheeses, see page 5.

• MAINS •

Sausages with Sprout Colcannon

SERVES 2 • PREP & COOKING TIME 40 minutes

- 4 pork and apple sausages
- 400 g (13 oz) floury potatoes, peeled and cut into chunks
- 50 g (2 oz) butter
- 200 g (7 oz) Brussels sprouts, thinly sliced or shredded
- ¼ teaspoon freshly grated nutmeg
- 1 tablespoon chopped chives
- 1 tablespoon wholegrain mustard
- 2 tablespoons crème fraîche
- salt and black pepper

Colcannon is traditionally made with cabbage, but this version adds pan-fried Brussels sprouts, chives and a hefty dollop of mustard to mashed potato to make it into something special.

- Arrange the sausages on a foil-lined baking tray and cook in a preheated oven, 190°C (375°F), Gas Mark 5, for 30 minutes or until cooked through, turning halfway through.

- Cook the potatoes in a pan of salted boiling water for 12–15 minutes, until tender.

- Meanwhile, melt half the butter in a frying pan and cook the sprouts with the nutmeg and a generous pinch of salt and pepper over medium-low heat for 5 minutes, stirring occasionally, until softened.

- Drain the potatoes, return to the pan and mash until smooth with the remaining butter. Stir in the chives, mustard, crème fraîche and sprouts and serve with the sausages.

V

• DESSERTS •

Orchard Fruit Crumble

SERVES 6 • PREP & COOKING TIME 45 minutes

- 2 dessert apples
- 2 ripe pears
- 400 g (13 oz) red plums, stoned and quartered
- 2 tablespoons water
- 75 g (3 oz) caster sugar
- 100 g (3½ oz) plain flour
- 50 g (2 oz) unsalted butter, diced
- 50 g (2 oz) desiccated coconut
- 50 g (2 oz) milk chocolate chips

A cold weather favourite, soft fruit baked beneath a crispy, golden topping spiked with sweet coconut and chocolate chips. Now the only decision is: do I want custard or cream?

- Peel, core and quarter the apples and pears. Slice the quarters and add the slices to a 1.2 litre (2 pint) pie dish. Add the plums and the measured water, then sprinkle with 25 g (1 oz) of the sugar. Cover the dish with foil and bake in a preheated oven, 180°C (350°F), Gas Mark 4, for 10 minutes.

- Put the remaining sugar in a bowl with the flour, add the butter and rub in with your fingertips or an electric mixer until the mixture resembles fine breadcrumbs. Stir in the coconut and chocolate chips.

- Remove the foil from the fruit and spoon the crumble over the top. Bake for 20–25 minutes until the crumble topping is golden brown and the fruit is tender.

V

• BREAKFASTS •

Mini Tomato & Feta Omelettes

MAKES 12 • PREP & COOKING TIME 20 minutes

- melted butter, for greasing
- 4 eggs, beaten
- 2 tablespoons chopped chives
- 3 sun-dried tomatoes, finely sliced
- 75 g (3 oz) feta cheese, crumbled
- salt and black pepper

These bite-sized omelettes are easy to make and portable, as well as a fun addition to the menu if you have friends coming round for brunch. Kids will love them too.

- Brush a 12-hole mini muffin tray lightly with the melted butter to grease.

- Mix together all the remaining ingredients in a large bowl until just combined.

- Pour the mixture into the greased holes and place in a preheated oven, 220°C (425°F), Gas Mark 7, for about 10 minutes until golden and puffed up. Remove from the oven and serve warm.

V

• LIGHT BITES •

Spinach & Red Lentil Soup

SERVES 4 • PREP & COOKING TIME 30 minutes

- 250 g (8 oz) dried red lentils
- 3 tablespoons sunflower oil
- 1 large onion, finely chopped
- 2 garlic cloves, crushed
- 2.5 cm (1 in) piece fresh root ginger, peeled and grated
- 1 red chilli, deseeded and chopped, plus extra to garnish (optional)
- 1 tablespoon medium curry powder
- 300 ml (½ pint) hot vegetable stock
- 200 g (7 oz) can tomatoes
- 100 g (3½ oz) baby leaf spinach
- 25 g (1 oz) chopped coriander leaves, plus extra to garnish
- 100 ml (3½ fl oz) coconut cream
- salt and black pepper
- 4 tablespoons natural yogurt, to serve

Comforting on a cold, grey day, this spicy vegetarian soup is packed with good-for-you ingredients including antioxidant ginger, fibre-filled lentils and iron-rich spinach. For a vegan-friendly soup, opt for a non-dairy version of the yogurt.

- Put the lentils into a medium saucepan and cover with 900 ml (1½ pints) cold water. Bring to the boil, skimming off the scum as it rises to the surface, and leave to simmer for 10 minutes until the lentils are tender and just falling apart. Remove from the heat, cover and set aside.

- Meanwhile, heat the oil in a large saucepan, add the onion and fry gently for 5 minutes. Add the garlic, ginger and chilli and fry for a further 2 minutes. Stir in the curry powder and ½ teaspoon black pepper and cook for a further 2 minutes.

- Add the stock, the lentils and their cooking liquid, the tomatoes, spinach and coriander and season with salt to taste. Cover and simmer for 5 minutes then add the coconut cream.

- Whizz the mixture with a hand-held blender, until the soup is almost smooth.

- Ladle the soup into bowls and garnish each with a spoonful of yogurt, the remaining coriander leaves, freshly ground black pepper and finely chopped red chilli, if desired.

· MAINS ·

Chicken & Mushroom Pies

MAKES 4 • PREP & COOKING TIME 1 hour 45 minutes, plus chilling

- 1 tablespoon olive oil
- 8 boneless, skinless chicken thighs, about |625 g (1¼ lb), cubed
- 1 onion, chopped
- 2 garlic cloves, finely chopped
- 2 tablespoons plain flour
- 150 ml (¼ pint) white wine
- 200 ml (7 fl oz) chicken stock
- few sprigs thyme or a little dried thyme
- 25 g (1 oz) butter
- 125 g (4 oz) closed-cup mushrooms, sliced
- beaten egg, to glaze
- salt and black pepper

FOR THE PASTRY
- 300 g (10 oz) plain flour
- 1½ teaspoons dry mustard powder
- 150 g (5 oz) mixed butter and white vegetable fat, diced
- 3 tablespoons cold water

Switch up the flavours of this dish by adding bacon – just reduce the amount of chicken to 500 g (1 lb) and add 125 g (4 oz) diced streaky bacon when frying the chicken and onion.

- Heat the oil in a large frying pan and fry the chicken, stirring, until it begins to colour. Add the onion and fry until the chicken is golden and the onion softened. Stir in the garlic, then mix in the flour. Add the wine, stock, thyme and a generous sprinkle of salt and pepper. Bring to the boil, stirring, cover and simmer for 30 minutes.

- Heat the butter in a small frying pan, add the mushrooms and fry until golden. Add to the chicken and leave to cool.

- Make the pastry. Add the flour, mustard and a little salt and pepper to a mixing bowl. Add the fats and rub in using your fingertips or using an electric mixer until you have fine crumbs. Gradually mix in enough of the water to form a soft but not sticky dough. Knead lightly, wrap in clingfilm and chill for 15 minutes.

- Reserve one-third of the pastry, then cut the rest into 4 pieces. Roll each piece out thinly, then line 4 greased individual springform tins, 10 cm (4 inches) in diameter and 4.5 cm (1¾ inches) deep. Roll out the reserved pastry thinly and cut out lids, using the tins as a guide.

- Spoon the chicken filling into the pies, brush the top edges with beaten egg, then add the lids and press the pastry edges together. Flute the edges and bake on a baking sheet in a preheated oven, 190°C (375°C), Gas Mark 5, for 30 minutes until golden. Leave to stand for 5 minutes, loosen the edges, transfer to a plate and remove the tins.

V

• DESSERTS •

Cranberry, Oat & Raisin Cookies

MAKES 12 • PREP & COOKING TIME 25 minutes

- 50 g (2 oz) butter
- 6 tablespoons golden syrup
- 125 g (4 oz) wholemeal plain flour
- 75 g (3 oz) rolled oats
- 1 teaspoon baking powder
- ½ teaspoon ground cinnamon
- ½ teaspoon ground ginger
- pinch of freshly grated nutmeg
- 50 g (2 oz) dried cranberries
- 50 g (2 oz) raisins

Wholesome, chewy and moreish, these are such a comfort. They'll still be soft in the centre when they are done – don't be tempted to cook them too long, as they will firm up as they cool.

- Heat the butter with the syrup in a saucepan over a low heat, stirring, until melted. Remove from the heat, add the remaining ingredients and mix well.

- Spoon the mixture on to a large baking sheet lined with baking parchment into 12 large mounds and press down slightly with the back of a spoon.

- Bake in a preheated oven, 180°C (350°F), Gas Mark 4, for 8–10 minutes until the edges are golden but the centres are still soft.

- Leave to cool for 2–3 minutes on the baking sheet before transferring to a wire rack to cool completely.

V

• BREAKFASTS •

Rosemary Panna Cotta with Apricot Compote

SERVES 6 • PREP & COOKING TIME 30 minutes, plus soaking and chilling

- 3 tablespoons cold water
- 1 sachet or 3 teaspoons powdered gelatine
- 450 ml (¾ pint) double cream
- 150 ml (¼ pint) milk
- 4 tablespoons thick honey
- 2 teaspoons very finely chopped rosemary leaves

FOR THE APRICOT COMPOTE
- 200 g (7 oz) ready-to-eat dried apricots, sliced
- 300 ml (½ pint) water
- 1 tablespoon thick honey
- 2 teaspoons very finely chopped rosemary leaves

TO DECORATE
- small rosemary sprigs
- caster sugar, for dusting

Fragrant rosemary brings a wonderful and unusual dimension to creamy panna cotta. The dried apricot compote is really versatile – spoon it over ice cream or Greek yogurt or swirl it through porridge or granola for a breakfast treat.

- Spoon the measured water into a small heatproof bowl or mug. Sprinkle the gelatine over and tilt the bowl or mug so that all the dry powder is absorbed by the water. Leave to soak for 5 minutes.

- Pour the cream and milk into a saucepan, add the honey and bring to the boil. Add the soaked gelatine, take the pan off the heat and stir until completely dissolved. Add the rosemary and leave for 20 minutes for the flavours to infuse, stirring from time to time.

- Pour the cream mixture into 6 individual 150 ml (¼ pint) ramekins or moulds, straining if preferred. Leave to cool completely, then chill for 4–5 hours until set.

- Put all the compote ingredients into a saucepan, cover and simmer for 10 minutes, then leave to cool.

- Turn the panna cottas out of their moulds on to serving plates by briefly immersing each ramekin in very hot water. Spoon the compote around them. Lightly dust the rosemary sprigs with caster sugar and use to decorate the panna cottas.

V

• LIGHT BITES •

Vegetable Samosas

MAKES 18 • PREP & COOKING TIME 1 hour 15 minutes

- 1 medium baking potato, about 150 g (5 oz) in total, scrubbed
- 2 tablespoons sunflower oil
- 1 onion, finely chopped
- 1 carrot, about 100 g (3½ oz), finely chopped
- 1½ teaspoons black mustard seeds
- 2 teaspoons cumin seeds, roughly crushed
- 2 Thai green chillies, with seeds, finely chopped
- 1 teaspoon coriander seeds, crushed
- 3 tablespoons chopped coriander
- ¼ teaspoon ground turmeric
- 75 g (3 oz) frozen peas, defrosted
- 1 litre sunflower oil, for deep-frying
- salt and black pepper

FOR THE PASTRY
- 200 g (7 oz) plain flour
- 50 g (2 oz) butter or ghee, diced
- 4–5 tablespoons cold water

Serve these spicy morsels warm with mango chutney or cucumber raita. To make your own raita, mix 175 ml (6 fl oz) of natural yogurt with 75 g (3 oz) deseeded and grated cucumber, 2 tablespoons of chopped mint, a squeeze of lemon juice and a pinch of cumin seeds.

- Cook the potato whole in boiling water for 15–20 minutes until tender. Drain and leave until cool enough to handle, then peel off the skin and dice the flesh.

- Heat the oil in the drained and dried potato pan, add the onion and carrot and fry for 3 minutes, add the mustard seeds, cumin seeds and green chillies and cook for 2 minutes.

- Mix in the crushed and chopped coriander and the turmeric, then the potatoes, peas and plenty of salt and pepper.

- Make the pastry. Add the flour, a little salt and the butter or ghee to a mixing bowl, rub in the butter with your fingertips until you have fine crumbs, mix in enough of the water to form a dough. Knead well until smooth and elastic.

- Cut into 9 pieces and shape into balls. Roll out to 12 cm (5 inch) circles, cut each in half, brush the edges with water, shape into a cone by folding one point to the centre of the curved top; do the same with the other point. Spoon the filling into the cone, then press the curved edges together to seal. Repeat to make 18 samosas.

- Half-fill a large saucepan with oil, heat to 180°C (350°F) on a cooking thermometer or until the oil bubbles when a samosa is dropped in. Cook the samosas in batches of 3 or 4 for 3–4 minutes until golden brown, then lift out and transfer to a plate lined with kitchen paper.

· MAINS ·

Pork & Red Pepper Chilli

SERVES 4 · PREP & COOKING TIME 40 minutes

- 2 tablespoons olive oil
- 1 large onion, chopped
- 2 garlic cloves, crushed
- 1 red pepper, deseeded and diced
- 450 g (14½ oz) minced pork
- 1 red chilli, finely chopped
- 1 teaspoon dried oregano
- 500 g (1 lb) passata
- 400 g (13 oz) can red kidney beans, drained and rinsed
- salt and black pepper
- soured cream, to serve

A quick and easy answer to 'What's for dinner?', this chilli is sure to become a family favourite. Serve it with brown rice or fresh, crusty bread.

- Heat the oil in a saucepan, add the onion, garlic and red pepper and cook for 5 minutes until soft and starting to brown. Add the minced pork and cook, stirring and breaking up with a wooden spoon, for 5 minutes or until browned.

- Add all the remaining ingredients and bring to the boil. Reduce the heat and simmer gently for 20 minutes. Remove from the heat, season well with salt and pepper and serve immediately with a dollop of soured cream.

V

• DESSERTS •

Chocolate Devil's Food Cake

SERVES 12 • PREP & COOKING TIME 1 hour, plus cooling

- 225 g (7½ oz) plain flour
- 1 teaspoon bicarbonate of soda
- 50 g (2 oz) cocoa powder
- 125 g (4 oz) butter
- 250 g (8 oz) light muscovado sugar
- 3 eggs
- 250 ml (8 fl oz) milk
- 1 tablespoon lemon juice

FOR THE FROSTING
- 175 g (6 oz) plain dark chocolate
- 75 g (3 oz) milk chocolate
- 3 tablespoons golden caster sugar
- 300 ml (½ pint) soured cream

Devilishly decadent, this is a cake that chocolate lovers will want to bake on repeat. Rich, moist cake layered with a luscious soured cream and chocolate ganache frosting, it explodes with chocolatey flavours.

- Sift together the flour, bicarbonate of soda and cocoa powder. Cream together the butter and half the sugar until soft and fluffy. Gradually whisk in the eggs, then whisk in the rest of the sugar. Mix the milk with the lemon juice to sour it, then fold into the flour mixture until smoothly combined.

- Spoon the mixture equally into 2 greased cake tins, 20 cm (8 inch) in diameter, their bases lined with nonstick baking paper, and level over the surface of both.

- Bake in a preheated oven, 180°C (350°F), Gas Mark 4, for 30 minutes until risen, springy to the touch and shrinking away from the edges of the tin. Cool in the tins for 10 minutes, then upturn the cakes on to a wire rack to cool.

- Melt the dark and milk chocolate together in a bowl over a pan of simmering water, then remove from the heat and whisk in the sugar and soured cream to make the frosting.

- Slice each cake in half horizontally to make 4 layers. Put one layer on the serving dish and spread with one-quarter of the frosting. Top with another cake layer, then some more frosting. Continue layering cake and frosting, ending with frosting on top.

• BREAKFASTS •

Bacon & Mushroom Frittata

SERVES 4 • PREP & COOKING TIME 30 minutes

- 8 portobello or flat chestnut mushrooms, about 500 g (1 lb) in total
- 1 garlic clove, finely chopped (optional)
- olive oil spray
- 4 lean smoked back bacon rashers
- 6 large eggs
- 1 tablespoon chopped chives, plus extra to garnish
- 1 tablespoon wholegrain mustard
- knob of butter
- salt and black pepper

Salty bacon and juicy mushrooms combine with eggs to make this fabulous frittata. A filling breakfast or brunch, served with slices of toasted sourdough, or serve it for lunch with a baby spinach salad.

- Put the mushrooms on a foil-lined baking sheet and scatter over the garlic, if using. Spray with a little olive oil, season with salt and pepper and place in a preheated oven, 180°C (350°F), Gas Mark 4, for 18–20 minutes or until softened. Leave until cool enough to handle.

- Meanwhile, lay the bacon rashers on a foil-lined grill pan and cook under a preheated medium-hot grill for 5–6 minutes, turning once or until slightly crispy. Cool slightly, then slice thickly.

- Put the eggs, chives and mustard in a bowl, beat together lightly and season with pepper.

- Heat a nonstick frying pan with an ovenproof handle, add the butter and melt until beginning to froth. Pour in the egg mixture and cook for 1–2 minutes, then add the bacon and whole mushrooms, stalk-side up. Cook for a further 2–3 minutes or until almost set.

- Place the pan under a preheated hot grill and cook the frittata for 2–3 minutes until set, then cool slightly, cut into wedges and serve, garnished with chives.

V

• LIGHT BITES •

Lemon & Green Veg Pasta Salad

SERVES 4 • PREP & COOKING TIME 20 minutes

- 375 g (12 oz) penne or rigatoni
- 150 g (5 oz) broccoli florets
- 100 g (3½ oz) frozen soya beans
- 100 g (3½ oz) frozen peas
- 100 g (3½ oz) sugar snap peas, trimmed
- 150 g (5 oz) soft cheese with garlic and herbs
- finely grated zest and juice of 1 lemon
- 4 tablespoons olive oil
- 1 red chilli, deseeded and finely chopped
- 100 g (3½ oz) grated pecorino or vegetarian hard cheese*
- 2 tablespoons chopped tarragon leaves
- salt and black pepper

Soft cheese with garlic and herbs is the clever ingredient in this recipe. It melts quickly into the hot pasta, providing a speedy, easy way to add creaminess and extra flavour.

- Cook the pasta in a large saucepan following the packet instructions, adding the broccoli florets, soya beans, peas and sugar snaps for the final 3 minutes of its cooking time.

- Drain the pasta and vegetables, saving a ladleful of the cooking water, then tip back into the pan.

- Stir in the soft cheese, lemon zest and juice, olive oil, chilli, pecorino, tarragon, some seasoning and a splash of cooking water.

- Serve the salad warm or at room temperature.

*For guidance on vegetarian cheeses, see page 5.

Goan Prawn & Coconut Curry

SERVES 4 • PREP & COOKING TIME 20 minutes

- 1 teaspoon cumin seeds
- 3 cardamom pods
- 2 onions, roughly chopped
- 4 tablespoons vegetable oil
- 1 bay leaf
- 6 curry leaves
- 2 cm (1 inch) piece fresh root ginger, peeled and chopped
- 3 garlic cloves
- ½ teaspoon ground turmeric
- 1 red chilli, deseeded and chopped
- 200 ml (7 fl oz) coconut milk
- 125 g (4 oz) tomatoes, halved
- 400 g (13 oz) raw prawns, peeled
- 1 tablespoon butter
- a handful of chopped coriander leaves

Friends coming for dinner and no time to cook? Here's your answer: a super-fast curry made with creamy coconut milk and sweet prawns that you can rustle up in hardly any time at all. All you need alongside is a bowl of fluffy basmati rice.

- Put the cumin and cardamom in a small frying pan and cook for 30 seconds until aromatic. Remove and set aside.

- Whizz the onions and 2 tablespoons of the oil in a food processor until smooth. Heat the remaining oil in a pan, add the onion paste, bay leaf and curry leaves and cook for 7–10 minutes until light brown.

- Meanwhile, whizz the ginger and garlic in a small food processor until smooth. Add to the pan with the toasted spices, turmeric, chilli, coconut milk, tomatoes and 150 ml (5 fl oz) water.

- Simmer for 5 minutes, then add the prawns and cook for 3 minutes until cooked through. Stir in the butter until melted. Scatter over the coriander leaves and serve with basmati rice.

v

• DESSERTS •

Chai Teabread

SERVES 10 • PREP & COOKING TIME 1½ hours, plus standing

- 5 chai tea bags
- 300 ml (½ pint) boiling water
- 225 g (8 oz) self-raising flour
- 1 teaspoon baking powder
- 150 g (5 oz) light muscovado sugar
- 300 g (10 oz) mixed dried fruit
- 50 g (2 oz) Brazil nuts, chopped
- 50 g (2 oz) butter
- 1 egg, beaten

Baked to soft, moist perfection, this cake uses chai tea to add a spicy complexity, though you can use regular black tea instead. Serve spread with butter or make a simple glaze by mixing 50 g (2 oz) icing sugar with 2 teaspoons of water and spreading over the cake while still warm.

- Stir the tea bags into the measured water in a jug and leave to stand for 10 minutes.

- Mix together the flour, baking powder, sugar, dried fruit and nuts in a bowl.

- Remove the tea bags from the water, pressing them against the side of the jug to squeeze out all the water. Thinly slice the butter into the water and stir until melted. Leave to cool slightly. Add to the dry ingredients with the egg and mix together well.

- Spoon the mixture into a greased and lined 1 kg (2 lb) or 1.3 litre (2¼ pint) loaf tin and spread the mixture into the corners.

- Bake in a preheated oven, 160°C (325°F), Gas Mark 3, for 1¼ hours or until risen, firm and a skewer inserted into the centre comes out clean. Loosen the cake at the ends and transfer to a wire rack. Peel off the lining paper and leave to cool.

V

· DESSERTS ·

Traditional Christmas Pudding

SERVES 12 • PREP & COOKING TIME 9–12 hours, plus cooling

- 125 g (4 oz) self-raising flour
- 175 g (6 oz) fresh white breadcrumbs
- 175 g (6 oz) currants
- 175 g (6 oz) sultanas
- 125 g (4 oz) pitted dates, chopped
- 250 g (8 oz) raisins
- 175 g (6 oz) shredded vegetable suet
- 50 g (2 oz) cut mixed peel
- 50 g (2 oz) blanched almonds, chopped
- 1 small apple, peeled, cored and grated
- grated zest and juice of 1 orange
- ½ teaspoon ground mixed spice
- ¼ teaspoon grated nutmeg
- ½ teaspoon salt
- 3 eggs
- 4 tablespoons brown ale or cider
- 250 g (8 oz) soft brown sugar
- 3–4 tablespoons brandy, to serve

Get that apron on because it's Stir-up Sunday and time to make the Christmas pud. It's traditional to allow everyone in the family a stir while they make a wish. This will keep, stored in a cool, dry, dark place for up to 6 months.

- Place all the ingredients in a large bowl and stir well to mix.

- Spoon the mixture into a liberally greased 1.2 litre (2 pint) pudding basin and a liberally greased 600 ml (1 pint) pudding basin. Spoon the mixture into each basin until just over three-quarters full, then cover with circles of greased greaseproof paper, then with foil or a pudding cloth. Fold a pleat in the centre and tie string securely around the rim.

- Place in the top of a steamer or double boiler, or put in a large saucepan and pour in boiling water to come halfway up the sides. Boil for 6–8 hours, depending on the size, topping up boiling water as necessary. Remove the puddings from the saucepan and leave overnight to cool.

- Remove the coverings and re-cover with fresh greased greaseproof paper and foil or a pudding cloth. Store in a cool, dark, dry place.

- On Christmas Day, reboil the puddings for 3–4 hours, depending on size, then turn out into a serving dish. Warm the brandy, pour over the puddings and set alight.

VG

• BREAKFASTS •

Homemade Baked Beans on Toast

SERVES 4 • PREP & COOKING TIME 20 minutes

- 2 tablespoons olive or vegetable oil
- 1 onion, thinly sliced
- 2 garlic cloves, crushed
- 500 g (1 lb) passata
- 100 ml (3½ fl oz) hot vegetable stock or water
- ½ teaspoon sugar
- 2 × 400 g (13 oz) cans haricot beans, drained and rinsed
- pinch of cayenne (optional)
- pinch of cinnamon (optional)
- salt and black pepper
- 4 thick slices of granary bread, to serve

Is there anything more comforting than beans on toast? Once you've tried these healthy homemade baked beans, there'll be no going back to shop-bought. Delicious for a warming breakfast or simple supper.

- Heat the olive oil in a heavy-based saucepan and cook the onion gently for 3–4 minutes. Add the garlic and cook for a further 2 minutes, until softened and golden.

- Add the passata, stock, sugar, beans and spices, if using, and season to taste with salt and pepper. Simmer gently for 12–14 minutes, until rich and thick.

- Meanwhile, toast the bread until golden and place on 4 serving plates. Serve the beans spooned over the toast.

• LIGHT BITES •

Croque Monsieur

SERVES 2 • PREP & COOKING TIME 15 minutes

- 4 thick slices of French country bread
- 25 g (1 oz) butter, melted
- 25 g (1 oz) Parmesan cheese, finely grated
- 2 large slices of roast ham
- 125 g (4 oz) Emmental cheese, coarsely grated

Literally 'Mr Crunch', this is a classic hot sandwich. The recipe uses a toasted sandwich maker but, if you don't have one, a hot frying pan will work just as well. Top each sandwich with a fried egg and you have croque madame.

- Use a pastry brush to brush one side of each slice of bread with the melted butter, then sprinkle with the Parmesan.

- Place 2 slices of bread on the worktop, with the Parmesan-coated sides face down and top each with a slice of ham and half the Emmental.

- Top with the remaining 2 slices of bread, Parmesan-coated sides on the outside, and toast in a sandwich grill for 4–5 minutes or according to the manufacturer's instructions until the bread is golden and crispy and the Emmental is beginning to ooze from the sides. Serve immediately.

• MAINS •

Stir-fried Lamb with Sugar Snap Peas

SERVES 4 • PREP & COOKING TIME 20 minutes, plus marinating

- 2 teaspoons cornflour
- 1½ tablespoons Chinese rice wine
- 2 tablespoons light soy sauce
- 2 garlic cloves, finely chopped
- 500g (1 lb) lean lamb steaks, cut into thin slices
- 1 teaspoon Szechuan peppercorns
- ¼ teaspoon rock salt
- 3 tablespoons groundnut oil
- 75 g (3 oz) sugar snap peas, sliced into 3
- 1 teaspoon sesame oil
- 1 red chilli, deseeded and finely chopped
- 1 spring onion, very finely shredded

A speedy stir-fry is a great choice for a healthy meal. If you don't have any rice wine, you can use dry sherry instead. Serve with egg noodles, if you like.

- Combine the cornflour with the rice wine to make a paste, then stir in the soy sauce and garlic. Add the lamb and stir to cover, then leave to marinate for 25–30 minutes. Drain.

- Place the Szechuan peppercorns in a dry wok and stir over a medium heat until they begin to pop and release their aroma. Transfer to a pestle and mortar and pound with the salt until coarsely ground.

- Heat half the oil in a wok over a high heat until the oil starts to shimmer. Add half the lamb and stir-fry for 3 minutes, then remove using a slotted spoon. Heat the remaining oil and stir-fry the rest of the lamb in the same way.

- Return all the lamb to the wok, add the sugar snaps and after 1 minute stir in the sesame oil, chilli, spring onion and the ground salt and pepper mixture. Cook for 1 more minute, then serve.

v

· DESSERTS ·

Pumpkin Pie

SERVES 6 • PREP & COOKING TIME 1 hour 45 minutes, plus cooling

- 500 g (1 lb) pumpkin or butternut squash, weighed after deseeding and peeling
- 3 eggs
- 100 g (3½ oz) light muscovado sugar
- 2 tablespoons plain flour
- ½ teaspoon ground cinnamon
- ½ teaspoon ground ginger
- ¼ teaspoon grated nutmeg
- 200 ml (7 fl oz) milk, plus extra to glaze
- 450 g (14½ oz) chilled ready-made sweet shortcrust pastry
- sifted icing sugar, for dusting

Thanksgiving means pumpkin pie. You don't need the leaf decorations but it does make the pie look extra special. Bring it proudly to the table and serve with a bowl of whipped cream sprinkled with cinnamon or nutmeg.

- Cut the pumpkin or butternut squash into cubes and cook in a covered steamer for 15–20 minutes or until tender. Cool, then purée in a liquidizer or food processor.

- Whisk the eggs, sugar, flour and spices together in a bowl until just mixed. Add the pumpkin purée, whisk together, then gradually mix in the milk. Set aside.

- Roll out three-quarters of the pastry on a lightly floured surface until large enough to line a buttered 23 cm (9 inch) × 2.5 cm (1 inch) deep enamel pie dish. Lift the pastry over a rolling pin, drape into the dish and press over the base and sides.

- Trim the excess and add the trimmings to the reserved pastry. Roll out thinly and cut out tiny leaves. Brush the pastry rim with milk, press on the leaves around the rim, reserving a few. Put the pie on a baking sheet.

- Pour the pumpkin filling into the dish, add a few leaf decorations on top of the filling, brush these and the dish edges lightly with milk. Bake in a preheated oven, 190°C (375°F), Gas Mark 5, for 45–55 minutes until the filling is set and the pastry cooked through. Cover with foil after 20 minutes to stop the pastry edge from overbrowning. Serve dusted with a little icing sugar.

Prawn & Rice Paper Wraps

SERVES 2 • PREP TIME 10 minutes

- 3 dried rice paper wrappers 20 cm (8 inches) in diameter
- ½ small carrot, cut into thin strips
- 2 Chinese leaves, shredded
- 25 g (1 oz) bean sprouts
- 4 tablespoons chopped coriander
- 125 g (4 oz) cooked peeled tiger prawns
- 1 tablespoon Thai fish sauce
- 6 mint leaves
- sweet chilli dipping sauce, to serve

The herbs in these wraps bring a strong hit of freshness to the crunchy veg and sweet prawns. Dried rice paper wrappers, also called bánh tráng, are available online and from Asian food shops. Thai fish sauce you'll find in any large supermarket.

- Place one of the wrappers in a bowl of warm water until softened and opaque. Shake off the excess water and lay on a plate.

- Place the carrot, Chinese leaves, bean sprouts, coriander and prawns in a bowl and mix well.

- Brush the middle of the wrapper with fish sauce, lay 2 mint leaves on it, then place one-third of the prawn mixture in a line down the middle. Fold in both sides of the wrapper, then roll up tightly.

- Cover with a damp cloth and repeat with the remaining wrappers and filling. Cut each roll in half and serve immediately with the dipping sauce.

· MAINS ·

Chicken & Barley Risotto

SERVES 4 · PREP & COOKING TIME 1 hour 30 minutes

- 2 tablespoons olive oil
- 6 boneless, skinless chicken thighs, diced
- 1 onion, roughly chopped
- 2 garlic cloves, finely chopped
- 200 g (7 oz) chestnut mushrooms, sliced
- 250 g (8 oz) pearl barley
- 200 ml (7 fl oz) red wine
- 1.2 litres (2 pints) chicken stock
- salt and black pepper
- parsley leaves, to garnish
- Parmesan cheese shavings, to serve

When the temperature tumbles, reach for this recipe. Swapping risotto rice for pearl barley creates a creamy, comforting texture with a nutty flavour. Serve as is or with a green salad or some garlic bread.

- Heat the oil in a large frying pan over a medium-high heat, add the chicken and onion and fry for 5 minutes, stirring until lightly browned.

- Stir in the garlic and mushrooms and fry for 2 minutes, then mix in the pearl barley. Add the red wine, half the stock and season with plenty of salt and pepper, then bring to the boil, stirring continuously.

- Reduce the heat, cover and simmer for 1 hour, topping up with extra stock as needed, until the chicken is cooked through and the barley is soft.

- Spoon into shallow bowls and garnish with the parsley and sprinkle with Parmesan.

• LIGHT BITES •

Cullen Skink

SERVES 6 • PREP & COOKING TIME 1 hour

- 25 g (1 oz) butter
- 1 onion, roughly chopped
- 500 g (1 lb) potatoes, diced
- 1 large Finnan haddock or 300 g (10 oz) smoked haddock fillet
- 1 bay leaf
- 900 ml (1½ pint) fish stock
- 150 ml (¼ pints) milk
- 6 tablespoons double cream
- salt and pepper
- chopped parsley, to garnish

It's St Andrew's Day so celebrate the patron saint of Scotland with the famous Scottish soup, cullen skink. It's a hearty and tasty blend of smoked haddock and potatoes finished off with rich double cream.

- Heat the butter in a saucepan, add the onion and fry gently for 5 minutes until softened. Stir the potatoes into the butter and onion then cover and cook for 5 more minutes. Lay the haddock on top, add the bay leaf and stock. Season with salt and pepper and bring to the boil.

- Cover and simmer for 30 minutes or until the potatoes are soft. Lift the fish out of the pan with a slotted spoon and transfer to a plate. Discard the bay leaf.

- Loosen the bones, if using a Finnan haddock, with a small knife, then lift away the backbone and head. Using a knife and fork break the fish into flakes and lift off the skin. If using haddock fillet, simply peel off the skin and then break the fish into flakes, double-checking there are no bones.

- Return two-thirds of the fish to the pan then purée the soup in batches in a blender or food processor until smooth. Pour back into the saucepan and stir in the milk and cream. Bring just to the boil, then simmer gently until reheated. Taste and adjust the seasoning if needed.

- Ladle into bowls and sprinkle with the remaining fish and the chopped parsley.

December

GOOD TO EAT THIS MONTH

beetroot * Brussels sprouts * butternut squash *
cabbage * carrots * cauliflower * celeriac * celery
* kale * leeks * mushrooms * parsnips * potatoes *
pumpkin * swede * sweet potatoes * apples * chestnuts
* cranberries * pears * quince * rosemary * sage

DATES TO LOOK FORWARD TO THIS MONTH

Winter Solstice
Christmas Day
Kwanzaa/Boxing Day
New Year's Eve

December should be the darkest and gloomiest month but is
actually full of celebrations, lights and sparkle and so much to
look forward to – parties and planning, shopping and wrapping
and, most important, time spent with family and friends.

The Christmas countdown has really began and this month's
recipes include four that make lovely homemade gifts: the
Cranberry & Almond Biscotti on page 383, the **Clove &
Cardamom Spiced Cookies** on page 399, the **Honeycomb** on
page 387 and the **Mint & Chocolate Fudge** on page 403. And
inspiration for Christmas treats comes from Europe: there's
marzipan-studded German favourite **Stollen** (page 391) and for
dessert on Christmas Day the stunning French classic **Bûche de
Noël** (page 404).

To help you make the most of the Christmas feast leftovers,
there's **Turkey & Chestnut Soup** on the menu for 28 December
(page 407).

But, to balance all the festive treats, there are also many good-
for-you options using seasonal veg, such as the **Beef, Pumpkin &
Ginger Stew** on page 390 and the **Carrot & Red Pepper Soup** on
page 397.

· BREAKFASTS ·

Herby Smoked Salmon Omelettes

SERVES 4 • PREP & COOKING TIME 25 minutes

- 8 large eggs
- 2 spring onions, thinly sliced
- 2 tablespoons chopped chives
- 2 tablespoons chopped chervil
- 50 g (2 oz) butter
- 4 thin slices of smoked salmon, cut into thin strips
- black pepper

Get the day off to a great start with these omelettes. Full of protein and flecked with chives and chervil, they are a good choice for a light supper too.

- Put the eggs, spring onions and herbs in a bowl, beat together lightly and season with pepper.

- Heat a medium-sized frying pan over a medium-low heat, add a quarter of the butter and melt until beginning to froth. Pour in a quarter of the egg mixture and swirl to cover the base of the pan. Stir gently for 2–3 minutes or until almost set.

- Sprinkle over a quarter of the smoked salmon and cook for a further 30 seconds or until just set. Fold over and slide on to a serving plate. Serve immediately and repeat to make 3 more omelettes.

• LIGHT BITES •

Beef & Barley Broth

SERVES 6 • PREP & COOKING TIME 2 hours 20 minutes

- 25 g (1 oz) butter
- 250 g (8 oz) braising beef, fat trimmed away and meat cut into small cubes
- 1 large onion, finely chopped
- 200 g (7 oz) swede, diced
- 150 g (5 oz) carrot, diced
- 100 g (3½ oz) pearl barley
- 2 litres (3½ pints) beef stock
- 2 teaspoons dry English mustard (optional)
- salt and black pepper
- chopped parsley, to garnish

Loaded with chunks of tender meat, plump barley and plenty of veg, this is pure comfort in a bowl. Easy to make – just a little chopping and stirring – it improves with keeping and freezes well so is a great make-ahead meal.

- Heat the butter in a large saucepan, add the beef and onion and fry for 5 minutes, stirring, until the beef is browned and the onion just beginning to colour.

- Stir in the diced vegetables, pearl barley, stock and mustard, if using. Season with salt and pepper and bring to the boil. Cover and simmer for 1¾ hours, stirring occasionally until the meat and vegetables are very tender.

- Taste and adjust the seasoning if needed. Ladle the soup into bowls and sprinkle with a little chopped parsley.

• MAINS •

Slow-cooked Aromatic Pork Curry

SERVES 4 • PREP & COOKING TIME 2½–3 hours

- 750 g (1½ lb) pork belly, trimmed and cubed
- 400 ml (14 fl oz) chicken stock
- 75 ml (3 fl oz) light soy sauce
- finely grated zest and juice of 1 large orange
- 1 tablespoon peeled and finely shredded fresh root ginger
- 2 garlic cloves, sliced
- 1 dried red Kashmiri chilli
- 2 tablespoons medium curry powder
- 1 tablespoon hot chilli powder
- 1 tablespoon dark muscovado sugar
- 3 cinnamon sticks
- 3 cloves
- 10 black peppercorns
- 2–3 star anise
- salt

Let this simmer away quietly on the hob and you'll be rewarded with a pot of steaming goodness. It's delicious served with steamed Asian greens and rice.

- Place the pork in a large saucepan or casserole, cover with water and bring to the boil over a high heat. Cover, reduce the heat and simmer gently for 30 minutes. Drain and return the pork to the pan with the remaining ingredients. Season to taste.

- Add just enough water to cover the pork and bring to the boil over a high heat. Cover tightly, reduce the heat to low and cook very gently for 1½ hours, stirring occasionally.

- Remove the lid and simmer, uncovered, for 30 minutes, stirring occasionally, until the meat is meltingly tender.

V

• DESSERTS •

Cranberry & Almond Biscotti

SERVES 4 • PREP & COOKING TIME 30 minutes

- 110 g (3¾ oz) caster sugar
- 110 g (3¾ oz) plain flour, plus extra for dusting
- 1 teaspoon baking powder
- grated zest of 1 lemon
- 50 g (2 oz) blanched almonds
- 15 g (½ oz) dried cranberries
- 1 egg, beaten

Baked twice for extra crunch, these are delicious dunked into a cup of tea or coffee. To ring the changes, swap in chopped unsalted pistachios and finely chopped dried apricot for the almonds and cranberries.

- Place all of the ingredients in a bowl and, using your hands, bring them together to make a stiff dough.

- Turn out on to a floured work surface and roll into a sausage shape about 28 cm (11 inches) long. Place on a baking sheet and bake in a preheated oven, 220°C (425°F), Gas Mark 7, for 15 minutes.

- Remove from the oven, leave to cool for 2–3 minutes and then gently slice into thin rusks.

- Lay the rusks flat on the baking sheet, return to the oven and cook for a further 2–3 minutes to crisp.

- Leave to cool on a wire rack.

V

• BREAKFASTS •

Creamy Mushroom & Walnut Bagels

SERVES 2 • PREP & COOKING TIME 20 minutes

- 1 tablespoon olive oil
- 150 g (5 oz) chestnut mushrooms, sliced
- 1 garlic clove, crushed
- 2 thyme sprigs, plus extra to garnish
- 150 ml (1¼ pint) cream
- 1 teaspoon soy sauce
- 50 g (2 oz) chopped walnuts, toasted
- black pepper
- 2 bagels, halved and toasted

Earthy mushrooms and crunchy walnuts combine beautifully in this dish. The soy sauce is salty, so you won't need to season with salt. Swap the cream for soya or oat cream for a vegan-friendly version.

- Heat the oil in a frying pan, add the mushrooms and cook over a high heat, stirring frequently, for 2 minutes until browned and softened.

- Reduce the heat and add the garlic, thyme, cream and soy sauce. Simmer, stirring, for 3 minutes, adding a little water if the sauce is too thick. Stir in the walnuts and season with pepper.

- Spoon the mushroom mixture over the toasted bagels and garnish with thyme sprigs before serving.

Bagna Cauda & Crudités

SERVES 4–6 • PREP & COOKING TIME 25 minutes

- 50 ml (2 fl oz) milk
- 6 garlic cloves
- 150 g (5 oz) anchovy fillets in olive oil, drained and roughly chopped
- 75 g (3 oz) butter
- 75 ml (3 fl oz) extra virgin olive oil

FOR THE CRUDITÉS
- 8 baby carrots, peeled
- 250 g (8 oz) cauliflower florets
- 4 celery sticks, cut in half
- ½ red cabbage, cut into thin wedges
- 5 baby fennel, cut in half lengthways

Meaning 'hot bath', bagna cauda is a great starter to share with family and friends. The crisp vegetables – add breadsticks if you like – are dipped into the robustly flavoured warm sauce, which is loaded with garlic and anchovies.

- Put the milk, garlic and anchovies in a small saucepan over a low heat and cook gently for 15 minutes, without letting the milk come to the boil, until the anchovies have melted into the pan and the garlic is soft.

- Use the back of a fork to mash the garlic against the side of the pan. Add the butter and oil and stir until the butter has melted. Transfer to a small serving bowl.

- Arrange the crudités in a large serving dish, leaving space for the bowl of sauce, and serve while the sauce is still warm for dipping.

Chicken Mole

SERVES 4 • PREP & COOKING TIME 1 hour

- 1 tablespoon sunflower oil
- 500 g (1 lb) minced chicken
- 1 onion, roughly chopped
- 2 garlic cloves, finely chopped
- 1 teaspoon smoked paprika
- ½ teaspoon chilli powder
- 1 teaspoon cumin seeds, roughly crushed
- 400 g (13 oz) can chopped tomatoes
- 400 g (13 oz) can red kidney beans
- 150 ml (¼ pint) chicken stock
- 1 tablespoon dark brown sugar
- 50 g (2 oz) dark chocolate, diced
- salt and black pepper

FOR THE TOPPINGS
- ½ red onion, finely chopped
- ½ red pepper, deseeded and diced
- 1 avocado, stoned, peeled and diced
- zest and juice of 1 lime
- small bunch of coriander, roughly chopped
- 100 g (3½ oz) mature Cheddar cheese, grated
- 100 g (3½ oz) tortilla chips

Mole is a Mexican classic – chillies and spices combined in a dark, rich, earthy sauce with a hint of bitter chocolate. It's wonderful. Put the toppings on the table to allow everyone to add their own combination to the mole.

- Heat the oil in a saucepan, add the chicken and onion and fry, breaking up the mince with a wooden spoon, until browned. Mix in the garlic, paprika, chilli and cumin seeds and cook for 1 minute.

- Stir in the tomatoes, beans, stock and sugar, then mix in the chocolate and seasoning. Cover and simmer gently for 45 minutes, stirring occasionally.

- Mix the onion, pepper, avocado, lime zest and juice and coriander in a small serving bowl. Put the cheese in a second bowl and the tortilla chips in a third.

- Spoon the mole into bowls and serve with the toppings.

V

• DESSERTS •

Chocolate Mousse with Honeycomb

SERVES 6 • PREP & COOKING TIME 30 minutes

- 200 g (7 oz) plain dark chocolate, broken into small pieces
- 4 eggs, separated
- 150 ml (¼ pint) double cream

FOR THE HONEYCOMB
- 5 tablespoons granulated sugar
- 2 tablespoons golden syrup
- 1 teaspoon bicarbonate of soda

Making your own honeycomb takes a bit of care and attention but is worth the effort, tasting so much better than shop-bought. Plus it makes a great homemade thank-you-for-having-me gift, broken into pieces and put in a pretty tin.

- To make the honeycomb, gently heat the sugar and golden syrup in a heavy-based saucepan until the sugar has dissolved, then boil until the mixture turns a deep golden caramel. Whisk in the bicarbonate of soda (this will make it foam up), then quickly pour it on to a greased baking sheet and leave to cool for 10 minutes.

- Meanwhile, melt the chocolate in a heatproof bowl set over a saucepan of gently simmering water. Leave to cool slightly, then stir in the egg yolks.

- Lightly whip the cream in a bowl with a hand-held electric whisk until it forms soft peaks and fold into the chocolate mixture.

- Whisk the egg whites in a clean large bowl with a hand-held electric whisk until stiff, then fold into the chocolate cream.

- Break the honeycomb into small chunks and fold most of it into the mousse. Pour into 6 glass tumblers or dishes and chill for 10 minutes until set. Sprinkle the leftover honeycomb over the top just before serving.

V

• BREAKFASTS •

Maple & Pecan Muffins

MAKES 8 • PREP & COOKING TIME 30 minutes

- 300 g (10 oz) self-raising flour
- 1 teaspoon baking powder
- 125 g (4 oz) soft brown sugar
- 1 egg
- 50 ml (2 fl oz) maple syrup
- 250 ml (8 fl oz) milk
- 50 g (2 oz) unsalted butter, melted
- 125 g (4 oz) white chocolate, finely chopped
- 75 g (3 oz) pecan nuts, coarsely chopped, plus extra to decorate

Studded with little chunks of white chocolate, these muffins make a special breakfast or mid-morning treat to enjoy with a cup of coffee. You can use chopped walnuts in place of the pecans.

- Line a 12-hole muffin tin with 8 paper muffin cases.

- Sift the flour and baking powder into a mixing bowl and stir in the sugar. Beat together the egg, maple syrup, milk and melted butter and beat into the dry ingredients until mixed. Fold in the chocolate and pecan nuts.

- Spoon the mixture into the muffin cases and top with some extra chopped nuts.

- Bake in a preheated oven, 200°C (400°F), Gas Mark 6, for 20–25 minutes until risen and golden. Transfer to a wire rack to cool.

• LIGHT BITES •

Chicken Dippers with Sweetcorn Salsa

SERVES 4 • PREP & COOKING TIME 25 minutes

- 2 eggs
- 2 tablespoons milk
- 100 g (3½ oz) fresh breadcrumbs
- 4 tablespoons freshly grated Parmesan cheese
- 3 boneless, skinless chicken breasts, about 500 g (1 lb) in total, cut into long, finger-like slices
- 25 g (1 oz) butter
- 2 tablespoons vegetable oil
- salt and black pepper

FOR THE SWEETCORN SALSA
- 2 tomatoes, diced
- ¼ cucumber, diced
- 75 g (3 oz) sweetcorn, defrosted if frozen
- 1 tablespoon coriander leaves, chopped

The whole family will love these crunchy chicken strips served with a colourful salsa. The dippers are also very good stuffed inside warmed pitta breads with a dollop of mayonnaise.

- Put the salsa ingredients in a bowl and mix together.

- Beat the eggs, milk and a little salt and pepper together in a bowl.

- Mix the breadcrumbs with the Parmesan.

- Dip one chicken strip into the egg, then roll in the breadcrumbs. Carry on doing this until all the chicken strips are well covered.

- Heat the butter and oil in a large frying pan and add the chicken strips. Cook for 6–8 minutes, turning a few times until they are brown all over. Serve with the salsa to dip into.

· MAINS ·

Beef, Pumpkin & Ginger Stew

SERVES 6 • PREP & COOKING TIME 2 hours

- 2 tablespoons plain flour
- 750 g (1½ lb) lean stewing beef, diced
- 25 g (1 oz) butter
- 3 tablespoons oil
- 1 onion, chopped
- 2 carrots, sliced
- 2 parsnips, sliced
- 3 bay leaves
- several thyme sprigs
- 2 tablespoons tomato purée
- 625 g (1¼ lb) pumpkin, peeled, deseeded and cut into small chunks
- 1 tablespoon dark muscovado sugar
- 50 g (2 oz) fresh root ginger, peeled and finely chopped
- small handful of parsley, chopped, plus extra to garnish
- salt and black pepper

This is a warming one-pot recipe for when the temperature takes a dip. Serve it in bowls with a side of crusty bread.

- Season the flour with salt and pepper and use to coat the beef. Melt the butter with the oil in a large saucepan and fry the meat in 2 batches until browned, draining with a slotted spoon.

- Add the onion, carrots and parsnips to the saucepan and fry gently for 5 minutes.

- Return the meat to the pan and add the herbs and tomato purée. Add just enough water to cover the ingredients and bring slowly to the boil. Reduce the heat to its lowest setting, cover with a lid and simmer very gently for 45 minutes.

- Add the pumpkin, sugar, ginger and parsley and cook for a further 30 minutes until the pumpkin is soft and the meat is tender. Check the seasoning and serve scattered with extra parsley.

V

• DESSERTS •

Stollen

SERVES 12 • PREP & COOKING TIME 1 hour, plus proving

- 175 g (6 oz) strong white bread flour, plus extra for dusting
- 1½ teaspoons fast-action dried yeast
- ½ teaspoon ground mixed spice
- 25 g (1 oz) caster sugar
- 40 g (1½ oz) salted butter
- 100 ml (3½ fl oz) warm milk
- 75 g (3 oz) sultanas
- 25 g (1 oz) chopped almonds
- 25 g (1 oz) chopped candied peel
- 150 g (5 oz) marzipan
- icing sugar, for dusting

This marzipan-filled delight is a German Christmas classic. It's traditionally dusted with icing sugar to create a snowy layer reminiscent of winter landscapes.

- Put the flour, yeast, mixed spice and sugar in a bowl. Melt 25 g (1 oz) of the butter, mix with the milk and add to the bowl. Mix with a round-bladed knife to make a soft dough.

- Turn out on to a lightly floured surface and knead until smooth and elastic. Place in a lightly oiled bowl, cover with clingfilm and leave to rise in a warm place for about 1½ hours or until doubled in size.

- Turn the dough out on to a floured surface and knead in the sultanas, almonds and candied peel. Cover loosely with a tea towel and leave to rest for 10 minutes.

- Roll out the dough on a floured surface to a 25 × 20 cm (10 × 8 inch) rectangle. Roll the marzipan to form a log shape about 23 cm (9 inches) long and flatten to about 5 mm (¼ inch) thick. Lay the marzipan down the length of the dough, and fold the rest of the dough over it. Transfer to a large greased loaf tin, with a base measurement of about 25 × 10 cm (10 × 4 inches), and press down gently. Cover loosely with oiled clingfilm and leave to rise in a warm place for about 30 minutes until slightly risen. Remove the clingfilm.

- Bake in a preheated oven, 220°C (425°F), Gas Mark 7, for 25 minutes until risen and golden. Leave for 5 minutes, turn out of the tin, place on a wire rack, cover with a sheet of foil and place a weight on top to keep the stollen compact while cooling. Melt the remaining butter and brush over the stollen. Dust with icing sugar.

v

· BREAKFASTS ·

Overnight Oats

SERVES 1 • PREP TIME 15 minutes, plus soaking

- 50 g (1¾ oz) rolled oats
- 120ml (4 fl oz) milk
- 1 tablespoon natural yogurt, plus extra to serve (optional)
- drizzle of honey or maple syrup
- fresh fruit of choice, to serve (optional)

FOR THE OPTIONAL FLAVOURINGS
- ¼ teaspoon cinnamon and a small handful of blueberries
- small handful of raspberries and chocolate chips
- ½ tablespoon cocoa powder and a few cherries
- ½ tablespoon desiccated coconut

Make this easy-to-prep and easy-to-transport breakfast vegan by using dairy-free milk and yogurt – oat and coconut both work well. You can experiment with flavourings to suit your taste; try adding seeds and nuts, chopped apple or pear, or dried fruit.

- Combine all the ingredients for the base of the overnight oats in a container or glass jar and stir. Add one of the optional flavourings, stir to combine, and leave in the fridge overnight.

- Add extra fruit or yogurt to serve, if desired.

v

• LIGHT BITES •

Goats' Cheese & Herb Soufflés

SERVES 4 • PREP & COOKING TIME 25 minutes

- 25 g (1 oz) butter
- 50 g (2 oz) plain flour
- 300 ml (½ pint) milk
- 4 eggs, separated
- 100 g (3½ oz) goats' cheese, crumbled
- 1 tablespoon chopped mixed herbs, such as parsley, chives and thyme
- 1 tablespoon grated Parmesan or vegetarian hard cheese*
- salt and black pepper

These light-as-a-feather soufflés make a lovely lunch with a peppery rocket salad alongside and work equally well as a dinner party starter. Serve them immediately while they are still perfectly risen.

- Melt the butter in a medium saucepan, add the flour and cook, stirring, for 1 minute. Gradually add the milk, whisking all the time, and cook for 2 minutes until the roux has thickened.

- Remove the pan from the heat. Beat in the egg yolks one at a time, then stir in the goats' cheese. Season well with salt and pepper.

- Whisk the egg whites in a large bowl until they form firm peaks, then gradually fold them into the cheese mixture with the herbs. Transfer to 4 lightly oiled ramekins, sprinkle over the Parmesan, then bake in a preheated oven, 190°C (375°F), Gas Mark 5, for 10–12 minutes until risen and golden. Serve immediately.

*For guidance on vegetarian cheeses, see page 5.

V

• MAINS •

Ratatouille Pie with Parsnip Mash

SERVES 6 • PREP & COOKING TIME 1 hour

- 5 tablespoons olive oil
- 1 red pepper, deseeded and cut into chunks
- 1 green pepper, deseeded and cut into chunks
- 1 yellow pepper, deseeded and cut into chunks
- 1 garlic clove, thinly sliced
- 1 large aubergine, trimmed and cut into chunks
- 2 courgettes, trimmed and cut into chunks
- 5 tomatoes, roughly chopped
- 150 ml (¼ pint) red wine
- 150 ml (¼ pint) water
- 1 vegetable stock cube
- 1.125 kg (2½ lb) parsnips, peeled and chopped
- 2 tablespoons butter
- 1 tablespoon chopped thyme leaves
- salt and black pepper

Bursting with flavour and packed with colourful veggies, this is a great way to head towards your five-a-day. The buttery parsnip mash adds a lovely note of sweetness. Serve with a simple green salad.

- Heat the oil in a large, heavy-based frying pan, add the peppers, garlic, aubergine and courgettes and cook over a medium-high heat, stirring and tossing occasionally, for 10 minutes until softened and lightly golden in places. Add the tomatoes and cook for 3 minutes. Pour in the wine and measured water and bring to the boil, then cover and simmer for a further 10 minutes.

- Meanwhile, bring a large saucepan of lightly salted water to the boil, crumble in the stock cube with the parsnips and mix well. Bring to a gentle simmer and cook for 10 minutes until the parsnips are tender. Drain well, return to the pan and mash with the butter, then stir in the thyme leaves.

- Transfer the ratatouille mixture to a large gratin dish. Spoon the mashed parsnips over the vegetables and season generously with pepper. Bake in a preheated oven, 200°C (400°F), Gas Mark 6, for 20 minutes until the top is lightly golden in places.

v

• DESSERTS •

Ginger & Hazelnut Ice Cream

SERVES 4 • PREP TIME 5 minutes, plus freezing

- 300 ml (½ pint) double cream
- 2 tablespoons milk
- 4 tablespoons icing sugar, sifted
- 50 g (2 oz) preserved stem ginger, drained and finely chopped
- 4 teaspoons ginger syrup
- 2–4 tablespoons finely chopped hazelnuts, plus extra to decorate

No ice-cream maker? No problem, with this creamy dessert which takes only minutes to prep – all you need is a whisk and a chilled bowl. Indulgent and velvety, it's wonderful by itself but also goes well with poached apples or pears.

- Whip the cream and milk lightly, then fold in the icing sugar. Pour into a shallow freezer container, cover and freeze for about 45 minutes, until the ice cream has frozen around the sides of the container.

- Turn into a chilled bowl and whisk until smooth. Stir in the ginger, syrup and hazelnuts.

- Return the ice cream to the container, cover and freeze until firm. Transfer to the refrigerator about 20 minutes before serving, to soften.

- Scoop into dishes and sprinkle with a few extra chopped hazelnuts to serve.

v

· BREAKFASTS ·

Bubble & Squeak Cakes with Poached Eggs

SERVES 4 • PREP & COOKING TIME 30 minutes

- 1 kg (2 lb) potatoes, peeled and quartered
- 40 g (1¾ oz) unsalted butter
- 500 g (1 lb) Brussels sprouts, trimmed and halved
- 50 g (2 oz) plain flour
- 3–4 tablespoons olive oil
- 4 eggs
- salt and black pepper
- chopped chives, to serve

Made from cooked potato and Brussels sprouts or cabbage, bubble and squeak – named for the sounds the ingredients make as they fry – is also a great way to use up vegetables left over from Christmas dinner.

- Boil the potatoes for 12–15 minutes, until tender, then drain and mash with the butter.

- Meanwhile, cook the sprouts in boiling water for 3–4 minutes, until just tender. Drain and refresh under cold running water.

- Mix the sprouts and potatoes together and season with salt and pepper. Shape the mixture into 8 round cakes and dust with the flour.

- Heat the oil in a frying pan over a medium heat and cook the cakes in 2 batches, for 2–3 minutes on each side, until golden.

- Meanwhile, poach the eggs in a frying pan of simmering water for 4–5 minutes, depending on how you like your eggs.

- Divide the cakes between 4 serving plates, top with a poached egg and sprinkle with chopped chives to serve.

v

• LIGHT BITES •

Carrot & Red Pepper Soup

SERVES 4 • PREP & COOKING TIME 1 hour

- 2 tablespoons olive oil
- 2 onions, finely chopped
- 1 garlic clove, crushed
- 3 red peppers, deseeded and roughly chopped
- 2 large carrots, peeled and diced
- 900 ml (1½ pints) vegetable stock
- salt and black pepper
- chopped chives, to garnish
- Greek yogurt, to serve

Warming, comforting and a beautifully vibrant colour, this soup is an ideal choice for lunch or supper to keep your energy up as midwinter draws near.

- Heat the oil in a large saucepan and fry the onions gently for 5 minutes or until softened and golden brown. Add the garlic and cook gently for 1 minute. Add the peppers and fry for 5–8 minutes or until softened.

- Add the carrots and stock to the pan, season to taste and bring to the boil. Reduce the heat, cover and simmer gently for 20 minutes.

- Allow the soup to cool slightly then blend in batches in a blender or food processor. Return the soup to the pan and gently reheat. Serve topped with chopped chives and with a dollop of yogurt.

• MAINS •

Creamy Lamb Korma

SERVES 4 • PREP & COOKING TIME 1 hour

- 4 tablespoons sunflower oil
- 750 g (1½ lb) lamb neck fillet, thinly sliced
- 1 onion, finely chopped
- 2 garlic cloves, finely chopped
- 2 teaspoons peeled and finely grated fresh root ginger
- 65 g (2½ oz) ground almonds
- 1 tablespoon white poppy seeds
- 5 tablespoons korma curry paste
- 150 ml (¼ pint) vegetable stock
- 250 ml (8 fl oz) single cream
- salt and black pepper

TO GARNISH
- slivered green pistachio nuts
- crispy fried shallots

White poppy seeds are traditionally used in curries, especially kormas, as a thickening agent. You can find them in large supermarkets, Asian grocery stores and online.

- Heat half the oil in a large, nonstick frying pan and brown the lamb in batches for 2–3 minutes. Remove with a slotted spoon and set aside.

- Add the remaining oil to the pan and add the onion, garlic and ginger and cook over a medium heat for 3–4 minutes. Stir in the ground almonds, poppy seeds and curry paste and stir-fry for 1–2 minutes.

- Add the reserved lamb to the pan with the stock and cream. Bring to the boil and season well. Reduce the heat and simmer, uncovered, stirring occasionally, for 30 minutes or until the lamb is tender.

- Remove from the heat and garnish with the slivered pistachio nuts and crispy fried shallots. Serve immediately.

v

• DESSERTS •

Clove & Cardamom Spiced Cookies

MAKES 30–40 • PREP & COOKING TIME 30 minutes

- 175 g (6 oz) unsalted butter, softened
- 200 g (7 oz) soft dark brown sugar
- 1 large egg, lightly beaten
- ½ teaspoon ground cinnamon
- ¼ teaspoon ground cardamom (or the ground seeds from 3 pods)
- ¼ teaspoon ground cloves
- 325 g (11 oz) plain flour, plus extra for dusting
- 1 teaspoon baking powder
- ½ teaspoon salt

Fill your kitchen with the amazing aroma of cinnamon, clove and cardamom as you bake these wonderful cookies. Full of festive flavours, they'd make a charming Christmas gift piled into a jar with a jaunty tartan ribbon tied around it.

- Place the butter and sugar in a large bowl and beat together with a hand-held electric whisk until light and fluffy. Add the egg and spices and beat well. Stir in the flour, baking powder and salt and mix until combined.

- Turn the dough out on to a floured surface and knead lightly until smooth. Roll out to 2–3 mm (⅛ inch) thick, then cut out about 30–40 shapes, such as stars, or stamp out rounds using a 6 cm (2½ inch) fluted cutter.

- Place the cookies on 3 baking sheets lined with nonstick baking paper and bake in a preheated oven, 180°C (350°F), Gas Mark 4, for 14–16 minutes until lightly golden and tinged brown around the edges. Transfer to wire racks to cool.

· MAINS ·

Sausage, Rosemary & Mixed Bean Hotpot

SERVES 4 • PREP & COOKING TIME 30 minutes

- 1 tablespoon olive oil
- 12 pork sausages
- 1 red onion, sliced
- 2 Romero red peppers, deseeded and cut into chunks
- 1 tablespoon rosemary leaves
- 400 g (13 oz) can adzuki beans (or any other canned pulse), drained and rinsed
- 400 g (13 oz) can butter beans, drained and rinsed
- 400 g (13 oz) can cherry tomatoes
- 150 ml (¼ pint) beef stock

It's the winter solstice, the longest night of the year and the official start of winter. You'll need something warming and a steaming bowl of this family favourite is just the thing. For extra comfort factor, serve with chunks of crusty bread.

- Heat the oil in a large, heavy-based frying pan and cook the sausages over a medium heat, turning frequently, for 10 minutes until browned all over and cooked through. Remove with a slotted spoon.

- Pour off most of the oil from the pan and discard, leaving about 1 tablespoon. Add the onion and red peppers to the pan and cook, stirring frequently, for 3–4 minutes until softened. Add the rosemary leaves and cook for a further 1 minute.

- Add the drained beans, tomatoes and stock and bring to the boil. Return the sausages to the pan, reduce the heat to a simmer and cook for 10 minutes until the beans and sausages are piping hot.

- Serve ladled into serving bowls.

v

• BREAKFASTS •

Carrot & Feta Potato Cakes with Eggs

SERVES 2 • PREP & COOKING TIME 30 minutes

- 150 g (5 oz) or 1 large carrot, peeled and diced
- 350 g (11½ oz) potatoes, peeled and diced
- 1 small egg, lightly beaten
- 75 g (3 oz) feta cheese
- 1 teaspoon ground cumin
- 1 tablespoon chopped parsley (optional)
- 2 spring onions, chopped
- flour, for dusting
- 3–4 tablespoons vegetable oil
- salt and black pepper
- 2 poached or fried eggs, to serve

Rise and shine with this delicious version of the traditional Irish potato cakes. The carrot adds a hint of sweetness that contrasts well with the salty feta. Combining crispy potato cakes and softly poached or fried eggs is a wonderful way to start the day.

- Bring a large pan of lightly salted water to the boil and cook the carrots and potatoes for about 12 minutes until tender. Drain well and mash together until crushed but not completely smooth. Set aside to cool, uncovered, for at least 10 minutes.

- While the potatoes and carrots are cooling, add the beaten egg, feta, cumin, parsley, onions and a pinch each of salt and pepper to the pan and mix well to combine. Use flour-dusted hands to form the mixture into 4 patties.

- Place the oil in a large nonstick frying pan and shallow-fry the patties gently for about 3 minutes on each side until crisp and golden. Drain on kitchen paper and serve with fried or poached eggs.

· MAINS ·

Garlic Butter-stuffed Chicken with Mixed Beans

SERVES 4 • PREP & COOKING TIME 1 hour

- 50 g (2 oz) coarse breadcrumbs
- 3 tablespoons olive oil
- 4 large skinned chicken breast fillets
- 25 g (1 oz) butter, softened
- 50 g (2 oz) cream cheese
- 2 garlic cloves, crushed
- finely grated zest of 1 lemon
- 4 tablespoons chopped parsley
- 150 g (5 oz) French beans, diagonally sliced into 3.5 cm (1½ inch) lengths
- 400 g (13 oz) can flageolet beans, drained
- 200 ml (7 fl oz) white wine
- salt and black pepper

Create a festive feast for friends on with this one-pot chicken recipe that you can take straight from oven to table. Stuffing the chicken fillets with garlicky filling is the only fiddly bit – and that can be done ahead of your guests arriving – yet it looks so impressive.

- Put the breadcrumbs in a flameproof casserole with 1 tablespoon of the oil and heat gently until the breadcrumbs begin to brown and crisp. Drain to a plate.

- Using a small knife, make a horizontal cut in each chicken breast to create a pocket for stuffing.

- Beat the butter with the cream cheese, garlic, lemon zest, 1 tablespoon of the parsley and salt and pepper. Pack the stuffing into the chicken breasts and seal the openings with wooden cocktail sticks.

- Heat the remaining oil in the casserole and fry the chicken on both sides until lightly browned. Drain. Scatter the French beans and flageolet beans into the casserole and add the wine and a little seasoning. Arrange the chicken on top.

- Cover and place in a preheated oven, 190°C (375°F), Gas Mark 5, for 20 minutes. Remove the lid and sprinkle the chicken pieces with the breadcrumbs. Return to the oven, uncovered, for a further 10 minutes until the chicken is cooked through.

- Transfer the chicken to serving plates. Stir the remaining parsley into the beans, then spoon around the chicken.

V

· DESSERTS ·

Mint & Chocolate Fudge

MAKES 800 g (1 lb 12 oz) · PREP & COOKING TIME 20 minutes,
plus setting

- 40 g (1½ oz) strong peppermints
- 500 g (1 lb) plain dark chocolate, chopped
- 400 g (13 oz) can sweetened condensed milk
- 50 g (2 oz) milk chocolate or white chocolate, melted

A homemade gift is the best kind of gift and this minty fudge will be appreciated by anyone with a sweet tooth. It will keep for up to 2 weeks in the fridge.

- Place the peppermints in a plastic bag and crush them with a rolling pin, breaking them into small pieces. Continue to roll and flatten the mints until they are ground to a powder.

- Put the plain dark chocolate and condensed milk in a heatproof bowl over a pan of gently simmering water. Leave until melted, stirring frequently. When melted, stir in the ground peppermints.

- Beat the mixture until the ingredients are combined then turn it into a shallow 18 cm (7 inch) baking tin lined with nonstick baking paper, spreading it into the corners. Level the surface and leave to cool. Chill in the refrigerator for at least 2 hours.

- Lift the fudge out of the tin and peel off the paper. Melt the milk or white chocolate in a heatproof bowl over a pan of gently simmering water, then place in a paper piping bag. Snip off the tip and scribble lines of chocolate over the fudge. When the chocolate is set, cut the fudge into 2 cm (¾ inch) squares.

V

• DESSERTS •

Bûche de Noël

SERVES 10 • PREP & COOKING TIME 1 hour, plus cooling

- 3 eggs
- 75 g (3 oz) icing sugar, plus extra for dusting
- 50 g (2 oz) plain flour
- 25 g (1 oz) cocoa powder
- 300 ml (½ pint) double cream
- 150 g (5 oz) canned sweetened chestnut purée
- 200 g (7 oz) plain dark chocolate, broken into pieces

As an alternative dessert on Christmas Day, try this French Christmas cake which is decorated to look like snow on a yule log. Don't be intimidated by rolling up the sponge, it's easier than you might think.

- Whisk the eggs and sugar in a heatproof bowl over a pan of hot water until the mixture leaves a trail when the whisk is lifted. Sift in the flour and cocoa powder and fold in.

- Pour into a greased 33 × 23 cm (13 × 9 inch) Swiss roll tin lined with nonstick baking paper tin and spread into the corners. Bake in a preheated oven, 180°C (350°F), Gas Mark 4, for about 15 minutes until just firm.

- Invert the cake on to a sheet of nonstick baking paper dusted with icing sugar. Peel away the paper that lined the tin, then roll the sponge in the fresh paper and leave to cool.

- Whip half the cream until softly peaking, then fold in the chestnut purée. Unroll the sponge and spread the chestnut cream over the top (don't worry if the cake cracks). Roll the cake back into a log shape.

- Bring the remainder of the cream almost to the boil. Remove from the heat and stir in the chocolate pieces. Leave until melted, then stir until smooth. Allow to cool.

- Arrange the cake, seam-side down, on a serving plate. Lightly whip the chocolate cream, then spread it over the top and sides of the cake, and mark to look like tree bark. Dust with icing sugar just before serving.

V

• DESSERTS •

Sweet Potato Meringue Pie

SERVES 6 • PREP & COOKING TIME 1 hour 30 minutes, plus chilling

- 500g (1 lb) chilled ready-made shortcrust pastry
- 500 g (1 lb) sweet potato, peeled and diced
- 150 ml (¼ pint) double cream
- 75 g (3 oz) light muscovado sugar
- 2 tablespoons runny honey
- 1 teaspoon ground ginger
- 1 teaspoon mixed spice
- 1 egg
- 3 egg yolks

FOR THE MERINGUE TOPPING
- 3 egg whites
- 50 g (2 oz) light muscovado sugar
- 50 g (2 oz) caster sugar
- ½ teaspoon ground ginger

Kwanzaa – an African-American holiday that celebrates community and culture – starts today. Make this meringue-topped take on sweet potato pie for Karumu, the community feast that marks the end of Kwanzaa on 31st December. Serving with scoops of vanilla ice cream make it even better.

- Roll the pastry out on a lightly floured surface until large enough to line a buttered metal pie dish, 20 cm (8 inches) in diameter and 5 cm (2 inches) deep. Lift the pastry over a rolling pin, drape into the tin then press over the base and sides. Trim the edges, then chill for 15 minutes.

- Put the sweet potato in the top of a steamer, cover and cook for 10 minutes or until tender. Mash with the cream, sugar, honey and spices, then beat in the whole egg and egg yolks. Pour into the pie case, level the surface, then bake in a preheated oven, 180°C (350°F), Gas Mark 4, for 40 minutes until set.

- Make the topping. Whisk the egg whites until you have stiff peaks, then gradually whisk in the sugars, a teaspoonful at a time, until all the sugar has been added. Add the ginger and whisk for a minute or two more until very thick and glossy.

- Spoon over the hot pie and swirl the meringue with the back of a spoon. Bake for 15 minutes until lightly browned and the meringue is crisp.

- Leave to cool for 30 minutes, then cut into wedges and serve.

• LIGHT BITES •

Marinated Prawn Skewers with Pickled Cucumber Salad

SERVES 4 • PREP & COOKING TIME 30 minutes

- 400 g (13 oz) raw tiger prawns in their shells
- finely grated zest and juice of 1 lemon
- finely grated zest and juice of 1 lime
- 1 tablespoon sesame oil
- 2 garlic cloves, finely chopped
- salt and black pepper
- coriander and lime wedges to garnish, optional

FOR THE PICKLED CUCUMBER SALAD
- ½ cucumber
- ¼–½ mild red chilli, deseeded and finely chopped
- 2 tablespoons chopped coriander
- 1 tablespoon white wine vinegar
- 1 teaspoon Thai fish sauce
- ½ teaspoon caster sugar

Soak the wooden skewers in cold water for at least 20 minutes to stop them burning when you grill the prawns. These skewers make a great alternative to burgers or sausages for a barbecue in the summer too.

- Divide the prawns between 8 wooden skewers.

- In a shallow ceramic dish long enough to hold the skewers, beat together the grated rind and juice of the lemon and lime, the oil and garlic. Season with salt and pepper, add the prawn skewers and coat in the marinade.

- Very thinly slice the cucumber and put into a shallow dish. Sprinkle with the chilli, coriander, vinegar, fish sauce and sugar. Spoon into small bowls set on serving plates.

- Place the skewers under a preheated hot grill with the exposed parts of the skewers away from the heat. Cook for 7–8 minutes, turning once, until the prawns are bright pink all over.

- Add 2 skewers to each serving plate, and garnish with coriander sprigs and lime wedges, if liked.

· LIGHT BITES ·

Turkey & Chestnut Soup

SERVES 6 • PREP & COOKING TIME 4 hours

- 1 turkey carcass
- leftover stuffing (optional)
- 2 onions, finely chopped
- 2 carrots, finely chopped
- 2 celery sticks, finely chopped
- 1.8 litres (3 pints) water
- cooked turkey, cut into bite-sized pieces
- 2 tablespoons olive oil
- 2 large potatoes, diced
- 475 g (15 oz) can whole chestnuts in brine, drained
- 3 tablespoons sherry or port
- salt and black pepper

A great way to make sure that not a scrap of the Christmas turkey is wasted. Don't worry too much about the quantity of turkey meat in the recipe – just use whatever you have.

- Break the turkey carcass into pieces and place in a large saucepan with the stuffing, if using, and 1 onion, 1 carrot, 1 celery stick and the seasoning. Add the measured water and bring to the boil. Cover and simmer for 3 hours. Add extra water as necessary.

- Remove the carcass and vegetables and discard. Strain the stock and add the turkey meat.

- Heat the oil in the rinsed-out pan, then add the potatoes and the remaining onion, carrot and celery. Cook gently, stirring, for 5 minutes.

- Pour in the turkey stock and bring to the boil. Simmer for 20 minutes, then add the chestnuts and sherry or port. Reheat and check the seasoning before serving.

V

• MAINS •

Frying Pan Macaroni Cheese

SERVES 4 • PREP & COOKING TIME 30 minutes

- 325 g (11 oz) macaroni
- 50 g (2 oz) butter
- 50 g (2 oz) plain flour
- 600 ml (1 pint) milk
- 100 g (3½ oz) Cheddar cheese, grated
- 25 g (1 oz) dried white breadcrumbs
- 25 g (1 oz) Parmesan or vegetarian hard cheese, grated*
- salt and black pepper

Creamy and comforting with a crunchy breadcrumb topping, does life get any more delicious than mac and cheese? This family favourite takes just half an hour to prep and cook.

- Cook the pasta in a large saucepan of salted boiling water according to the packet instructions until al dente.

- Meanwhile, melt the butter in a large, ovenproof frying pan and stir in the flour to make a smooth paste. Cook until golden, then gradually whisk in the milk. Bring to the boil over a medium heat, then simmer for about 3 minutes until slightly thickened. Remove from the heat, stir in the Cheddar cheese and season.

- Drain the pasta, then tip into the frying pan. Stir into the cheese sauce until well combined. Scatter over the breadcrumbs and Parmesan.

- Place in a preheated oven, 190°C (375°F), Gas Mark 5, for 15 minutes or until golden brown and bubbling.

*For guidance on vegetarian cheeses, see page 5.

VG

• LIGHT BITES •

Pea & Potato Tikkis

MAKES 25 • PREP & COOKING TIME 50 minutes

- 1 tablespoon sunflower oil, plus extra for deep-frying
- 4 teaspoons cumin seeds
- 1 teaspoon black mustard seeds
- 1 small onion, finely chopped
- 2 teaspoons peeled and finely grated fresh root ginger
- 2 green chillies, deseeded and chopped
- 625 g (1¼ lb) potatoes, diced and boiled
- 200 g (7 oz) fresh peas
- 4 tablespoons lemon juice
- 6 tablespoons chopped coriander
- 100 g (3½ oz) gram flour
- 25 g (1 oz) self-raising flour
- 50 g (2 oz) rice flour
- large pinch of ground turmeric
- 2 teaspoons crushed coriander seeds
- 350 ml (12 fl oz) water
- salt and black pepper

These lovely little balls of lightly spiced pea and potato make great snacks. And, as a bonus, they're vegan. Serve warm with mango chutney or try the **Autumn Harvest Chutney** on page 324.

- Heat the oil in a large saucepan over a medium heat.

- Add the cumin seeds and mustard seeds and stir-fry for 1–2 minutes. Add the onion, ginger and chillies and cook for 3–4 minutes.

- Add the cooked potatoes and peas, and stir-fry for 3–4 minutes. Season well and stir in the lemon juice and coriander leaves. Divide the mixture into 25 portions and shape each one into a ball. Chill until ready to use.

- Make the batter by mixing together the gram flour, self-raising flour and rice flour in a bowl. Season and add the turmeric and coriander seeds. Gradually whisk in the measured water to make a smooth and thick batter.

- Pour sunflower oil into a large saucepan until one-third full and heat to 180–190°C (350–375°F), or until a cube of bread browns in 30 seconds. Dip the potato balls in the batter and deep-fry in batches for 1–2 minutes or until golden. Drain on kitchen paper and serve warm.

v

· LIGHT BITES ·

Three Cheese Filo Bites

SERVES 6 • PREP & COOKING TIME 30 minutes

- 125 g (4 oz) feta cheese
- 125 g (4 oz) ricotta cheese
- 50 g (2 oz) grated pecorino or vegetarian hard cheese*
- 2 eggs, beaten
- 100 g (3½ oz) butter, melted
- 4 tablespoons olive oil, plus extra for greasing
- 4 large sheets of filo pastry
- salt and black pepper

Filled with oozy warm cheese, these will go down a storm at your New Year's Eve celebrations. They can be made the day before and stored, covered in clingfilm in the fridge, and then simply popped in the oven to warm through when your guests arrive.

- Drain any excess water from the feta and ricotta, then mix together with the pecorino and eggs. Season to taste.

- Stir together the butter and olive oil. Unwrap the filo pastry, keeping any pastry you are not using covered with a damp (but not wet) tea towel.

- Cut each pastry sheet into thirds lengthways and brush all over with the butter mixture. Place a heaped spoonful of the cheese mixture at one end of a strip of pastry. Fold one corner of the pastry diagonally over the filling to meet the other side, then continue to fold all the way down the strip to create a triangular parcel. Repeat with the remaining pastry and ingredients.

- Place the parcels on a lightly greased baking sheet, brush over again with the butter and oil and bake in a preheated oven, 200°C (400°F), Gas Mark 6, for 12 minutes or until golden and crisp. Serve warm from the oven.

*For guidance on vegetarian cheeses, see page 5.

• DRINKS •

Bellini

SERVES 2 • PREP TIME 5 minutes

- 4 measures peach juice
- 8 measures chilled Champagne
- 2 dashes grenadine (optional)
- peach wedges, to decorate

Served in an elegant flute, this classic cocktail is a great way to kick off any party. It was created in the 1930s by the founder of iconic Harry's Bar in Venice and named after Venetian artist Giovanni Bellini.

- Mix together the peach juice and chilled Champagne in a large mixing glass. Add the grenadine, if using.

- Pour into 2 Champagne flutes, decorate each glass with a peach wedge and serve.

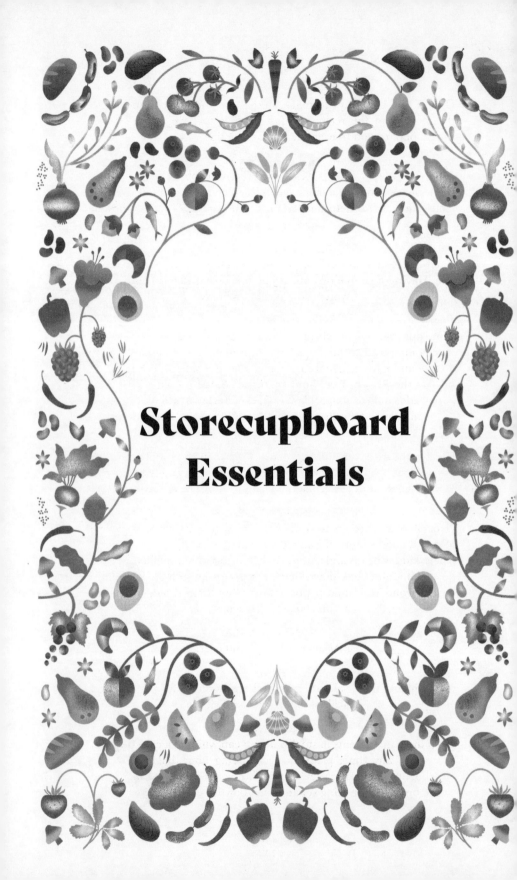

Storecupboard
Essentials

One of the best ways to make life easy in the kitchen and to get the most from the recipes in this book is to have a well-stocked storecupboard and freezer. Here are some tips:

DRIED PASTA AND NOODLES
Endlessly versatile for a quick meal. Keep an assortment of different kinds, such as spaghetti, macaroni, penne and fusilli pasta, and rice and egg noodles.

RICE
Keep a selection of brown, jasmine, basmati, risotto and pudding rice. Having a couple of pouches of precooked rice is handy when you need a meal in a hurry.

GRAINS
Couscous and bulgur wheat are super-quick to prepare – just pour over boiling water. Quinoa is high in protein and has a lovely nutty texture and flavour. Use it in place of rice as a side dish or in salads such as the **Prawn, Pea Shoot & Quinoa Salad** on page 140. Pearl barley adds bulk to soups (like the **Beef & Barley Broth** on page 381) and stews and is great as an alternative to rice in risottos.

TOMATOES
Possibly the most versatile ingredient to have in your cupboard. Buy cans of chopped and whole tomatoes for sauces, soups and stews. Tomato purée is brilliant for adding a punch of flavour.

PULSES AND BEANS
Cans of pulses are great as the base for speedy meals so it's worth having a good supply of canned chickpeas, cannellini beans, butter beans, kidney beans and lentils. Packets of dried red split lentils need no soaking and cook down quickly in soups and dhals. Puy lentils have a wonderful, mild peppery taste. Buy them dried, canned or precooked in pouches.

COCONUT MILK
For Asian-style soups and curries.

FISH
Good-quality tuna, salmon, mackerel and sardines for pasta dishes, fishcakes, salads and sandwiches.

BAKING
Keep these ingredients in stock and you can whip up a cake or batch of cookies any time: plain and self-raising flour, baking powder, bicarbonate of soda, caster sugar, granulated sugar, soft light and dark brown sugar, icing sugar, cocoa powder and vanilla extract.

STOCK CUBES OR POWDER
Vegetable, chicken and beef stock cubes or powder for soups, stews, sauces and gravies. Buy the low-salt ones if you can.

DRIED HERBS AND SPICES
These make all the difference in cooking. While some recipes in the book need a particular spice, like the ras el hanout in the **Moroccan Baked Eggs** on page 50, these are the ones you are most likely to use on a regular basis: chilli (flakes or powder), Chinese five-spice, paprika, curry powder, cumin, cinnamon, oregano, mixed herbs, rosemary, thyme.

OILS
Groundnut, vegetable oil, rapeseed or olive oil for frying, plus extra virgin olive oil for salad dressings and drizzling over food.

VINEGARS
Balsamic and red or white wine vinegar for dressings and marinades.

HONEY AND/OR MAPLE SYRUP
For baking, desserts, pancakes, sauces, marinades and drizzling over porridge or yogurt.

ROLLED OATS
Not just for morning porridge but to add to homemade granola and muesli (see pages 148, 248 and 294) and for baked treats such as in the **Banana & Honey Flapjacks** on page 32.

PEANUT BUTTER
Delicious spread on toast but also the star ingredient in the **Banana & Peanut Butter Smoothie** on page 96, the **Gado Gado Salad** on page 232, the **Peanut Butter Swirl Brownies** on page 317 and the **Thai Chicken Burgers with Coconut Satay Sauce** on page 225.

MUSTARD
Loved as a condiment for meat but also adds a kick to salad dressings and sauces. Our recipes use English, Dijon and wholegrain.

PASTES
Ready-made pastes are a simple way of adding exciting flavours. Fiery North African harissa paste, curry paste, red and green Thai curry paste and chipotle paste are good ones to have to hand.

SAUCES
Every family has its own favourites but it is useful to have tomato ketchup, mayonnaise, Worcestershire sauce, soy sauce – the low-salt version preferably – and sweet chilli sauce.

NUTS AND SEEDS

For healthy snacking and to add crunch to salads or sprinkle over yogurt or porridge. Keep a few packets of your favourites in the cupboard.

A WORD ABOUT HERBS

Many recipes in this book use fresh herbs as they give such a lift to food. Growing some in a pot by the back door or on the kitchen windowsill is easy and looks pretty. And you'll always have a ready supply for a garnish or to add extra flavour.

FROZEN FRUIT

Can be defrosted to use in warming crumbles or pies or to top yogurt or porridge. It is often cheaper than fresh fruit and is flash-frozen within hours of picking so as healthy. Frozen fruit is also super-useful for making smoothies as it's already peeled and chopped and can be chucked in the blender without defrosting.

FROZEN VEGETABLES

Peas are the definitive frozen veg but frozen spinach and sweetcorn are also very handy.

PASTRY

Frozen pastry is essential for easy pies and tarts – you'll find several in this book. Just remember to take it out of the freezer in good time to defrost.

FISH & MEAT

Fish fillets, prawns, chicken pieces, sausages and minced beef or lamb are great for when the fridge is looking bare.

VANILLA ICE CREAM

A tub of good-quality vanilla ice cream to serve with desserts like pies and crumbles.

Index